THE ART OF WARFARE
IN BIBLICAL LANDS

In the Light of Archaeological Study

By YIGAEL YADIN

Professor of Archaeology at the Hebrew University, Jerusalem

Major-General, former Chief of the General Staff, Israel Defense Forces

VOLUME ONE

McGRAW-HILL BOOK COMPANY, INC.

New York   Toronto   London

*In memory of my brother
Matatyahu, who died defending
the State of Israel*

Printed and bound in Great Britain
by Jarrold and Sons Ltd., Norwich

THE ART OF WARFARE
IN BIBLICAL LANDS

Translated from the Hebrew
by M. PEARLMAN

CORRIGENDA

Y. Yadin: The Art of Warfare in Biblical Lands

p. 48 (fig.) read "to fight" instead of "to light".

pp. 79 and 206 (bottom) read "1307–1275" instead of "1310–1280".

p. 126 read "Ein Gedi" instead of "Ei Gedi".

    read "see page 125" instead of "see page 124".

pp. 130, 136, 150, 173 read "Telloh" instead of "Lagash".

p. 154 read "Tehutihotep" instead of "Tehutitep".

    "(cf. 169)" to be omitted.

p. 159 read "(20th century B.C.)" instead of "(c. 1900 B.C.)".

p. 168 read "left" instead of "above" and "above" instead of "left".

    Same correction in index, p. 473, No. 168.

p. 174 read "at Ginossar" instead of "of Ginossar".

    read "above and left" instead of "above".

    read "spear head" instead of "javelin head".

p. 180 read "The Palestine Archaeological Museum" instead of "The Rockefeller Museum".

    Same correction in index, p. 474, No. 180.

p. 187 read "The Ugaritic hunting charioteer (above)" instead of "The Canaanite hunting charioteer".

p. 191 read "1·69 ms." instead of "1·47 ms."

p. 195 read "from a tomb at Thebes" instead of "from a tomb of Iamanezeh, Sheikh Abd el-Gurnah".

p. 197 (bottom) read "14th century" instead of "17th century".

p. 224 read "The city of Hattussas" instead of "The city of Boghazköy".

p. 229 read "on page 347" instead of "in the opposite illustration".

p. 237 read "pages 103 ff." instead of "following page 107".

p. 354, the words "National Museum, Athens" refer to the Warriors' Vase.

p. 397, Nos. 13 and 14 read: "*xiii*" instead of "*viii*".

p. 473, No. 168 read "The Palestine Archaeological Museum" instead of "Dept. of Antiquities, Archaeological Museum, Jerusalem."

p. 473, No. 172 read "Virolleaud" instead of "Viroelleaud".

Where Rockefeller Museum is mentioned read Palestine Archaeological Museum.

CONTENTS

VOLUME ONE

PREFACE

This book—which is a first attempt to discuss all the facets of the art of warfare, its implements, techniques and strategy in all Biblical lands—requires a few explanatory words as to its structure and method of presentation to the reader. Although the book discusses a variety of subjects, each of which is in a sense independent, it is the interweaving of the various themes that makes the harmonious whole at which I have aimed.

The book covers all lands of the Bible—from Anatolia to Egypt and from Palestine to Mesopotamia—a part of the world containing nations and countries that had been fighting each other over long periods of history. Only a complete analysis from both the military and archaeological point of view will enable us to comprehend the development of warfare in all its aspects: weapons, fortifications, army organization, and tactics.

The book is, in fact, composed of three parts: the text accompanied by line drawings, the color plates, and explanatory captions. This arrangement is necessitated by the fact that the principal sources for the subject are pictorial in character, consisting of thousands of carved and painted monuments, together with other remains of an archaeological character, which must first be set in their proper historical and geographical setting through archaeological and chrono-logical analysis before it is possible for one to draw military conclusions.

The object of the text is to define the historical and archaeological background, to describe the various elements in the art of war and weave them into a single pattern which will make evident their mutual relationship and their connexion with the different warring nations. The accompanying line drawings should at this point assist the reader to visualize the subject without undue reference to the color plates. The subjects are discussed here within their archaeological period, and in each period the individual aspects are dealt with separately. This seemed to me preferable to discussing any one element (e.g., the bow) from its very beginning to the end of the period discussed in the book. The latter may perhaps be a suitable method for a book which aims merely at presenting a body of data for reference purposes, but, in my opinion, it is unsuitable for a book whose aim it is to emphasize the inter-relationship among the many elements which compose the art of warfare, this being the only satisfactory way to grasp the development of this art or science.

The plates are put at the end of each part, according to the archaeological periods. In this kind of book, which is based to a large extent on archaeological finds, it is imperative, I believe, to present visually to the reader the many sources in as clear and faithful a manner as possible. The choice of suitable subjects out of thousands of documents, the collection of colored and other pictures, and the arrangement of this abundant material on plates, by their geographical provenance, their archaeological periods, and their relation to the various elements of war, has necessitated considerable efforts, which often surpassed anything I had anticipated when I first started the book. Nevertheless, I believe this to have been worth while, since the pictures will not only aid the reader to understand many things that are impossible to describe in mere words, but will enable him to read critically and come to his own conclusions. Moreover, much of the material published here is scattered in scores of museums and hundreds of publications (some of them quite rare). I have made a special point of presenting material from these sources (such as the rare publications of Layard, Botta, and Flandin) and at the same time trying to show them in conjunction with their places of discovery. I have made it a rule to present, whenever possible, the pictures of the objects themselves, together with the monuments describing them. I have sometimes preferred a certain monument to others, not because of its absolute importance, but on the basis of its relative artistic value or its rarity. As for the written documents—Egyptian, Accadian, etc.—which I have incorporated into the text, I have of course used translations and, unless otherwise indicated, I have mostly followed those in Pritchard's book (see bibliography). These translations do not pretend to be literal; their purpose is, in general, to give a clear understanding of the contents of the documents.

As for the explanatory captions, I thought it best not to include too many descriptive details of the monuments and finds in the text proper, lest it distract the reader from the main points and hinder him from seeing the wood for the trees. On the other hand, it is frequently these fine differences in details which make it possible to follow clearly the essential interrelationship between the various aspects of warfare and the development of the science as a whole. That is why I have paid particular attention to the captions of the more complex monuments which embody several subjects simultaneously.

The reader who wishes to explore more thoroughly the whole subject, or that of a particular chapter, has but to turn to the last pages for the very extensive bibliography on every find and monument depicted in the book. I have not spared details there, since I wished to provide the reader with ample opportunity for studying and comparing various opinions in regard to the objects.

Only seldom have I touched on actual battles, the reason being that here, more than on any other topic, the sources are very scant and are subject to speculations and interpretations so extremely divergent that it is impossible to present the problem satisfactorily from a scientific viewpoint. Moreover, the details of the battles depend mainly on our knowledge of the topographical factors which determined the tactical and strategical moves. In most of the famous battles this element is completely lacking, and often scholars cannot even identify with certainty the places named. Any change in identification of a site—a matter which is of primary importance to our understanding of a particular battle—alters, in fact, our grasp of the whole situation. Schematic maps, so often brought forth to explain the battles in Biblical lands, may be useful to explain a war as a whole and the lines of the "grand strategy", but not more than that, and are therefore liable to mislead the reader who is not familiar with the topographical problems. Nevertheless, we have enough details about some battles, and the most important of those are discussed here. Even this, however, is not done just for their own sake, but in order to illustrate the principles, techniques, and implements of warfare which are the subject of this book. In a few instances I have described Biblical battles, but only where I thought the data were sufficient to clarify their main problems and, perhaps, to stimulate other scholars to give the matter more thought.

I have no illusions that I have succeeded in exhausting the subject. This may be possible in the future, when primary and basic work on the subjects discussed will have been done separately for each period and each country. I hope I may succeed in rousing scholars in various fields to devote their abilities and energies to further research, and thus prepare the way for still other scholars to complete the job. My debt to previous research on every subject mentioned in this book can be realized from the long bibliography at the end, which can also serve as a guide to readers who may wish to delve more deeply into the subject.

It gives me great pleasure to acknowledge my gratitude to all those who helped me to bring this book into being. First and foremost I want to thank Mr. Y. Makavi, the general manager of the International Publishing Company, who urged me a number of years ago to put into writing some of the data I had been collecting, and has spared no effort in helping me to acquire photographs and publish the book in its present elaborate format. I am deeply indebted to his daring and able execution.

I am particularly thankful to the many museums and their directors who have permitted me to check their collections and sometimes employ special photographers for my purposes. Amongst them I would like to thank Professor A. Parrot and the Louvre; Dr. D. R. Barnett and the British Museum; Dr. W. C. Hayes and the Metropolitan Museum of Art; Professor P. Delougaz and Dr. W. Boyd of the Oriental Institute, University of Chicago (especially for permission to use the magnificent colored drawings from Medinet Habu); to the museums of Florence and Bologna; to the University Museum, University of Pennsylvania (and particularly to Mr. A. R. Schulman who kindly allowed me to study his manuscript on the organization of the Egyptian army); to the Hittite Museum in Ankara; to the Archaeological Museum in Istanbul; to Miss W. Needler and the Royal Ontario Museum; the Prince of Wales Museum in Bombay; to the Ashmolean Museum, Oxford; to the Archaeological Institute, London University, and particularly to Dr. K. Kenyon; and also to the Museum of the Department of Antiquities, government of Israel, and the Museum of the Hebrew University, Jerusalem.

May I also record my thanks to Miss A. Pesin of the editorial staff of *Horizon*, who allowed me to use a color transparency of the Tutankhamun chest; to Mr. J. Perrot for a photograph of a gate at Boghazköy and Yazilikaya; to Mr. E. Erickson for permission to reproduce an ivory panel from his collection; to Dr. E. Borowsky for permission to reproduce a sickle sword of his; to Mr. A. Sorrell and Dr. R. D. Barnett for permission to reproduce the drawing of the reconstruction of the Lachish siege; to Miss T. Kish for her color reconstruction of several drawings; to Mr. P. Bar-Adon for the photograph of an axe from the Judean Desert; to Mr. B. Rothenberg for a photograph of Ein Qadis, and to Messrs. S. Smilan, D. Ussishkin, W. Marmot, Colonel M. Michael, Lieutenant-Colonel A. Perry, and Major A. Aran, for their help in procuring colored photographs during their travels. I also thank the Oriental Photographic Company for preparing several colored photographs from various sources, and copies of all the photographs for the purpose of the layout.

I am deeply indebted to Lord Marks, who kindly put at my disposal the photographic laboratories of Marks and Spencers and the services of its chief, Mr. Baynton, who, together with his assistants, worked tirelessly to photograph many objects from the British Museum. To my good friend Mr. L. Shalit I am grateful for help, as usual, in more ways than one. Mr. Zim and Mr. Bengum kindly helped in many phases of the work of preparing the layout.

I should also like to express my deep appreciation to Clichés Schwitter AG, Zürich, who with much patience prepared the illustrations, as well as to Jarrold & Sons, Norwich, England, for their high standard of printing.

I thank most heartily my friend Mr. Pearlman for his painstaking translation of the manuscript from the Hebrew.

I am grateful to Mr. H. Raviv of the scientific staff of the Views of the Biblical World for his help in selecting the pictures and preparing the index of sources, and to Mrs. I. Pomerantz for much help in editing the bibliography and index of sources.

I wish to thank McGraw-Hill editorial staff for much help, and particularly Mr. D. Scott.

Lastly, I wish to thank my wife, who not only took upon herself the extensive correspondence with museums and individuals, but also gave me the benefit of her advice throughout.

Yigael Yadin

Jerusalem

I

INTRODUCTION

THE ART OF WARFARE

War is the attempt by one nation to impose its will on another by force. This breakdown in human association has been a recurring feature in the history of man since the very beginning. Human conflict finds expression in the first pages of the Bible. Hardly has man begun life on earth when, as the Biblical narrative records with unadorned simplicity, "Cain rose up against his brother Abel and killed him." The chain reaction to this event has continued right up to the 20th century. A study of human history cannot therefore be complete without a study of the military events of the past and of the means conceived by nations to secure their own military aims and thwart those of their enemies. Moreover, in ancient times, as today, men devoted much of their technical genius to perfecting weapons and devices for destruction and defense. Weapons of war thus serve as an enlightening index of the standards of technical development reached by nations during different periods in history.

Since war always involves at least two sides, the development of the art of warfare of one nation can only be fully evaluated in the light of the art of warfare conducted by its enemy, in attack and defense.

As an object of military study, a single land or nation is too limiting and confining—and can be misleading. The smallest unit of such a study is a region or a group of peoples who battled each other at some period or another in their history. One must examine the reciprocal effects of such encounters, which enabled each side to gain knowledge of the weapons and fortifications of the other, to copy them and improve upon them. And these effects are often evident in the relics laid bare by the spade of the archaeologist. But—and here is an example of how a limited study can mislead—these ancient weapons may be and have often been found far from their land of origin, carried there as war booty by a victor or left behind by a powerful nation waging war beyond its own frontiers. Such war material, found in archaeological excavations, sheds much light on the art of warfare of a particular period and in a particular region, but not necessarily of the nation in whose land it was discovered. The study of warfare must clearly cover both rivals.

There is a reciprocal impact on nations who come into conflict with each other. There are similar reciprocal influences, inevitable and consistent, which the different weapons, fortifications, tactics, and military organizations make upon each other. The progressive developments in each branch and instrument of war during successive periods in history become clear only when examined in the context of enemy opposition at the time. New tactics introduced by one side prompted new counter-tactics by the other. These in turn produced further tactical innovations by the first. Weapons development followed the same process. The appearance of the composite bow, for example, with its increased power of penetration, led to the invention of the coat of mail for defense. This in turn provided a further challenge for a weapon to defeat armor. And so the process continued, leading to advances in both offensive and defensive battle devices. Similarly, the various types of city fortifications can be understood only in the light of standard patterns of attack on cities prevalent during the different periods, and in particular of the use of the battering-ram.

The study of military development is in large measure the study of the unending process of reaction of each element in warfare to its counterpart. But all elements must be considered as an integrated whole, and the relationship of each to the other properly examined. The development of weapons must be studied against the background of the development of tactics, army structure, and the systems of fortifications. To study each element in isolation would be superficial and sterile, and as unrewarding as the study of military developments of a single nation without reference to those of its neighbors. But account must also be taken of a human feature which has affected the rate of military development among different peoples—inertia, or conservatism. There are countless examples throughout history, right up to the present time, in which military innovations, proved in battle, have been spurned by other armies who have preferred to adhere to traditional patterns, and have been finally introduced only after long delay. There is often a considerable time-lag between the appearance of an improved weapon in one country and its adoption by another.

Moreover, even when some technical improvement gradually becomes accepted in the military scheme of things, it suffers for a time by being considered in the obsolete terms of patterns prevalent before its introduction. These complex factors must always be borne in mind when we come to study the monuments left behind by the nations of antiquity. These monuments relate mostly to warfare, since war was a regular part of the lives of these people.

Military action may be classified in several ways. But none is completely satisfactory. The most general classification, for example, is by the character of the operations, either offensive or defensive. But in every operation there is usually a concern both with offense and defense. Even an army initiating an assault must be organized to defend itself against surprise or counterattack. This is also true of the individual soldier, who must be armed with both offensive and defensive weapons.

Military action may be classified according to forms of warfare—battle in open terrain and battle on a fortified city. But here, too, each side must be armed and organized in a manner suited to both types of warfare. For it may have to move from the city to the plain, or from the plain to the city, during the course of the fighting. An army mauled in an open battlefield may seek to retreat behind a fortified base—as did the Canaanites when beaten by Thutmose III in the celebrated battle near Megiddo. And an army that may be expected to sit behind the defensive walls of its city may break out and attack the enemy in the open plain—as happened with the counterattack of the King of Samaria on the armies of Aram who sought to besiege him.

And there is yet a further classification. A military action can be analyzed in the light of strategy and tactics. Basically, strategy is the art of war. Tactics is the art of battle, concerned with the movement and operation of fighting units on the battlefield.

But however military action may be classified and defined, in the final analysis the art of warfare is to seek to achieve supremacy over the enemy in three fields: mobility, firepower, security. To put it another way, it is the ability to move troops to engage and injure the enemy without serious injury to oneself.

The principles of warfare discussed in the following chapters, as they emerge from the military record of ancient peoples, reflect the attempt of each warring faction to achieve this triple supremacy over the enemy, or the action taken after its successful achievement. These principles, often regarded as the basis of strategy and tactics, may be broken down into surprise; maintenance of aim, economy, and concentration of force; coordination of arms; security, mobility, and the offensive spirit.

Incidentally, surprise is generally accepted as the most important of these factors. Surprise is, in fact, the ability to move one's forces to engage the enemy at a time, place, and under conditions which he does not expect, for which he is unprepared, and to which he cannot, therefore, react by the most effective application of his own forces and weapons.

These principles are illustrated in cameo form at any boxing match, in which the contendors are even unarmed. The constant movement of the body has a single purpose: to put the boxer in the most advantageous position from which he can both attack and at the same time evade the blows of his opponent. The predominant role of one fist is to attack—firepower; of the other, to parry—security. To gain this advantageous position, the boxer has to know where his opponent is—or is likely to be at a given moment—and to seek out his weak spots. In this he is served by his senses—sight, sound, and touch. His eyes, ears, and hands provide him with the intelligence which, in battle, is provided by reconnaissance units on patrol or at forward observation posts. The action of his fists and other parts of his body is directed by his brain, through the medium of nerves and muscles. Their counterpart in warfare is the military commander and his staff, as the brain; their nerves—the communications network; their muscles—trained and disciplined troops.

Mobility, firepower, and security, as the three basic elements in the art of

3

warfare, are appropriate headings under which the nature of ancient warfare and the weapons used in antiquity may be examined. The three groups we shall be considering are therefore:

1. Means whose purpose was to offer mobility, such as chariots, cavalry, and the capacity of the foot soldier to move far and fast.
2. Means of firepower, namely weapons whose purpose was to hit the enemy at various ranges.
3. Means of security, namely protective devices such as the helmet, shield, and armor, whose purpose was to parry or blunt the effectiveness of the enemy's weapons.

Fortifications are a subject in themselves. For, though they may be classed as a security device against the designs of an enemy, their structure must be such as to offer their own troops mobility and freedom of action in addition to security both for soldiers and civilians.

Before proceeding to a description and analysis of these means of warfare, it is perhaps worth underlining that in the final resort it is not weapons alone which determine the issue in battle, but often, particularly where both sides are evenly matched, the spirit of the commander in the direction of his forces and the spirit of the troops in the handling of their weapons. These have been the decisive factors in fateful wars throughout history.

MOBILITY

The Chariot   The chariot in battle is basically a mobile firing platform. It is not, primarily, a means of transport from a distant base to the battlefield. Its principal purpose is to serve as a movable platform within the battlefield, from which relatively limited firepower can be rushed to and brought to bear on decisive spots in the midst of the fighting. A secondary and by no means negligible purpose is its shock value as it charges into the enemy ranks.

To fulfil its major function, the chariot must offer speed and maneuverability as well as stability for the firing of weapons. These needs are contradictory. For speed and maneuverability are best provided by a small and light chariot. But a stable firing platform demands a heavier vehicle, capable of supporting and providing operational space for at least one weapon-carrying soldier in addition to the driver. The rival claims of these two considerations exercised the minds of military planners throughout the generations. Different solutions were devised at different times. And these are reflected in the variety of ancient battle chariots. At times speed was sacrificed to stability. At other times stability gave way to speed. Eventually the chariot became a finely balanced war instrument, serving both needs equally effectively. In its complete form, it was a complex vehicle, comprising the following carefully designed parts: body, wheels, axle, chariot pole, yoke,

An Egyptian chariot of the XVIIIth Dynasty

and fittings for weapons such as quivers, bow cases, and sheaths and stands for axes and spears.

To give it strength and lightness, the chariot was built largely of wood—special kinds for each part—strips of leather, and various metals. It was not an instrument common to the equipment of all armies. It could be fashioned only by nations commanding rich resources and advanced techniques. Technique was important. For, as we shall see later, the turning-point in the development of the chariot came with the lighter body, the introduction of the light, spoked wheel, and the technical knowledge which enabled the axle to be set farther to the rear. For only with the rear axle could the chariot be completely maneuverable even on sharp turns. But this required lightness. For a rear axle on a heavy chariot, made heavier by the weight of the military team, would have been too great a strain on the draft animals. It was the combination of the rear axle plus the design of a light body and light wheels, as well as powerful and swift draft animals, which brought about the perfect chariot: stable, fast, and highly maneuverable.

Cavalry

Like the chariot, the primary purpose of the cavalry horse was also to serve as a mobile firing platform, though here, too, the panic and confusion induced in the enemy by a cavalry charge was not without importance. The advantage of the horse over the chariot was its ability to move over almost any ground, whereas a wheeled vehicle was limited to comparatively level and unbroken terrain. Against this, the horse offered a poor and unstable firing platform. In a chariot, there was the driver, concerned solely with controlling the horses, and a fighting soldier, free for operational action. In the cavalry, rider and soldier were one. If his weapon were the bow, requiring two hands to operate, his control of the horse in action was correspondingly reduced. Even if armed with a spear, which needed only one hand and left the other free for the reins, he lacked a third to hold a shield. The effectiveness of the mounted horse in battle in earliest times was thus limited. Only with the very late introduction of improved saddles, stirrups, and spurs, making it possible to control the horse with thigh, knee, and ankle, was the cavalry-man free to fight with both hands. Small wonder that the cavalry made its serious appearance on the battlefield only some 1,500 years after the chariot.

FIREPOWER *Personal Weapons*

Every fighting commander since the beginning of time has dreamed of possessing a weapon which could out-range anything in the armory of the enemy. With such a weapon he could not only surprise his foe, but could do so without harm to himself and his men, for they could remain out of reach of enemy missiles.

But long-range weapons do not obviate the need for medium- and short-range instruments of war. Their key importance is at the start of hostilities. But as the battle progresses, medium-range weapons must be brought to bear on the enemy, giving way finally to the weapons used in hand combat.

It was clearly impossible for the individual soldier to carry at all times the weapons for all ranges required at progressive stages of battle. And so even the most ancient armies were organized in units linked to specific types of weapons: the long-range-weapon troops were used at the start of the battle; the follow-up units were armed with medium-range weapons; and the hand-to-hand fighters engaged in the final phase of battle.

Range, as a basic factor in the use and development of weapons, can serve as a convenient criterion in weapons classification. The major weapons in use in ancient times were the bow and the sling for long range; the javelin and the spear for medium range; and the sword, the axe, and the mace for short range.

The bow is one of the earliest known weapons of war. It was in use in prehistoric times and was, because of its range, the most convenient weapon also of the hunter. The bow may well have been the first composite implement devised by man, and definitely the first method of concentrating energy.

Since we shall be discussing its development in some detail, let us first record its component parts and action. It consists of two basic elements: the body, which is of wood, and the string. The surface of the wood farthest from the string is called the back; the inner surface is called the belly. The point on the wood at which the bow is held, near its center, is called the grip. The parts of the wood on either side of the grip are called arms, or limbs. The string is attached to the extreme ends of the arms. The bow is operated by placing the base of the arrow against the string, putting the string under maximum tension by pulling it as far as possible from the wood, and suddenly releasing it. The act of drawing the string brings the ends of the body closer together and puts the wood under tension. The wood, which should be both pliable and tough, springs back to its former position the moment tension on the string is released, and this brings back the string with a snap, propelling the arrow sharply forward as it does so. The bowman holds the wood with his left hand—the bow arm—at the grip, and draws back the string with his right, by which he also holds the base, or hook, of the arrow. To protect his left arm from the blow of the string as it snaps back on release, the bowman often wore an armguard on the inside of the bow arm.

The range of a bow depends on one or all of the following factors—its size, shape, and the pliability and toughness of the wood. The bigger the bow, the greater its pliability and consequently its range. But a large bow was more unwieldy to operate and it also hampered mobility.

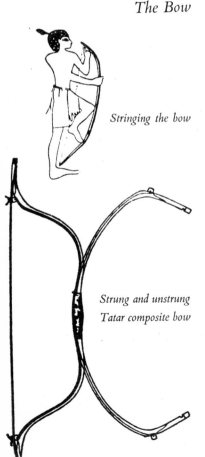

A simple double-convex bow of a Semite. XIIth Dynasty

The Bow

Stringing the bow

Strung and unstrung Tatar composite bow

The shape of the wood in the early simple bow was a single convex arc, so that the distance between string and body was widest at their respective centers. Maximum tension was reached when the hand on the string was pulled as far away as possible from the hand on the grip. But it was found that this did not exploit the maximum pliability from the wood to produce the deserved tension. This, it was found, could be achieved by reducing the distance between both fists in the start position, that is, between the grip on the body and the center of the string. This led to the invention of the double-convex or double-span bow—like the shape of a Cupid upper-lip—which brought the grip closer to the spring, and, when fired, increased the distance between the string and the peaks of both arcs. The archer was thereby able to bring his weapon under greater tension and give it greater range.

The emergence of the bow as a battle weapon of first importance came with the introduction of the composite bow. This weapon proved decisive in numerous campaigns in ancient days.

There was no single natural element which could give a bow wood the required toughness and elasticity. But gradually the idea was developed of combining several available natural materials which, together, could meet all needs. Thus was born the composite bow. It was made of four materials—wood, sections of animal horn, animal tendons and sinews, and glue. Even the wood—the skeleton of the bow—was sometimes not made from a single block but comprised pieces of wood from different trees with varying pliability suited to the different tension demands at different parts of the limbs and the grip. The back of the bow was covered with strips and bands of sinews. The belly was reinforced with two sections of animal horn, one on either side, the inner curve of the horn facing the belly.

All these materials were stuck or bound together to form a single integrated body. And they were so bound that before the string was attached, the arms of the body tended to bend the other way. To pull them round for the attachment of the string, or the bracing, so that the wood assumed the shape of a bow, required great strength. This, of course, put it under great tension even in its position of rest, and, when operated, greatly increased its propulsive power. The composite structure made possible for the first time the production of a bow which, though comparatively small, and therefore light and mobile, nevertheless had considerable power. It was well described by an Arab author of the 15th century A.D. He wrote: "The structure of the composite bow is not unlike that of man. The human body is made up of four basic elements—bones, flesh, arteries, and blood. The composite bow has the same four counterpart elements: wood—its skeleton; horns—its flesh; tendons—its arteries; glue—its blood. Man has back and belly. So has the bow. And just as man can bend forward but is likely to damage himself by bending too far backward, so with the operation of the bow."

The height of perfection of the composite bow was reached when, to endow it with greater power, it was given a double-convex form.

The composite bow could have had an effective range of some 300 to 400

The Composite Bow

Parts of a Turkish composite bow. From left to right: first and second, pieces of thin wood formed the core of the bow, and the pieces glued together—surface view. Third from left: the pieces glued together—side view. Fourth: the strip of sinew that was glued to the core, and which formed the back of the bow when strung. Fifth: sections of horn, which formed the belly

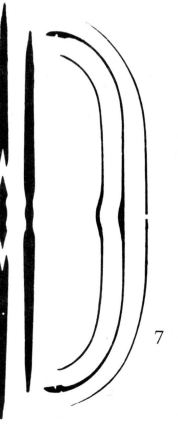

7

Forms of bows: the triangular, the curved, and the double concave, or the recurved ends, as depicted on Egyptian monuments

yards, though its absolute range was about two times that distance. For the first time in history, it was possible with this weapon to surprise the enemy and attack him from beyond his range of retaliation, of hearing, and, on occasion, of vision. Its power also had a revolutionary impact on the art of warfare, and was directly responsible for the introduction of the coat of mail for personal protection.

Somewhere between the simple and the composite bow came the compound bow. This was stronger than the first but less complex and of course less powerful than the second, and was in wide use among armies who had not reached the technical standards demanded by the manufacture of the composite bow. The body of the compound bow was made of two or more strips of wood partially overlapping, glued together or bound with tendons and cord.

Much of our knowledge of bows used by early warriors in Biblical lands comes from ancient drawings and bas-reliefs. The simple, reinforced, and composite bows are depicted in the works of ancient artists, both in their single-span and double-convex forms. The composite bow is always easy to pick out. For, as we have observed earlier, in this bow, there was a tendency for the ends of the arms to recurve and bend outwards before, and often even after, they were bound to the string. This feature is usually evident in the artistic representation of this type of bow, giving it almost a double-concave rather than convex appearance. Moreover, the form of attachment of the horns beneath the arms gave the composite bow, with the string as base, a triangular form. We are indebted to the ancient artists, who paid meticulous attention to detail, for the certainty with which we can recognize the different bows used in antiquity.

The Arrow

None of the improvements to give the bow greater range would have been of any value without comparable advances in the development of the arrow, which is, after all, the offensive element of this weapon. The arrow is made up of three parts, each of a different material to suit its special function. The arrowhead, which is the destructive part, had to be of the hardest possible material—flint, bone, or metal. The body of the arrow, whose function is to direct the energy transmitted from the string on release, had to be long, thin, hard, straight, and light, and was made of wood or reed. The tail, designed to keep the arrow on its course in smooth and straight flight, was made of feathers. The feathers of an eagle, vulture, kite, or sea fowl were found to be the most effective. The tail, without which the arrow could not reach its target, was so important that its feathers were aptly described by the Persians as "messengers of death."

Forms of arrowheads

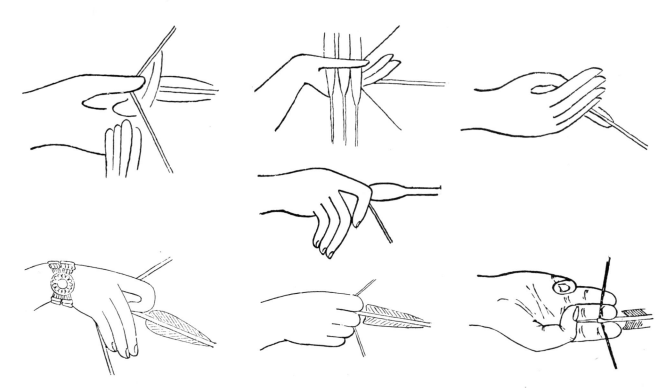

Special technical difficulty was experienced in the attachment of arrowhead to body. If the base of the head was inserted into the body, the arrowhead was known as a tang. If the body was fitted into the base of the head, it was known as a socket. The effectiveness of the arrow to pierce armor was determined by the shape and structure of its head. Arrowheads may be classified as leaf-shaped, or triangular, etc., and as flat or with a central spine or rib. The form was not the fruit of caprice but was dictated by the nature of the defense and armor of the enemy.

Methods of release as depicted on Egyptian and Assyrian monuments. Top four drawings depict Egyptian, bottom three Assyrian

The Quiver

Since the bow was required to fire numerous arrows during the course of battle, the archer had to have some means of carrying a reasonable complement of arrows in a handy manner which would put them within easy reach and facilitate speedy reloading. In this he was served by the quiver. The quiver had to be capable of holding between twenty and thirty arrows and to be made of lightweight material. It was carried either on the back of the bowman or over his shoulder so that both hands were free to fire the bow.

Of the bow, as of the chariot, it can be said that no other weapon in ancient days required so high a technical capacity to produce and such skill to operate. These two qualities in combination were decisive on more than one occasion in determining the course of history.

The Sling

The sling, devised by ancient shepherds to scare predatory animals from attacking their flocks, gradually made its appearance on the battlefield as a weapon of war. For it enabled a missile to be thrown a considerable distance—considerable for those days—in any terrain, hilly as well as flat. Its capacity to fire up a slope, indeed, gave it some importance in assaults on fortified cities.

9

A slinger from a painting in Beni-hasan

The sling had the supreme advantage of simplicity of structure, which made it easy to produce, and its ammunition, slingstones, was provided by nature.

Its principal disadvantage was that considerable training and experience were required to operate it with effective accuracy.

The early sling looked rather like a large eye-patch. It consisted of a small piece of leather or cloth with two cords attached to opposite edges. The stone missile was placed on the material and the cords pulled taut so that the material became a kind of bag containing the stone. The bag was held by the left hand and the ends of the two cords held together by the right. The bag was then swung round and round several times above the head until it gained the required momentum, at which point one of the cords would be released, thereby releasing the missile which would be flung forward.

The function of the sling was often complementary to that of the bow. Whenever they were used in battle, the slingmen always served close to the archery units.

The Javelin and the Spear

These two weapons are similar in appearance but differ in size and in the way they are operated. The javelin was like a large arrow and served as a medium-range weapon. It was hurled by hand, and the soldier would be armed with several javelins which would be carried, like arrows, in a quiver. To increase its range of throw, a cord with a loop on the end would on occasion be added, giving the weapon the appearance of a weaver's leash rod. The cord would be wound round the javelin and the loop retained by the fingers of the warrior, so that as the javelin was hurled, the swift unwinding of the cord would give it a spin and therefore a steadier flight.

Like the arrow, the javelin consisted of a body, made of wood or reed, and a head of metal, either provided with a socket or tang, and its shape was suited to the nature of the enemy's armor. Often, to enable the javelin to be stuck in the ground during a rest period, its base would be fitted with a metal point. The weight and form of this metal tip were such that not only did it not interfere with the propulsion of the weapon, but contributed to the speed and balance of its flight.

The spear, a replica of the javelin in shape, was much bigger and heavier, and pierced by thrust. As a thrusting weapon it was thus not unlike a very long stabbing sword. It consisted of a stout staff and a metal head, with either tang or socket, and was sometimes tipped at the base with a metal point.

The Sword

The sword has always been the principal weapon for hand-to-hand combat. There were two main types of sword, each serving a specific function: the sword for stabbing and the sword for striking. Both consisted of two main parts, a handle or hilt and a metal blade. The stabbing sword had a long straight blade tapering toward the point. To give it strength, the blade was thickest along its center and tapered toward the edges. This straight sword, sharp at the edges and at the point, served equally to cut as to stab.

The striking sword, on the other hand, had only one sharp edge, and the

A Canaanite sickle sword from Gezer (14th century B.C.)

thickest part of the blade was not along the center but along the opposite or blunt edge. This type of sword could also be curved, the sharp edge being the convex, or outer edge. Sometimes the curve was slight, sometimes so considerable as to give it the appearance of a sickle. It is, indeed, often referred to as the sickle sword. But this may be misleading, for in a sickle the inner or concave edge is sharp, whereas in the sword it was the outer edge.

The curved sword underwent changes during the different periods in history, notably in the relationship between hilt and blade. At times, the hilt was long and the blade short; at other times the short hilt and long blade were preferred. These changes reflected the exertions of the armorers to fashion a sword light enough to be brandished easily, but without shortening considerably the blade.

It may seem strange, but the sword was never a decisive weapon in ancient campaigns—except on a few isolated occasions—and became important only in comparatively later periods in history. Unlike the arrow, javelin, and spear, where the metal portion was comparatively small, the sword required a long metal blade to give it effective range. But before man had learned the secret of producing perfect hard metals, the long sword was doomed to failure when put to the test. Alternatives to the sword were therefore sought for close-contact battle, weapons which required relatively small metal parts, or which could use a substitute for metal. These alternatives were the mace and the axe.

The common factors in the mace and the axe are that both were designed for hand-to-hand fighting and both consisted of a relatively short wooden handle, one end of which was fitted with the operative lethal part which was either metal or stone. The weapons were swung by the handle, and the head brought smartly down on the enemy. The key problem in the manufacture of both was the fitting of head to handle in such a way that it would not fly off when swung nor break off when struck.

The difference between the two weapons was the difference in function. The purpose of the mace was to beat and smash. The purpose of the axe was to pierce and cut. This difference determined the different shapes of their respective heads. The head of the mace was heavy and blunt. The blade of the axe was light and sharp. To prevent the weapon from leaving the soldier's hand when swung, in both mace and axe the handle was widest at the point of grip, tapering toward the head, or it was curved. Sometimes the handle was both curved and tapered.

The head of the mace, which was usually of stone but occasionally of metal, was shaped like a pear, an apple, or a saucer, or it could be oval. Each shape had its advantages and drawbacks. The saucer-shaped head, for example, turned the mace also into a cutting instrument, but weakened its striking power. The head of this weapon was always of the socket type, into which the handle was fitted.

The effectiveness of the mace as an instrument of war declined sharply when it was met by enemy troops clad in armor, and particularly when they were helmeted. With the development of armored devices for defense, the mace virtually disappeared from the battlefield.

The problems involved in the manufacture of the axe were more complex

The Mace and the Axe

Types of maceheads: apple-shaped, pear-shaped, and saucer-shaped. The handled mace is one depicted on Egyptian monuments

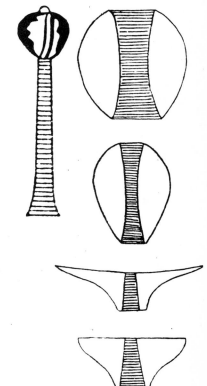

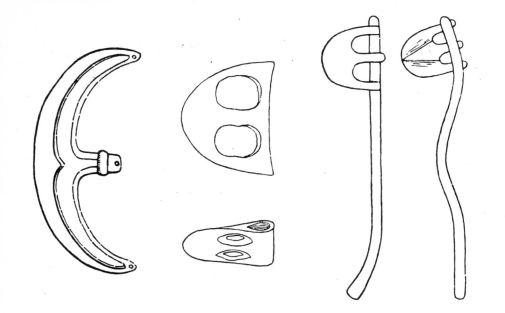

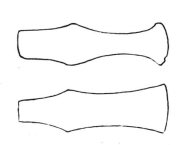

Types of axes: far left, epsilon; next left, top: eye; and below it, duck-bill. The next pair are tang and socket axes, and far right: lugged axeheads

than with the mace. And the varied attempts to find solutions led to the variety of shapes devised for the blade during the different periods in history.

Since the axe was conceived, as the sword, for hand-to-hand fighting its development was guided by the same alternate purposes of the sword—to pierce (paralleling the sword's function of stabbing) and to cut. The priority of one purpose over the other during a specific period was determined by the quality of the enemy's armor at the time. This, too, influenced the form of the axeblade. The cutting axe was effective against an unarmored enemy. Against armor, the piercing axe was required, with deep power of penetration. Axes may therefore be broadly classified according to shape, which also coincides with their respective functions: the axe with a long blade ending in a short sharp edge, for piercing; and the axe with a short blade and a wide edge, for cutting. There were also variations within each type.

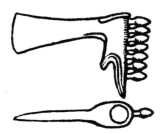

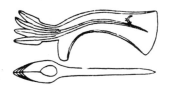

Upper two drawings, socketed axe with mane-like back. Below, socketed axes with finger-like backs

A problem facing its manufacture, which often influenced the form and development of the axe, was again the problem of fitting blade to handle in such a manner that it would not fly off in action. This, of course, is a danger in all such instruments, even the axe used by the laborer. And the Bible draws attention to it in Deuteronomy 19:5: "And when a man goeth into the wood with his neighbor to hew wood, and his hand fetcheth a stroke with the axe to cut down the tree, and the head slippeth from the helve, and lighteth upon his neighbor, that he die. . . ."

The axe may therefore be further classified according to the way its blade is joined to the handle: the socket type, in which the handle is fitted into a socket in the blade; and the tang type, in which the rear of the blade is fitted into the handle. In the latter type, the join was strengthened by binding or intertwining with cord. In some tang-type cutting axes, with the short blade and wide edge, the rear of the blade had three projections or tangs by which it was fitted to the handle, giving it the appearance of the figure 3, or—it depends how you look at it—of the Greek letter epsilon. This axe is therefore known as the epsilon axe. Another blade of the same type had a somewhat longer central tang projection from its rear fitted with a crossbar, by which it was fitted better to the handle. This projection and bar and the shape of the blade gave it the outline of an anchor, and it is therefore called the anchor axe.

The socket type also had its variations. There was the axe with two large holes in the blade, known as the eye axe; the duck-bill axe, with the longer blade and two smaller holes; axes with blades whose rear part was decorated with the likeness of animal heads, the fingers of a hand, a horse's mane.

The variety of axes reflected the attempts of armorers at successive periods to meet the new technical and tactical demands of the times. Each will be studied in detail in the context of its appropriate period.

SECURITY *Personal Protection*

Of the three basic elements in the art of warfare—mobility, firepower, security—the third is the most passive. But without it, the other two cannot be fully exercised, and at times not at all. A weapon cannot be fired if its wielder is put out of action, through lack of secure defense, before he begins. Security is a factor of warfare not only at the strategic and tactical levels but also at the level of the individual soldier.

One of the most absorbing chapters in the story of warfare is the search through the ages for devices which would offer personal security to the soldier on the battlefield without limiting his mobility or firepower. There was a constant struggle for priority among the three. A large and heavy shield could give excellent security—but at the expense of mobility. Protective devices for ears and eyes would hamper both mobility and the efficiency to direct fire. A shield which required to be held by one hand left only the other free to operate a weapon. And a coat of mail which freed both hands was unwieldy and slowed movement. In determining which of the three factors should be emphasized in the planning of a protective instrument, account was taken of the character of one's own offensive weapons, those of the enemy, and of the forms of mobility available to both—chariots, cavalry, or infantry. The appropriate solution was sought by the appropriate adaptation of the shape of the protective device and the material from which it was to be made.

Instruments for personal defense fall into two categories—shields and armor.

Three types of shields. From top to bottom: a round "Sea Peoples" shield; long Egyptian shield; and figure-8 Hittite shield.

The shield is simply a device to serve as a barrier between the body of a soldier and the weapon of his enemy. For reasons we have already considered, no shield could be completely satisfactory. If it was large enough to give complete protection, it was too heavy to permit free movement. If it was small enough to give easy mobility, it was inadequate to offer the body full cover.

The Shield

13

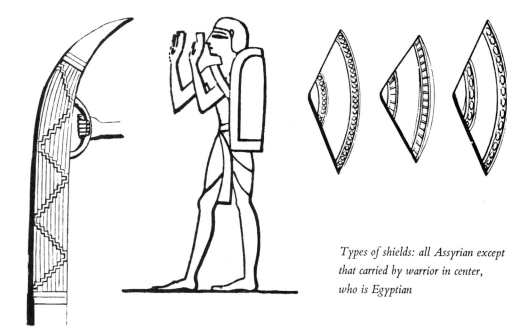

*Types of shields: all Assyrian except
that carried by warrior in center,
who is Egyptian*

The ancient armorers sought compromise solutions to these conflicting considerations, experimenting with different shapes, or different materials, or both. Their efforts are reflected in the numerous shapes of shields which have been found —long, short, rectangular, circular, triangular, shields shaped like a figure 8, flat shields, and convex shields. Each provides its own clue to the reasoning behind its design. The long shield served the soldier who fought without armor and needed maximum body protection. The short, usually round, shield was for the armored fighter who required protection for his face alone. The figure-8 shield was simply an economy form of the long shield, with superfluous parts cut out to save material and weight. The convex shield gave slightly more protection to the sides of the body, and was also designed to deflect arrows.

These were all personal shields, carried by the fighter himself. But also in use in ancient times was the very large shield. This was carried by a special shield-bearer who was constantly at the side of the fighter he was protecting.

Ancient designers were as concerned with the choice of material as they were with shape in the search for the ideal shield. The ideal was of course material which was both light and tough, and easily available. Most early shields were of wood, leather, plaited twigs or reeds, or of metal. The metal shields were very heavy, but they gave better protection. Some shields, as a compromise between

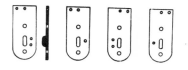

*Types of armor scales and method of
fastening and lacing—from Cypress*

14

strength and lightness, were made of wood or leather and stiffened with metal plates and studs. All these variants are fully depicted in several illustrated monuments.

Armor

The twin advantages of personal armor were that it covered the body of the fighter and left his hands free to operate his weapon. Its drawbacks were that it was difficult and expensive to manufacture and its weight hampered movement. The simplest solution was a uniform made of leather or some tough fiber. This would not give perfect protection, but it could give some, was simple to manufacture, and was light to wear. It could, in a way, serve as a substitute for the long shield, and only a short shield would be required for protection of the face, though this would not help the bowmen or cavalry who needed two free hands. The simple solution was not therefore the ideal solution.

The big advance toward perfection came with the coat of mail. This consisted of hundreds of small pieces of metal, like fish-scales, which joined together and attached to the surface of a cloth or leather cloak. Whereas armor made of plates of metal was excessively heavy to wear and interfered with movement, the coat of mail was relatively light and afforded easier movement. It was certainly the best protective device conceived at the time. But even the coat of mail had its disadvantages. Its manufacture demanded high technical skills and was very costly. It also had its points of weakness at the join of the sleeves and between the scales.

The Helmet

The most vulnerable part of the soldier in battle was his head. And so the search for protection by means of some form of helmet goes back to early times. Interestingly enough, because of the climate in the lands of the Middle East in Biblical times, the development of the helmet never reached the stage achieved in Europe, where it also covered the face. The only improvements in the Eastern helmet were the armored neckband, which protected the gap between the original helmet and the coat of mail, a collar made of scales. Neither of these hampered movement or vision.

Different armies during different periods favored special shapes for their helmet. In some cases, such as the round- or cone-shaped helmet, the consideration was functional: to deflect the arrow and make difficult its penetration. In most cases, the reason was quite different. One was to facilitate identification between friend and foe in the midst of the anarchy of battle. The head of the soldier stands out more than any other part of his body, and so each army would equip its troops with a specially shaped or specially decorated helmet. Some went further, and equipped different units of the same army with different helmets so that the commander in the field could quickly identify the position of each at all times. And there were also instances in which the shape of the helmet and its decoration had their origin in some tribal or other tradition and served no military purpose. Some of these types of helmets have provided us with a safe clue in determining the periods of ancient illustrated monuments, such as the monuments of the Assyrian period.

An Assyrian helmet

FORTIFIED CITIES IN ATTACK AND DEFENSE

The art of warfare knows no more illuminating example, on so large a scale, of the characteristic "chain reaction" feature of military developments than the history of the fortified city in defense and attack. The battle on such a city produced special and conflicting problems for the attacker and the defender. And the actions of one were a direct response to the actions of the other. The study of the systems of defense and the methods of attack, the problems of each and the various solutions conceived during the different periods, is therefore of great interest to the student of military history. Such study also sheds much light on the history of man, for human beings, from earliest times, sought shelter from their enemies, both man and beast, and devised some system of fortifications. The development of such systems and the innovations introduced at different times are indices of both the technical advances registered by one period over its predecessor and also of new means and methods of assault which they were devised to counter.

Fortifications are basically an artificial barrier, whether or not they are built around naturally defensive terrain, whose purpose is to deny the enemy the two important advantages in assault, mobility and firepower, and to provide a foundation of security for the defender. This dual purpose cannot, as may be supposed, be achieved by the erection of a simple barrier, but by designing it in such a way as to afford freedom of movement and firepower to the defenders behind it.

To follow the reciprocal developments in the methods of attack and defense, let us first consider the various ways of conquering a fortified city.

Attack and Penetration   There were five possible ways of conquering a fortified city. Sometimes one was enough. At other times a combination of two or more was necessary. The five methods were: penetration by force from above the fortifications, penetration through the barrier, penetration from below, siege, penetration by ruse.

The first three methods demanded sufficient resources at the disposal of the attackers to enable them, at specific stages of the battle, to cover their penetration units, so that they could work without interference, by maintaining steady fire on the defenders and preventing them from using their weapons.

Penetration from above the fortifications was achieved by scaling the walls, mostly with the aid of ladders.

Direct penetration through the fortifications could be gained in several ways. It could be effected by breaching the wall, either by primitive methods using hammers, axes, spears, and swords, or by a special instrument called the battering-ram. It could also be done by demolishing the doors of the gate or setting them on fire.

The battering-ram is an interesting object of study, for it was, in fact, a special invention, technically complicated to manufacture, and requiring, for its operation, both engineering skill and the capacity to give effective and sustained cover to its operators.

In its elemental form, the battering-ram was a long beam with a sharp metal head. It would be thrust with force against the wall to be breached so that its head was lodged deeply between the stones or bricks. It would then be levered right and left, thereby dislodging the stones or bricks and causing part of the wall to collapse. The beam and its sharp head represent the firing power of the battering-ram.

In action, the penetration unit handling the battering-ram had to reach the wall, bringing them close to the defenders above—and to their missiles. To protect them, an early improvement was introduced. The battering beam was carried beneath a long wooden box-like structure, similar to the top half of a covered wagon, its surface strengthened with leather or shields, its forward part open to allow the beam to be swung.

A primitive battering-ram operated by three soldiers from behind cover. Beni-hasan, 20th century B.C. See page 159

But only in the more primitive battering-ram was this structure used solely for protection. In later periods, with more advanced engineering skills, it was adapted to serve also the technical purpose of easing the movement of the beam and giving it a more powerful thrust. The method most commonly used was to drop a rope from the "ceiling" of the structure and tie it to the beam at an appropriate spot, so that it became a kind of pendulum. It could then be swung backward and forward, gathering momentum, so that, when released, it would fly forward with greater force and wedge itself more firmly in the wall. The special shape of the structure stems from this second function. Its forward portion was higher than the rest of its body, rather like a tower, and it was within this tower that the rope hung from the top and was tied to the beam.

The battering-ram, complete with structure, was heavy. It had to be brought from great distances to the proximity of the city under assault, and then right up to the walls. The more advanced types were therefore equipped with wheels, and this indeed gave it the appearance of a complete covered wagon and not just the top half.

From the rear base to the battlefield, it would often be drawn by draft animals. But in the final phase, it would have to be moved to the city wall by the soldiers themselves. This was a tough task, for the ground was usually rough, rocky, and steep. To make it easier, the assaulting force would try to lay an improvised track, often of earth occasionally strengthened with wooden planks, to serve as a smooth ramp of gentle gradient along which the battering-ram could be moved from the foot of the slopes to the city wall. When it had been brought within appropriate range for the battering operation, it would be braked at the spot to prevent its rolling back.

Often, to give the penetration unit additional protection, the covering fire from the regular infantry was strengthened by fire from special troops who would accompany the battering-ram, walking at its sides or even inside the structure. At a later period, such troops were moved in high, mobile, wooden towers from which they could fire at the defenders upon the walls.

Penetration from beneath the fortifications was perhaps less dangerous for the assault group, but technically more difficult. The tunneling could be started outside the range of the defenders' weapons, and could be done in darkness. But it was a lengthy process. Moreover, if at some stage the operation should become known to the defenders, they could offer a warm welcome to the attackers as they emerged from the other end of the tunnel. However, with the discovery of destructive

An Assyrian battering-ram

devices which could be placed beneath the foundations of the wall, this penetration from beneath the fortifications became in a much later period extremely dangerous for the defenders.

The siege, as a method of conquering a fortified city, was by its very nature the most protracted of all, and the least dangerous to the attacker. Its aim was to encircle the city and so prevent supplies from reaching the defenders within. But it demanded of the besieging army special measures for its own defense. For it became, in great measure, a passive force, and one which was exposed to attack at any point by allies of the besieged city who might come at them from any direction. It might also be attacked by the defenders themselves who, when their plight became desperate, might venture forth from their beleaguered positions and attempt to break through the ring. To meet these possible threats, a besieging army would establish fortified camps. This also enabled them to prevent outside armed assistance from reaching the city and the defenders from leaving it.

The lengthy process of siege was resorted to by a hostile army when time was on its side and it could afford to wait, or when it lacked the means of penetration by force, or when the fortifications of the city were too powerful to overcome. Some sieges lasted several years.

Penetration by ruse had as its aim the conquest of a city without the dangers of the first three methods and without the delay of the fourth. Men of a hostile army would seek to infiltrate into the city by cunning, using some trick to gain the confidence of the defenders. Once inside, they would overpower the guards and open the city gates to the waiting attackers.

Fortifications and Defense

The fortifications of an ancient city and the principles governing its defense were determined primarily by its topographical position, and its shape and size. And, apart from certain subsidiary considerations, the nature and siting of most of the cities of Palestine, Syria, and Anatolia, and of many other parts of Biblical lands, were themselves determined by two basic factors: strategic and tactical on the one hand, and the sources of water on the other.

Most cities were established only at sites whose natural conditions met these two basic needs. But in many parts of the Middle East, both needs could be met only by diametrically opposite conditions. For tactical considerations usually demanded the siting of a city on the top of a hill or mountain, whereas the sources of water—springs, streams, or rivers—were most often to be found in the valley. To resolve this objective contradiction of nature, fortifications had to be planned so as to encompass at least part of the sources of water; or else some suitable system had to be devised for ensuring that water flowed into the city.

Additional security considerations, particularly in lands ruled by powerful central authority, dictated the establishment of cities at sites which were of country-wide or even regional strategic importance, in order to protect main lines of communications, highways, routes to supply bases, or distant sources of water.

The nearest approach to complementary natural conditions to satisfy both security and economic needs was to be found only at specific places. Since their topography remained virtually unchanged throughout the periods under review, it is not strange for us to find a general continuity of settlement at each site, with a new city built on the ruins of the old.

This process, which led to the creation of the celebrated "tell," or mound, of the Middle East, created in time its own special problems of defense. At first, it gave the new city an advantage. For its new construction raised it above the level of its predecessor, and gave it a commanding defense position over the surrounding country. But later, as the tell got higher and higher, after hundreds or thousands of years of settlement, it produced two great disadvantages. The higher the tell, the softer its slopes. For now they were not of rock but simply the sides of a huge heap made up of the crumbled ruins of dead cities. They were easier now to penetrate by anyone seeking to undermine the foundations of the wall at the top. This problem was to exercise the minds of planners of fortifications in the later periods. Moreover, the higher the tell, the smaller the area of the city built on its crown. This in turn led to a more reduced population, with a corresponding reduction in the number of fighters to defend it. In time, these two defense disadvantages often prompted the inhabitants to make one of two far-reaching decisions: either to build an "extension" of the city at a lower level, or to abandon the site altogether. Where it was decided to build an extension, it meant the virtual construction of a new lower city on level ground. This required an artificial system of defense in place of the natural topographical defense advantages enjoyed by the original city on the tell. These are the major premises in any analysis of the defense problems of fortified cities. They made their impact on the character of the city. More important, they determined its size in most of the Biblical lands. In the earliest periods, the average area of most cities in Palestine, Syria, Anatolia, and Mesopotamia ranged from 5 to 10 acres. There were also, of course, a number of principal cities covering an area of hundreds of acres. On the reasonable assumption that there were roughly 240 inhabitants to an urban acre, the population figures of most of the cities of the ancient Middle East ranged from 1,000 to 3,000, with some cities boasting a population of between 5,000 and 10,000. There were a few exceptions where the population reached scores of thousands. The proportion of fighters among the inhabitants averaged 25 per cent. So that the small cities had about 300 fighting men, the medium-sized cities about 1,000 to 2,000, and the large cities several thousand.

In the organization of the defense of these ancient cities, there was a concentration of three major elements: the walls and subsidiary fortifications; the inner citadel; and the supply of water.

The City Walls

The primary purpose of the city walls was to prevent the enemy from breaking into the city, to deny him, that is, his advantage of mobility. But a passive barrier could only hold him up temporarily. For, as we have observed, the walls could be scaled or breached. They had therefore to be so built as to enable the defenders to fire their weapons from the top, and so frustrate the enemy design.

The wall and its fortifications comprised three principal components: the wall itself—the barrier; its upper structures, to enable the defenders to fire their weapons and to give them protection while doing so—the firing platform and defensive

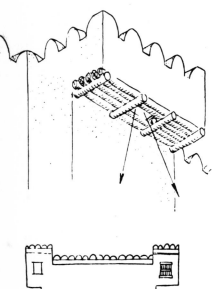

An Egyptian representation of an Asiatic city (top) and a reconstruction of crenelation and balcony

cover; forward obstacles and traps, set up in front of the wall to keep the enemy archers as far away as possible and to prevent battering-rams from being brought into action. The city gate posed a special problem. For by its nature it was the weakest point in the system of fortifications.

To make scaling difficult, the wall had to be high. To prevent breaching, it had to be thick. And to withstand undermining or tunneling below it, its foundations needed to be deep and broadly based. A wall which is both high and thick, whether built of stone or brick, or a combination of the two (bricks upon a base of stones), requires additional strengthening by a series of regularly spaced buttresses of considerable thickness.

The defenders on the ramparts had to be free to fire on the enemy in three directions: forward, to direct frontal fire on the approaching attackers; right and left, to bring flanking fire to bear on the enemy; downward against troops attempting to bring up ladders and battering-rams. The top of the walls had therefore to be wide enough to give sufficient freedom of movement to the defenders, and to be so designed as to offer them fields of fire in the required directions while at the same time giving them protection from enemy arrows.

The architectural solution to meet these needs was the battlement. This was a crenelated parapet built along the top of the walls facing the enemy. It looked from a distance like a row of teeth with gaps between them. The teeth are known as caps or merlons. The gaps are called embrasures or crenels. The defending soldier would fire his weapon through the embrasure and find protection from enemy missiles by dodging behind the merlon. Special towers or bastions built as an integral part of the wall at regular intervals, and protruding from its outer face, enabled the defenders to direct flanking fire on enemy troops. The distance between the towers was never more than double the range of the defenders' bows, and often less. In this way, fire from any two towers could cover the ground between them. An inferior alternative was to give a stepped line to the wall itself, but this was not as effective as the tower or bastion. The shape of the tower was square or semicircular. The latter was technically more difficult to build, but it had the advantage of commanding a wider field of fire and eliminating "dead" areas.

To enable the defenders to deal with troops who had managed to reach the wall, the towers were built with balconies which had holes or slots in the floor through which vertical fire could be directed down upon the heads of the enemy. Sometimes the fortifications were so built that the dead ground at the foot of the vertical wall was wiped out completely. This was done by filling it in with an embankment. This is called a glacis, a bank sloping down from a certain point in the wall and broadening its base. It exposed the attackers to the defenders' fire and made it difficult for them to breach the lower part of the wall by battering-ram.

The security of the wall itself was effected in one or both of two ways. One was the construction of an outer or advance wall. This was particularly necessary where the main wall was at the top of a high hill or tell. The outer wall was then lower than the main wall but within range of its weapons, so that, when attacked, it could be covered by the fire of the main defending units. An alternative to the outer wall was an obstacle of the reverse kind—the digging of a wide and deep moat running round the base of the main wall. This had the advantage, especially when filled with water, of denying to the enemy the use of his battering-ram unless he was powerful and skilled enough to bridge the moat or fill it up at certain points—all under fire. The ideal security for the main wall was a combination of glacis, moat, and outer wall.

The gate was inevitably the weakest point in the system of fortifications. It was, indeed, a gap in the wall, deliberately left in order to allow entrance into the city of inhabitants and friends. It was natural that the attacker should also seek to gain entrance through this gap. And so the gate was always the focus of action in battle, receiving the concentrated attention of both attackers and defenders.

The Gate

It was also the central problem engaging the minds of those who planned the fortifications. And the most imaginative ingenuity and the finest engineering talent were mobilized over a long period to design a city gate which would give maximum trouble to an attacking army and maximum help to its defenders. The result was a series of devices, each serving a limited purpose but together providing a formidable defense complex.

Primary attention was given to the planning of the approach path to the gate. The gate, like the wall of which it was a part, was usually situated high up on a hill or tell. To reach it from the bottom, a path had to be laid in gentle gradients, climbing the slope obliquely either from the right or left. For a direct road would be far too steep even for the defenders themselves, whether in chariots or wagons or on foot. Wherever possible the approach road was planned so as to reach the gate from the right—from the point of view of those facing the gate from the outside, or left from the point of view of the defenders. This produced the first difficulty for the attacker. For it meant his having to move up the incline with the right side of his body nearest to the wall. Since he carried his shield in his left hand, he was exposed to the fire of the defenders without cover.

This principle in planning was followed with even greater effectiveness where the fortification system included a lower outer wall. This wall, too, would have a gate. And it was sited to the right of the gate in the main wall (from the point of view of one facing the main wall). The two gates were usually linked by a broad wall. So, again, if the attacker succeeded in gaining entrance through the gate of the outer wall, he would have to approach the main gate with the right side of his body exposed to the defenders' weapons.

The second and principal barrier to an attacking force were the doors of the

Defenders of a fort operating from behind the crenelated parapet, and from balconies. Beni-hasan, c. 1900 B.C.
See pages 158–159

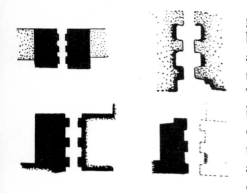

Types of City Gates.
Above: Middle Bronze gates from
Syria and Palestine
Below: Late Bronze and
Iron Age gates from
Anatolia, Syria, and Mesopotamia

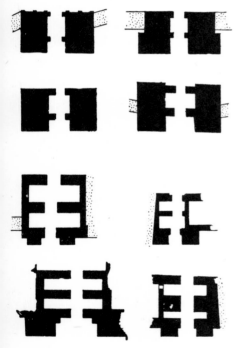

gate. These were made of wood and usually plated with metal to prevent their being set on fire by enemy torches. Since the entrance had to be wide enough to allow the passage of chariots, double doors were required. This meant, however, that the barrier was weakest at its center, along the line where the two doors met. To strengthen it against an attempted enemy breakthrough, it was fitted with huge bolts. These usually took the form of a heavy beam which ran right across the back of the double doors, and was held in position by sockets in both doorposts. One of these sockets was a very deep recess into which the beam would be moved to allow the doors to be opened. The other socket was just deep enough to hold the other end of the beam after the doors were closed.

The third element in the defense complex of the gate was devised to meet a situation in which the enemy had succeeded in penetrating the outer defenses and had come near enough to try and smash the doors and their hinges with his axes and firebrands. This called for some means—as with the wall itself—to enable the defenders to engage the enemy from above, both directly above and from the sides. It was met by building two towers, one on either side of the gate, which protruded from the outer surface of the wall and which enabled fire to be directed at the attackers from the sides. Direct fire from above was made possible by the construction of a roof above the gate, complete with crenelations and balcony. These auxiliary structures virtually turned the gate complex into an almost independent fortress, with its battlements and often two or more stories.

The additional buildings also determined the form of construction of the gate itself. The roof above the gate and the additional stories required strong supports in and around the entranceway. These were provided by pilasters, rectangular columns engaged in the walls on either side of the entrance. The number of pilasters depended on the depth of the gate. Some had one pair of pilasters, some two, and some three. They naturally narrowed the entrance at the points where they were erected. Where there was more than one pair of pilasters, the spaces between them on each side were either left open, so as to give the defenders more room to engage the enemy who would be crowded in the narrower part of the entrance between the first two pilasters, or they were closed in to serve as guard-rooms for the sentries. The part of the gate giving out on to the inside of the city was of course much broader, allowing the defenders greater maneuverability in engaging the enemy emerging through the narrowed entranceway.

This type of gate structure was characteristic of fortified cities built on the top of a tell, and where the approach route followed an oblique incline up the slope compelling the assault troops to leave their right sides exposed. But in the very earliest cities, built on sites with no previous ruins to form a tell, neither wall nor gate was very much higher than the surrounding land. The problem here, of dictating the direction of the enemy approach to put him at a disadvantage, was partly solved by designing an angular gateway which could be traversed only by passing through a turning. The entrance of the gateway was so positioned that the approaching troops had to expose their right sides, and even when they succeeded in moving through the first opening, they found themselves in a turning of the gateway which cramped their freedom of action, while the defenders could operate under no such disability. But this type of gateway became fairly obsolete with the emergence of the chariot. For the entranceway had then to be wide enough to take the vehicles of the inhabitants in peacetime. In some cases, the type was retained but the entrance and turnings were made wider.

The Inner Citadel

The main weakness of the perimeter fortifications, even though they were formidable, was the magnitude of their circumference. Even a city of average size had a perimeter of some 700 meters, and in the big cities it was often several kilometers. Feinting or diversionary attacks by the enemy compelled the defenders to man every meter of the wall, while the assaulting army could concentrate its main striking force against one point alone. And once the wall at this point was breached, the rest of the wall served no further defense purpose, even though it might be intact and its guards unharmed. To meet this weakness of the outer fortifications, several additional defense systems were devised. The most common was the division of the city into several sections, each capable of independent defense, by the construction of an additional wall, an inner citadel, or both.

The citadel usually included the palace of the governor or the king and the dwelling-houses of his ministers, and sometimes also the temple. It was built on the

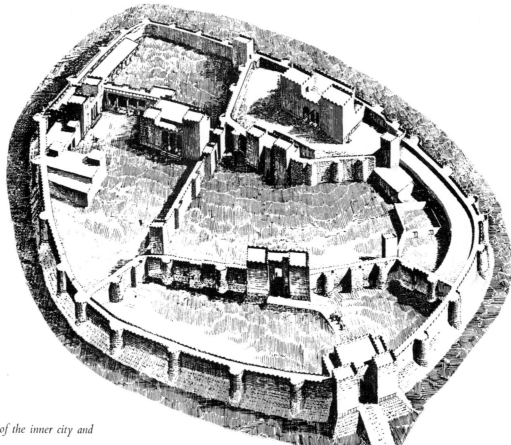

A reconstruction of the inner city and citadel of Zinjirli

23

highest part of the city to give it additional natural protection. It was constructed as a self-contained defensive unit, even though, on occasion, one or more of its sides was based on and contiguous to the city wall. The citadel was a replica of the fortified city, having its main wall, gateway, outer wall, and sometimes even a moat. It was small in area, and was usually the scene of the city's last stand, with the governor and the surviving inhabitants who had taken refuge therein fighting to the end. In the fight on the citadel, the defenders had an advantage in that the assault troops, to reach the fort, had to batter their way through the built-up area of the city, with its tortuous alleyways convenient for ambush. In the large cities, where the original city on the heights had been extended by the building of a fortified lower city at its foot, the original city became a kind of double inner citadel, serving as the inner citadel of the entire combined-cities area, and having its own inner fort which housed the governor.

Water Supply during Siege The various systems of fortifications had as their purpose the prevention of the enemy from breaking into the city. But the planning of the fortifications had also to take account of the need to keep both troops and civilians supplied with water even during a siege. It was comparatively easy to store food. But this was not true of water. A partial solution was the cistern. And this served for long periods as the sole solution. But it could not be the decisive answer, particularly in time of drought. It has already been observed that the siting of a city was largely determined by its proximity to sources of water. If the source was a stream, the city might be built on one of its banks, and this afforded easy access to the water supply in time of siege. The stream could also serve as part of the city's defense system. But the problem arose where the city was built on a hill or tell and was dependent for its water supply on a spring which, naturally, would be found nearer to the foot of the hill, and outside the city wall. The solution here was to block its mouth and camouflage it from the enemy, while safeguarding access to its source by the inhabitants of the city.

This could be, and was, done in one of two ways, and sometimes both: either by cutting a tunnel at a gradient from the spring or well through to a cistern inside the city into which the water would flow by gravity, and which would be reached by a pit equipped with a staircase; or by digging a pit inside the city, and, at its bottom, tunneling a passageway through to the outside near the spring, which could then be reached without detection by the besiegers. These were tunneling projects of considerable complexity. But, as we shall see later, we have evidence of extraordinarily advanced engineering knowledge and skills displayed by the people of antiquity in the construction of such tunnels. And, indeed, if it were not for such engineering feats, these cities would not have been able to hold out against lengthy siege.

Yet despite powerful fortifications and highly developed systems of defense, we know that many fortified cities were vanquished. This underlines the point that, in the final analysis, what counts is not the strength of the defenses nor the power of the assault weapons but the spirit of the man behind the wall and the man behind the battering-ram.

ARCHAEOLOGICAL SOURCES

The sole evidence in our possession which can help us to trace the pattern of life in ancient days are the *material* remains left behind by ancient peoples. Their thoughts, feelings, moods, and aspirations are lost to us forever unless they found expression in tangible relics, and we can only seek to recapture them by analogy and inference from the remains which have been brought to light. Archaeological discoveries are thus our main sources for an investigation of the art and methods of warfare in Biblical lands in ancient times.

Thanks to the revolutionary development of archaeological research in the Biblical lands in the last hundred years, and particularly in the last few decades, we now have a wealth of finds which shed light on most of the subjects dealt with in this book. Moreover, since, as we have observed, warfare played no less formidable a role in the lives of ancient peoples than it does in those of the nations of today, many of the material legacies laid bare by archaeological expeditions relate to war. For convenient study, this archaeological evidence will be discussed under three headings: illustrated monuments, both sculptured and drawn; ruins of fortifications and actual weapons found by excavation; written documents.

Illustrated Monuments

This group of relics is, in some ways, the most important for a study of ancient warfare. For on many of these monuments are graphic representations of military events which cannot be reconstructed by an examination of other relics nor given such tangible expression by literary description alone. They are of immense help to an understanding of several branches of warfare—tactics, weapons, and fortifications.

Of special value are the drawings and reliefs of military articles and weapons which were made of perishable materials, such as wood, leather, or textiles. Such materials defy preservation, except under special conditions, and rarely have they figured among the finds of the archaeologist. Our knowledge of them would be incomplete without the designs on ancient monuments. And even if, for example, a reasonably preserved part of a chariot is discovered, it will tell us nothing of how the horses were harnessed or how the chariot was used in battle. But the drawing on a monument may. The same is true of instruments fashioned from harder material which preserves longer. A few metal scales will tell us something about the coat of mail. But only through monuments do we know what the garment looked like and how it was worn. We would know almost nothing of the development of the bow through the different periods and in the different countries if it were not for its reproduction on monuments. The battering-ram, made of many parts, most of them perishable, would be a mystery to us today if we had no ancient picture showing the complete implement in action. And the same, of course, is true of fortifications. Most of the fortified walls were either destroyed or fell into ruin already in ancient times, with almost nothing left above their foundations. Yet it was precisely their upper portions, the towers, battlements, ramparts, and balconies, which were the vital functional features of the defense system. Only by their visual representation on monuments are we able to restore them in our minds and understand clearly their form, shape, character, and function.

The monuments also shed light on the principles of tactics and methods of warfare by presenting, albeit in isolated instances, the battle array of armies and the position of units on the battlefield. The graphic presentations of the Battle of Kadesh and the battle with the Philistines, and the Assyrian sculptured reliefs, are priceless sources, indeed the sole sources, of much of our knowledge of the art of ancient warfare.

Monuments have an additional importance, rarely found in other relics, in that they quite often bear the name of the person who ordered their erection. This provides us with a documentary description which can be dated with absolute certainty, and is of great chronological value.

But drawings and reliefs are not the font of all our knowledge. There is much that we know about ancient times which derives solely from other sources.

Finds at Excavations

It is only through the spade of the archaeologist which laid bare the foundations of fortifications in ancient cities of the Middle East that their plan and the methods of construction are known to us. Only by excavation do we see, for example, that they were built of brick or stone and sometimes of both. Such archaeological discovery also enables us to fill in the gaps in our information about fortifications of cities during specific periods which boast no illustrated monuments or whose monuments bear no illustration of a fortified city. The most enlightening example of the contribution of archaeology to our body of knowledge is the excavation which uncovered the earliest known system of fortifications in the world, in Jericho, which is the subject of a special chapter.

Similarly, it is only through archaeology that we have details of the various forms of the different weapons used in ancient days, and particularly of the materials of which they were made.

And, finally, it is only by scientific excavation that we have been able to establish the relative chronology of a particular site and follow consistently the changes it underwent throughout history. Since we can assume that the topography of the site remained constant, the changes in the planning of fortifications and the system of defense in cities at different times, as revealed in the different strata, are clearly reflections of the changes in the character of warfare, both in defense and attack.

It is important to remember, however, that archaeology is not yet so exact a science as to make possible the precise dating of every artifact. Often the best that can be done is to place the period of a weapon within a relatively wide range of dates.

Written Documents

The abundance of written material, apart from the Bible, which has been discovered in the last few decades, does much to complete our information on a number of military subjects which cannot be gleaned from either illustrated monuments or excavations. Such subjects include the names of weapons, types of soldiers and fortifications, structure and size of battle units, organization of armies, centers of arms production, systems of intelligence, and auxiliary services. We would certainly be ignorant of the dates and details of important campaigns of ancient days if it were not for written records.

Apart from the numerous inscriptions of monuments and such voluminous archives as the records of the Assyrian and Babylonian kings, we have been vastly enriched in recent years by the discovery, in particular, of five huge archives and collections of writings from ancient times. These are the texts of Boghazköy, capital of the Hittites; of Ugarit, in Syria, known also as the Ras Shamra texts; of Mari on the Euphrates, where more than 20,000 documents were found belonging to the end of the 18th century B.C., a period particularly poor in illustrated monuments; of Tell el-Amarna, in Egypt, whose archive from the first half of the 14th century B.C. includes the letters sent to the Egyptian Pharaoh by the kings of the various cities in Palestine, Syria, and the neighboring region, and which deal, in part, with military problems; and the large collection of texts from Nuzi, in Mesopotamia, dating mostly to the 15th century B.C.

Since the subject of this book is concerned primarily with monuments and archaeological discoveries, we shall have recourse to these ancient documents only for important information which cannot be gleaned from purely archaeological sources.

CHRONOLOGY AND TERMINOLOGY

Chronology is the skeleton of historical research. It would be impossible in our case to discuss the development of the art of warfare or the reciprocal effects of fortifications in one land upon the weapons of its neighbor, if we were unable to determine the dates of ancient relics. Each monument and archaeological artifact mentioned in this book will therefore be given its estimated period. But we must issue a word of warning to readers who may not be familiar with archaeological literature: the solution to the problem of absolute dating is not completely satisfactory for certain periods or for certain countries, and many given dates are no more than estimates. To make matters even more complicated for the non-professional historian or archaeologist, there is no uniformity in the names given to the various archaeological periods of the lands of the Bible with which we shall be dealing. This confusion of chronological terms stems from the special history of each land and also from the different approaches and methods used by different scholars. It may therefore be helpful to describe briefly the methods of dating and the nomenclature of the archaeological periods.

Relative Chronology

Relative chronology—that is, which of two sets of ruins is earlier—is easily determined. For the clues are contained in the special character of the tell, which was a feature of most ancient lands of the Middle East. In fact, there were tells formed by ruined village settlements even in prehistoric times. Since communities settled at sites which offered natural obstacles to an attacker and which were close to sources of water, the same sites were settled over and over again during successive periods in history. In most of these periods, the upper part of the houses were built of brick and mud. Their collapse into ruin, either as the result of enemy destruction of the city by fire, or through the ravages of time, left little more than a deposit of rubble covering the floor to a height of about one or two meters. When the city was rebuilt, either by returning original settlers who may have fled during an attack or by later settlers, they rarely removed the debris but simply leveled it and built their houses on top, having no need to construct new or deep foundations. And so the tell was born. The tell is thus simply an artificial mound, consisting of successive layers of ruined cities. It is this process which makes it easy to determine the relative chronology of ruins and artifacts: the lower the level, the earlier its history. The exceptions are, of course, wells, pits, or underground silos, which were dug at depth and whose level alone would be a misleading pointer as to date.

Absolute Chronology

Far more difficult is the determination of absolute chronology. And it must be done separately for each country.

The key for period-dating in all the Biblical lands is to be found in Egyptian archaeology, thanks to the special system on which the Egyptian calender is based and which was developed in the very earliest times. Egyptian monuments bear inscriptions of the dates and names of the kings who erected them. The lists of the pharaohs and dynasties are preserved in ancient Egyptian written documents. These two sources of illumination enable us to determine the absolute dates of the Egyptian kings within a specific range of time. (Excluded from this range is the very earliest period, at the beginning of the Dynastic line, on which scholars differ. The difference in their estimates is as much as 200 to 300 years.)

How does the absolute dating in Egypt help us to fix the dates in the other countries of the early Middle East? Well, from the dawn of recorded history, Egypt alternately traded and warred with all the Biblical lands. Egyptian artifacts are therefore often found in the strata of ruined cities in these lands. Since the date of the artifact is known, it provides the clue to the date of the stratum. On occasion, during an archaeological dig, an Egyptian sculpture or seal bearing the name of an Egyptian Pharaoh may have been found in one of the strata. The dates of the Pharaoh are known. And it was possible, therefore, to fix the absolute dates of the stratum, and consequently the dates of the strata below it and above it.

It also became possible to determine the dates of ruins of neighboring tells, and even of tells in neighboring countries. For with the absolute chronology fixed for each stratum, the other artifacts found therein became, in their turn, additional aids to date-fixing. By comparing them with artifacts found in ruined cities elsewhere, even when no Egyptian relics of absolute date were present, it was possible to give an absolute date to these cities.

Perhaps the best example of this is pottery. A minute examination of ancient pottery revealed that there were relatively rapid changes in the style, form, and shape of vessels from one period to another. Moreover, a particular type of vessel of a particular period found in one city was also found to be common to a large

28

group of cities within the same geographical or political frontiers. Once, therefore, this vessel was dated by reference to an artifact whose absolute date was known and which was found in the same stratum, the vessel itself became a key to date-determination. And wherever its type was found, it was possible to date the stratum accordingly. Furthermore, one of the results of commercial relations between the Biblical lands in ancient times was that the vessels of one would be found in the ruin-level of a tell in a neighboring country. The pottery of one land was thus of help in the dating of archaeological strata in another.

To a lesser degree, though on occasion they could be decisive, weapons also served as an index to the absolute chronology of ruins in neighboring lands. For the weapons of one country were indeed likely to be found among the ruins of a city in another country, taken there as war booty, or left behind on the battlefield, or presented as a votive offering to the local temple.

In the last few years, a completely new method of determining absolute chronology has been discovered which is of particular importance for dating prehistoric or very early periods where the Egyptian chronological system is of no help. This is known as the carbon-14 method, and its discovery is the practical exploitation of the following scientific reasoning. Atomic particles known as carbon 14 are to be found in all organic matter. Carbon 14 is radioactive, and when the organism dies, the particles begin to lose their radioactivity at a regular rate. With modern advance in nuclear science, it became possible to ascertain the degree of radioactivity of the live atom and its annual rate of loss after death. Thus by measuring the degree of radioactivity of the carbon 14 in an ancient organic relic like wood or bones, we arrive at the total amount of radioactivity lost. Dividing this figure by the figure of the regular annual loss gives a result which is the number of years that have passed since the death of the organism, providing, in other words, the absolute date of the relic.

The only drawback to this method is that it lacks split-second precision, and the results with ancient organic matter are always subject to an adjustment of plus or minus about 200 years. This is good for the absolute dating of prehistoric periods. But a range of inaccuracy of some 400 years is of little value to the study of the more advanced periods of history, periods which can be dated by the purely archaeological methods we have already described. There is, however, one section of our subject, dealt with in the next chapter, in which the carbon-14 test proved invaluable, making possible the absolute dating of the immensely important ancient fortifications of Jericho.

Archaeological Terms and Periods

The study of archaeological remains from countries so different from each other as Egypt, Palestine, Mesopotamia, and Anatolia is fraught with complications arising out of a non-uniform archaeological terminology for the different historic periods. Each scholar used his own special terminology in dating the periods of his discoveries in the country of his research, which was different from the terminology of his fellow-scholars operating in other countries. There is thus almost no all-embracing standard terminology covering all four countries. This makes especially difficult a comparative examination of artifacts found in these lands. For example, how are we to define the period of a Sumerian socket-type axehead, belonging to Early Dynastic times in Mesopotamia, which was discovered in a tell in Syria in a stratum belonging—in the Syrian-Palestinian terminology—to Early Bronze Age III? And what of an Egyptian sword from the period of the Egyptian New Kingdom, discovered in Palestine in a stratum belonging to Late Bronze II?

The basic division of history into the Stone, Bronze, and Iron Ages, to mark off the great epochs in the development of man, is not accepted in all countries and certainly not for those specific periods in history which could be named after emperors, kings, or dynasties. To complicate matters further, some countries use several different designations for the same period. And there is, in addition, the widespread practice of naming a period or a culture after the place where the signs of that culture were first discovered.

In our descriptions of the relics which are illustrated in this book, and in the reference to them in the text, we have followed the archaeological terminology used by the scholars of the particular land under consideration. But we have sought, at the same time, to indicate their absolute date whenever that was possible. In this way, the reader is enabled to compare them with relics of the same period in other countries.

In tracing the development of a particular weapon or system of fortifications, we have not always circumscribed ourselves rigidly within the artificial time frontiers of an accepted historic period—nor indeed did the people who lived at the time! On occasion, when we felt it would be helpful we have "encroached" on another period.

The broad archaeological periods cover the main phases in the development of the art of warfare. These periods, and their dates, are as follows:

Neolithic   8000 to 4000 B.C.
Chalcolithic
     transition period from the Stone Age to the Copper or
     Bronze period   from   4000 to 3200 B.C.
Early Bronze
     corresponding in Egypt, to the end of the Pre-Dynastic
     period, the Old Kingdom and the First Intermediate
     periods and, in Mesopotamia, to the Proto-Literate,
     Early Dynastic, and Accadian periods   3100 to 2100 B.C.
Middle Bronze
     The Patriarchal Age, including the Hyksos period   2100 to 1570 B.C.
Late Bronze
     In Syria and Palestine, corresponding to the period of the
     New Kingdom in Egypt; the Hittite Empire; and cover-
     ing the period of the Israelite Exodus from Egypt and
     conquest of the Land of Canaan by the Tribes of Israel   1570 to 1200 B.C.

This last date, 1200 B.C., marks a turning-point in the development of warfare in the lands of the Bible. These lands experienced a powerful military intervention by European elements, the "Sea Peoples" of the time, who left their imprint on, among other things, forms of warfare. The year 1200 B.C. also marks the end of the Bronze and the beginning of the Iron Age. The introduction of iron and its widespread use in the daily life of the people also had a far-reaching impact on various branches of warfare.

At a later phase of this period, all the lands of the Bible were faced with the rising and expanding power of the Assyrian Empire. The Assyrians left many monuments. And it is not surprising that war figures prominently as the subject of their illustrations. These monuments are indeed highly illuminating guides to the art of warfare of the period, and are particularly rich in detail. They enable us to follow the development of warfare during a series of brief, specific spans of time, depicting the patterns under each king with the monuments of his reign.

II

THE FORTIFICATIONS
OF JERICHO

7000 B.C.

The Most Ancient Fortifications in the World

Had this book been written in the year 1951, or even in 1955, it would have begun with a description of the artifacts and monuments belonging to the second half of the fourth millennium, 3500 to 3000 B.C. This would correspond to the end of the Pre-Dynastic period in Egypt, the beginning of the Proto-Literate period in Mesopotamia, and the end of the Chalcolithic period in Palestine and Syria.

But now, thanks to the amazing archaeological discoveries in Jericho in the last ten years, we can start with the earliest known fortifications in the world, dating back to about 7000 B.C., the beginning of the Neolithic period.

The discovery of these groups of ancient fortifications, whose standards of planning and construction almost match many of the powerful fortifications of later periods, despite the 4,000-year gap, also had the effect of changing all our previously held concepts about the beginnings of the urban settlement.

Before these discoveries, the term "the walls of Jericho" was automatically associated with the walls of the city, which, we are told in the Bible, fell mysteriously before the hosts of Joshua some time between 1300 and 1200 B.C. Now, however, certainly for archaeologists, the walls of Jericho are intimately bound up with the Neolithic fortifications built some 6,000 years before the time of Joshua. Unfortunately we cannot go into as much detail as we should like on these Neolithic structures, since this book is primarily concerned with relics from the later periods. But a brief account will be helpful to our understanding of later fortifications.

The tell of Jericho—Tell es-Sultan—lies in the Jordan Valley just north of the Dead Sea, close to a running spring which is popularly known as the Spring of Elisha. Whatever the reason for Jericho's ancient existence—it is the oldest known city in the world—one thing is clear. It was the spring which drew the earliest settlers and prompted them to build their city near by.

The Neolithic culture in Jericho prevailed for a long time and covered the transition from the Pre-Pottery culture to that of Pottery. It was thus possible to divide the Neolithic strata of Jericho into Pre-Pottery (which is the true Neolithic) and Pottery Neolithic (which might be called Ceramolithic). Moreover, the meticulous excavations by Kathleen Kenyon, who directed the expedition, enabled her to make accurate subdivisions of each of these two periods, which she called, provisionally, Pre-Pottery A, Pre-Pottery B, and Pottery A and Pottery B.

The first shock waves reached the scientific world with the preliminary discovery of Neolithic city fortifications dating back to the Pre-Pottery B period. The absolute date of this wall was determined by the carbon-14 test as 5859 B.C. (plus or minus 100 years), making it about 8,000 years old. Before this discovery, the earliest known fortified city, or indeed, any city, belonged to the period some 3,000 years later.

When it was laid bare, the Jericho wall still stood some $2\frac{1}{2}$ meters high and was built of large slabs of undressed stone. Its lower part also served to buttress structures inside the city. The full height of its external face, as seen by the enemy, is estimated to have been at least 5 meters.

The span of settlement during Pre-Pottery B was long. The archaeological excavations revealed twenty-six strata of building in some places during this period alone, strata, that is, which showed the raised floor built on the debris of earlier ruins. The wall itself was built some time corresponding to the thirteenth to fourteenth level of settlement. We still do not know enough about the character of the fortifications. But the very fact of their construction is evidence of an organized society, capable, either from desire or compulsion, of carrying through an impressive collective engineering project. And the need to build this fortified wall also indicates the presence of an organized neighboring society capable of launching a powerful assault.

The next shock wave to the world of archaeology was even more stunning. This came in 1954 when it was found that the previously discovered wall was neither the oldest nor the finest in the history of Jericho. Beneath it, at a considerably lower depth, a series of fortifications were discovered which were staggering in their power and the ingenuity of their planning.

The core of this fortifications system was the wall. Part of it, on the western edge of the tell was still standing, to a height of 7 meters! Moreover, it was possible to establish that this wall encompassed the entire city, which at that period extended over some 10 acres. Its population thus numbered between about 2,400 to 2,600 inhabitants, of which some 500 to 600 were fighting men. This means that it was possible to station about one soldier to every meter of fortifications.

This wall, too, was built of undressed stone, though the slabs were smaller than those in the later wall.

Even more surprising was the second discovery. The excavations revealed a large moat scooped out of the rock at the foot of the wall, 9 meters wide and 3 meters deep. How the inhabitants of ancient Jericho managed to cut this ditch out of the rock when the only tools they had were of flint is still a mystery. Equally mystifying is their need for a moat. What kind of powerful assault did

33

they dread from their neighbors that could demand the continuous application of a large labor force for a project that must have taken thousands, perhaps tens of thousands, of workdays?

The third surprise was the discovery of a building which shows the very high standards of planning and constructional engineering achieved by the inhabitants of Neolithic Jericho (115). This is a huge stone circular tower, 10 meters high, seemingly attached to the inner or city side of the western part of the wall. It is 13 meters in diameter at its base and 10 meters at its crown. Inside it was a hollow shaft containing twenty-two steps of dressed stone, each 75 centimeters wide. The bottom of the staircase led to a passage which ended in an opening at the foot of the tower. The steps gave access to the top of the tower. Was it to give the inhabitants a defensive position from which they could engage the enemy? This could not have been the tower's main purpose. Unlike the towers of later periods, this one did not abut against the outer side of the wall which would have enabled the defenders to harry the flanks of an attacking enemy. Instead, the entire building was inside the city, even though apparently attached to the wall. Could it have served as an observation post? Or was it built to defend some near-by installation for securing water or structure of special importance inside the city? One can only speculate, but there can be no definite answer without further excavations of the surrounding area.

The shaft inside the tower contained human skeletons, apparently flung there in a heap at some time, one on top of the other. These could not have been skeletons of city defenders who had made a last stand, for they were found on top of the debris by which the shaft was blocked and which filled it to a height some 60 centimeters from the top of the tower. They must certainly have been brought there long after the shaft had fallen into disuse. The purpose of the tower remains a riddle.

But there is no mystery about its chronology. The excavations established that there were at least three technical phases in the construction of the complex tower and fortifications. First came the tower. Then came a stone wall around the tower. And last came the outside wall. Also built during the first phase was an early compact wall slightly nearer to the center of the city than the later wall.

After the completion of the third phase, namely the construction of the out-side wall, several buildings were constructed inside the city and partly buttressed by the wall. The excavations revealed that the structures built during this third phase were destroyed by fire. The ashes were subjected to the carbon-14 test and the result was startling. It put the date of the fire at 6770 B.C., plus or minus 200 years. Since the main fortifications, as we have indicated, were built a consider-able time before the fire, the date of their construction can reasonably be presumed to have been about 7000 B.C.

Even with the necessary reservations with which the carbon-14 test must be accepted, it is clear in the light of both absolute and relative chronology that here were the earliest known attempts on the part of man to build a city and to fortify it with wall, tower, and moat.

The inhabitants of this city had certainly advanced beyond the stage where men just plucked their food from nature. They had started to work for their daily bread by some form of farming and by other means. Flint arrowheads found on the site show that they also used the bow. And the fortifications themselves, particularly the tower and the moat, indicate that the bow was the decisive weapon in warfare, out-ranging the javelin and the spear. But the character and pattern of attack and defense in this period was still beyond the scope of our knowledge. Nor do we have the answer to the enigma of what took place during the fantastic gap—a gap of 4,000 years—between these and the next most ancient systems of fortifications known to us.

We can only proceed, without lingering over this baffling hiatus, to a consideration of the art of warfare from the beginning of the historic periods, as revealed by illustrated monuments and archaeological remains.

III

THE PERIOD BEFORE
ABRAHAM

4000–2100 B.C.

During the second half of the fourth millennium, and more markedly during the third, the foundations were laid for the principles of warfare and the basic types of weapons and fortifications which prevailed during the succeeding 3,000 years—indeed, right up to the discovery of gunpowder in the 15th century A.D. This is clearly shown in the monuments and archaeological discoveries from the fourth and third millennia.

Apart from cavalry units, which appeared on the battlefield only at the end of the second and beginning of the first millennium, the means of mobility, attack, security, and defense all have their origin in the earlier period. Naturally many of them were developed and considerably improved in later ages. But they were all based on prototypes which had been introduced earlier. In some cases there was a marking-time, and even a retrogression, with the original standards remaining unmatched by the later armies who operated in the lands of the Bible.

Not that these lands can be lumped together in a generalization about military progress, especially during this period. Indeed, one of the strange features of this epoch is the vast difference in the standards of weapons and methods of warfare between the different lands of the Bible. At this time, for example, the forms of warfare among the Sumerians were highly advanced, whereas in Egypt they were very primitive. The most striking instance of this difference is the use of the chariot. Chariot units were being widely used in battle in Mesopotamia already in the first half of the third millennium. Not until 1,200 years later do we find the battle chariot first being used in Egypt.

It may be appropriate, therefore, to start our review of this period with the chariot. Its invention and development were without doubt the most significant contributions to the art of warfare in the third millennium, thanks, as we have observed, to the inhabitants of Mesopotamia at that time.

MOBILITY

The first half of the third millennium in Mesopotamia, which saw the introduction of the battle chariot, is also known as the Early Dynastic period. The military impact of the chariot was revolutionary. Its appearance cannot be associated with any special city or king. It was in general use, as a basic instrument of war, throughout Mesopotamia at this time.

Before describing its form and the illustrations which appear on ancient monuments, it is worth noting that in one of the comparative dictionaries of the Sumerian and Accadian languages, there is a comprehensive list of terms relating to the chariot which almost certainly were in use in this period. In this dictionary, about a hundred terms are preserved which are concerned with types of chariots, materials of which they were made, chariot parts, whips, and so on. There are terms for chariots made of reeds, for those strengthened with metal, and for the leather covering. Chariot parts listed in the dictionary include the platform, body, dust-shield, front, tail, pole, yoke, axle, and wheels. This detailed terminology indicates both that the manufacture of chariots was well developed and that a wide range of types was in use, for battle, racing, and transport. The abundance of terms and the large number of chariot illustrations on ancient monuments make it possible, with pleasing frequency, to identify the parts with accuracy.

The legacy of illustrated monuments which feature the chariot is rich and varied. It includes drawings of chariots (128); reliefs (130, 134); mosaics (132–133, 138–139); and models (129, 130, 131, 132). Archaeological excavations have also brought to light parts of chariots, notably wheels and metal portions of the body (131). Here is what the archaeologist who excavated at Kish had to say about the chariot parts he found in tombs belonging to the Early Dynastic period (see accompanying drawing).

"Three of the tombs contained chariots. Two two-wheeled chariots, or possibly one two-wheeled and one four-wheeled . . . only . . . (one) specimen . . . could be studied in detail. . . . Towards the front on each side of the pole there were two pairs of skeletons of equines with their leather harnesses. . . . The platform of the chariot was made of wood, 45 cms. wide, terminating at the rear in a second small platform surrounded under the back end by a copper band. On each side of the platform attached to the tail stood stout spokes attached to an arc band to protect the load of the vehicle from rubbing against the wheels. I am unable to give the length of the platform, since it was totally decayed in front. The wheels fitted on to the ends of the axles have a diameter of 50 cms. The axles are 90 cms. long and have a diameter of 8 cms. The wheels were kept in position by wooden pegs and are made of irregular pieces of boards held together by transverse boards attached to them by wooden pegs.

". . . The copper nails of the felloes are 4 cms. long and 2 cms. thick at the head. They are driven into the wood obliquely and there are about 55 on the circumference, 1·52 meters in length. . . ."

The Chariot

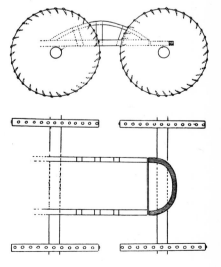

A drawing of a four-wheeled chariot from Kish, described on this page

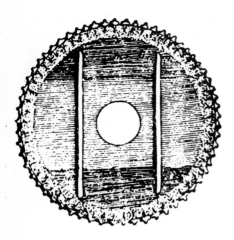

A solid wheel with nails of a chariot from Susa

This quotation underlines the point that information on the nature of the materials and the detailed measurements of the parts of a chariot can be gained only by an examination of its physical remains. We can now proceed to a review of what we know of the chariot from illustrated monuments which are enlightening on many additional details upon which the remains themselves are inevitably silent.

There were two basic types of battle chariots—two-wheelers and four-wheelers. This we know not only from the above archaeological discoveries but also from ancient models and monuments. The battle chariot which appears in the Standard of Ur (132–133) is a four-wheeled vehicle, capable of carrying two soldiers, the fighting man and his driver. A similar chariot appears in the design on the vase from Khafajah (128). The lighter, two-wheeled chariot is the subject of ancient models (129, 130), and part of a relief on a limestone plaque from Ur (130). These light chariots also served, without doubt, on the battlefield, and were probably used chiefly for command errands and communications.

The chariots were usually harnessed to four draft animals. These were apparently not horses but wild asses or onagers or some other animal close to the horse breed. The fact that four such animals were required suggests that they were not very robust, that the chariot itself must have been relatively heavy, and that its traction system was not very advanced, so that the haulage power of the beasts was not fully exploited.

On the two-wheeled chariots, they had not yet succeeded in placing the axle at the rear of the carriage. This was no doubt due to the weight of the chariot, for a rear axle would have put too heavy a load on the animals. But this certainly meant that these vehicles could not maneuver at speed on turns. However, the danger of overturning on a sharp curve was considerably reduced by linking the wheels to a long axle-rod so that they were well clear of the sides of the body. The length of the axle-rod was double the width of the carriage platform, 90 centimeters to its 45. The wheels themselves were all, without exception, heavy, solid, and spokeless, and were no doubt liable to break when the chariot took a curve at speed.

To give them greater strength, these solid wheels were usually made not of a single wooden plank but of several boards, either straight (129), fitted side by side with simply the edges curved to take the line of the wheel, or crescent-shaped (130). The join of these boards with wooden pegs is characteristic of every representation of these chariots in the monuments of the period. The rims or "tires" of the wheels were mostly secured by nails (128–129) which appear to have covered some two-thirds of the surface of the tire. From the remains found at Kish, we see that there were fifty nails, each with a 2-centimeter broad head, covering a rim whose circumference was $1\frac{1}{2}$ meters. These nails served not only to strengthen the wheel but also to give greater stability to the chariot by acting as studs which gripped the earth. On occasion, instead of nails, the wheel was fitted with a broader rim to protect the wood on rough ground (130, 132–133). The front of the chariot was shielded by a high upright panel which gave protection to the soldiers from frontal missiles.

This shows that these chariots were used mainly for direct assault on the enemy, and not for movement at medium ranges along the flanks. Moreover, as we shall see later, the fighting men in these chariots were armed with the javelin and spear and not with the bow, which indicates that the security they required was against weapons of similar medium and short ranges.

The reins, from the animals' heads to the hands of the charioteer, passed through two special rein guides. The rein guides were generally two hoops or rings, one for the right and one for the left group of reins (131, 132–133). They were fitted to the chariot pole, which was either curved or straight, close to the yoke. This system prevented entanglement of the reins and also no doubt enabled the single charioteer to release them or tie them to the breast of the chariot (135) when he needed both hands to operate his weapon.

The carriage of the chariot was usually made of a frame of wooden poles or canes covered with panels of wood or leather. At the rear of the heavy chariot was an additional small platform, a kind of extension to the main platform, which gave more room for the fighting man and enabled him to operate more freely without jostling the driver. The main platform alone, just 45 centimeters wide, would not have been enough to hold both driver and fighter standing side by side.

The four-wheeled chariot offered more space for its two passengers. But its nature certainly gave it a reduced speed and maneuverability over those of the two-wheeled vehicle.

The weapons carried by the chariot were in the main a spear and a quiverful of javelins (132–133, 135) and occasionally an axe. The absence of the bow from the armament of the Sumerian charioteer or even from that of the infantryman is more instructive. For the bow, in the latest periods, was most definitely the weapon of the chariot. This indicates that the bow, the only accurate long-range weapon, was not yet in wide use during this period. It shows, too, that the primary function of the Sumerian chariot was to charge and panic the enemy and engage him at medium range with the help of the javelins, and then at short range with the spear.

With all its shortcomings, the Mesopotamian chariot was assuredly a formidable and decisive instrument of warfare in this region. And it was used continuously in its basic original form throughout the whole of the third millennium (131). Only in the first half of the second millennium did it undergo a revolutionary development which turned it into an effective mobile firing platform. This change came with the mastery of the two basic problems of mobility and firepower. Effective mobility was achieved with the discovery of the light, spoked wheel and the means of making a light body, which made possible the shifting of the axle to the rear, to give it maneuverability. It was aided by the use of fast horses in place of the former onagers. Strengthened firepower was provided by the

A drawing of the model from Tell Agrab. Cf. page 129

39

composite bow. Strangely enough, the spear continued to be included, as a kind of third-millennium hangover, among the weapons of the charioteer in Mesopotamia and neighboring lands even in the later periods, long after the bow had become the principal armament of the chariot. As against this, the spear was never one of the weapons of the charioteer in Egypt, where the chariot made its appearance only very much later.

WEAPONS SHORT-RANGE *and Hand-to-hand Fighting*

The Mace

It is perhaps natural that among the most important weapons used in hand-to-hand fighting during Chalcolithic and the first half of the Early Bronze periods (3500 to 2500 B.C.), pride of place should have been taken by the mace. And indeed the mace in its various forms was a weapon of much striking power in wide use during this period in all lands of the Bible, notably in those places and at those times where the helmet had not yet made its appearance. Long after it had become obsolete as a battle weapon, the mace continued to serve as the symbol of authority of the king and the god. Some of the most interesting specimens of ancient mace-heads are to be found in the Chalcolithic collection discovered a few years ago in the excavations near Beer-sheba. Even more spectacular are the magnificent variety brought to light by the Israel archaeological expedition to the caves of the Wilderness of Judea, near Ein Gedi, in the spring of 1961. Many of them are made of a hard, heavy stone, like hematite, similar to maceheads found at other sites from the same period. (Hematite is a blood-colored stone containing iron oxide.) But there were also many made of copper (like those from Beer-sheba, 120). Now in this period, copper was just becoming known. The fact that maceheads were molded from copper is explicable only in terms of the high importance of this weapon, so much so that neither resources nor efforts were spared to strengthen its striking power.

These maceheads, as in other countries, were of the socket type, the hilt being inserted into the head and tightened by strips of cord.

In Egypt, too, the mace was in wide service. At the beginning of the Pre-Dynastic period, a rather strange type of macehead was found, shaped like a disk and slightly concave (120). This type gradually disappeared, as did many other weapons which were designed to fulfil two different functions and ended up by fulfilling neither. It is clear that the designers of the disk-shaped (or saucer-like) macehead sought to make it also a cutting instrument by giving it a sharp edge, but this necessarily reduced its smiting power. Eventually they realized that the two aims could not be achieved through a single instrument, and apart from isolated experiments here and there, they settled on the mace for striking and the axe for piercing and cutting. And so, beginning with the latter part of the Pre-Dynastic and continuing through the early part of the Old Kingdom, the mace-heads were either pear-shaped or round (124–125). These maces were found in excavation relics and are depicted in the monuments of the period. Two of the

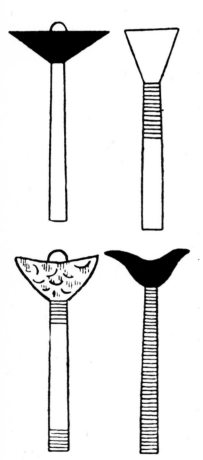

Pre-Dynastic Egyptian saucer-shaped maceheads

most important monuments from the end of the Pre-Dynastic period present with graphic clarity the mace in the act of operation both in hand-to-hand fighting (116) and in hunting (119, top). This weapon was so characteristic of the time that it even became the symbol of the pharaoh's might. The ceremonial macehead of King Scorpion (120), just before the Dynastic period, is one of the most interesting art objects of ancient Egypt. And at the beginning of the Dynastic period, the pharaohs are shown smiting their enemies with a mace (10–11). These monuments also show us the shape of the hilt, which was tapered toward the head and broadened at the base to prevent the weapon from flying out of the hand when swung. A further device to prevent the handle from slipping was to bind it with a rough cord (124).

In Mesopotamia, too, we find the mace in wide use during the Chalcolithic, Proto-Literate, and Early Dynastic periods. At first it was egg-shaped, then pear-shaped, and finally it was fluted (120). This last type, which was also found in Syria, succeeded in some measure in giving the mace a cutting function with the sharp edges between the grooves, without reducing its power to stun. Two handsome ceremonial maceheads, encrusted with precious stones and gold, dating back to 2500 B.C., are illustrated on page 142.

The mace, then, was an effective weapon so long as the enemy was not armored and his head, in particular, was unhelmeted. But as soon as he appeared on the battlefield with these means of security, another weapon had to be invented which could be swung with force and which had the power to penetrate. This was the axe.

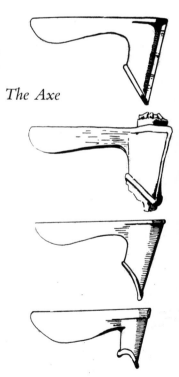

The Axe

No weapon seems to have taxed the inventiveness of armies and technicians more heavily than the axe. And none is so integral to the various traditions which mark the character of these armies. The period which best reflects the ingenuity of the military artificer is the third millennium. This period saw the emergence of every type and prototype of axe which was in use in all subsequent periods right up to the end of the Iron Age. Apart from the early experiments in all lands of the Bible with the primitive stone axes, both single- and double-bladed (118, bottom right-hand corner), the two main families of axe referred to in the Introduction, the tang type and the socket type, already appear in the first half of the third millennium. In this period, too, we also find two distinct functional forms of axe —the axe for piercing and the axe for cutting.

It is no exaggeration to claim that one of the most remarkable technical achievements of the Sumerians was their use of an axe with a pipe-like socket, its blade narrow, long, and very sharp-edged. In this, they exploited to the maximum the already existing prototypes of such axes, as was recently shown by the dramatic discovery of a great number of copper axes in a cave in the Judean Desert, in the Dead Sea in Israel (see pages 126–127). The appearance of this type of piercing axe precisely among the Sumerians and the Early Dynastic period is no accident. For it is at this time and in this land that we find our first evidence of a high-standard metal helmet (see page 49). Such helmets could be rendered ineffective only by a piercing axe which could be swung with force, by an axe, that is, whose

Types of Early Dynastic Sumerian socket axes

41

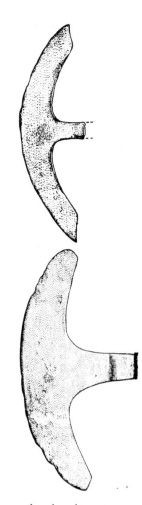

Two epsilon-shaped tang-type axes from Palestine (Early Bronze III, 26th–23rd century B.C.). Upper: Jericho. Lower: Tell el-Hesi

handle was very firmly attached to the blade. The Sumerian axeblade (134, 136, 137, 139) was made of copper. It was long and narrow, getting slightly wider and rounder near the edge. Its socket was rather like a pipe, and set at an acute angle, so that the handle, which fitted into it, sloped forward. To give a better grip and prevent its slipping out of the hand, the handle was slightly curved toward the bottom, where it was also thickened (137). The axe was the personal weapon of the spear-carrying infantry (bottom of 134, top of 132) and of the charioteers (bottom of 135, bottom of 132).

From the illustrated monuments and from the axeheads themselves which archaeologists have brought to light, we are now familiar with their detailed characteristics and their methods of use. The Sumerian axe continued to be used right into the Accadian period, particularly in Syria at the end of the third millennium, as we can see from the magnificent collection of axes discovered in the celebrated tomb of Til Barsip (148). It underwent improvements from time to time. There was the later addition of a small blade or a lub (in the form of an animal head) at the rear of the socket, which was accordingly shortened. And of particular interest were the changes in the shape of the blade which made it a more effective piercing instrument. On occasion, the blade was much narrower and tapered toward the edge, giving it almost the form of a large peg (top left of 148). This type, together with the beautiful axe of Naram-Sin—a long, narrow-bladed weapon and a socket no longer in the form of a pipe—are the prototype of many of the axes which appear in the Middle Bronze period, which we shall discuss later.

Another type of piercing axe in use at the time was the axe of Anatolia. This could almost be called a double-bladed weapon. Its main blade, long and narrow, was similar to the Sumerian blade. On the other side of the socket was a smaller blade whose primary function was to add weight to the swing and to increase thereby the penetration power of the first blade. Some excellent examples of ceremonial axes of this very type, made of precious stones and metals, were discovered in Troy at the end of the last century by the celebrated archaeologist Schliemann in a stratum belonging to the middle of the third millennium. More recently, a similar collection was found in the royal tombs at Dorak, not far from the southern coast of the Sea of Marmara, and they are even finer and richer than the Trojan axes. They can be more precisely dated because of the name of Pharaoh Sahure which appears on some of the objects found in the same tombs. This then in the first half of the 25th century B.C. Drawings of these axes are to be found on page 143.

The socket-type piercing axe spread from Mesopotamia to several lands of the Bible, but did not reach Egypt. Egyptian armies always made do with the tang-type axe, primarily a cutting instrument, even during much later periods when they, too, had started using the piercing axe. But the tang-type cutting axe, notably the triple-tang epsilon form, also made its first appearance not in Egypt but in Mesopotamia, Syria, and Palestine. This axe, as we have observed, was strange to the conditions of warfare in Sumer. Yet we have several examples from that region and during the period under review, particularly during the succeeding

Accadian period. Thus we find a tang-type cutting axe in the hand of a soldier on a monument of the period (151). This, in fact, is similar in character to the curved or sickle sword which, as we shall see, also had its origin in this period. This axe, however, was not in wide use in this region, and its birthplace was probably Syria and Palestine. The best example of this kind of curved axe with a well-made central tang was found at Tell el-Hesi in Palestine (149). It was found at a time when the methods of archaeological excavation were not as developed as they are today, and it was not possible therefore to date it definitely within the third millennium. But recently an identical type was found in Jericho, together with pottery which was established as belonging to the Early Bronze III period (2600 to 2300 B.C.). This shows that the Palestinian relics were at least of the same period as the Mesopotamian, or even earlier. Additional examples of these axes from the second half of the third millennium were discovered in Syria and southern Anatolia (see also 150, right), and from there the type spread to Egypt at the end of the third and beginning of the second millennium (154, 155).

It is worth recording that already in the Accadian period we find efforts to strengthen the attachment of handle to blade in the epsilon type by adding to the central tang a vertical bar parallel to the handle. This weapon, prototype of the socketed "eye axe" which appears in the beginning of the Middle Bronze period, is commonly known, because of its shape, as the "anchor axe."

Egypt

We have seen that, throughout Egyptian history, the socket-type axe was never brought into use. This is explicable by the fact that, as we shall show, the Egyptian axes in the third millennium were always wide-edged cutting weapons, and it was clearly difficult to fit such blades with a long socket. Moreover, it was comparatively easy to attach the handle to the blade by means of a tang or by cords run through holes in the rear of the blade. But this explanation does not meet the point that when the first piercing axe was introduced into Egypt in a much later period, even then it was socketless. Perhaps the reason is to be found in the conservatism of the ancient Egyptians, which is also noticeable in other fields, and in their laggardly absorption of new methods of warfare. But it may be also that throughout the third millennium, Egypt had no need for a piercing axe. For no evidence has been found of the use in Egypt or in its immediate neighborhood, during the third millennium, of the helmet or coat of mail, against which a piercing weapon would have been needed.

The cutting axe was an efficient weapon and was the standard type of axe used in Egypt throughout the third millennium. We finds signs of early experiments to produce a hybrid weapon by fitting a metal blade to a macehead, but they failed. In the first half of the third millennium, the axeblades were mostly semicircular and often were fitted with lugs at the rear, on either side, to enable the handle to be bound more firmly. But starting from about 2500 B.C. we find the gradual introduction of the narrow blade, shaped like a slice of an orange. This was attached to a wooden handle by cords which were drawn through holes in its neck and fastened securely round lugs on either side.

43

The siege and battle scene depicted on limestone in the tomb of Anta, at Deshashe in Upper Egypt (146), is most instructive on the functioning of the axe in battle. It shows very clearly the shape of the "slice axe" used by Egyptian soldiers and it also shows how it was used: it was swung with both hands and brought smartly down to deliver a sharp blow. In a scene from the wall painting at Saqqarah, the semicircular bladed axe is well depicted. Here it was used mainly for tearing down the wall of a besieged city (147).

The illustration of a triple-tang crescent, or epsilon, axe in the hands of a warrior, discovered on a fragment of a stone jar, and attributed to the end of the Pre-Dynastic period, is an anomaly. Even in Mesopotamia and Palestine, it appears in a slightly later period, and in Egypt itself not before the end of the third millennium. For the moment, we must reserve judgment, for neither its origin nor the method of its discovery is yet sufficiently clear.

The Sword Unlike the mace and axe, whose compatatively small operative head or blade could be easily attached to a long wooden handle, the sword could be fashioned only after a mastery of the art of producing hard metals. For a long and tough blade which would not break or bend on impact could be made from hard metal alone. This technical limitation, together with the existence of the mace and the piercing and cutting axe, explain the time-lag behind the appearance of the sword as a decisive weapon of warfare in the third millennium.

When they did appear during this period, the swords were usually straight, double-edged, sharp, and very short, more like daggers designed mainly for stabbing (144–145). Since they were not made of hard metal, there was the constant fear that they would break or be blunted by a heavy blow. This, however, was partly overcome by thickening the center of the blade throughout its length, giving it a protuberant spine (140, 141). The hilt was not an extension of the blade but was usually made of some other material, either wood or bone, secured to the blade by nails. This attachment would have been ineffective with a weapon that needed to be swung downward, putting too great a pressure on the join, but served this kind of sword, whose function was stabbing, so that hilt and blade followed the same line of movement (145).

The swords shown on pages 140–145 are the most splendid and typical specimens ever found in Mesopotamia, Anatolia, and Palestine. The pommel was ball-shaped or carved into an animal head, or, as we found among the swords in Ur (140, 141) and Alaca Hüyük in Anatolia, crescent-shaped. A sword with a crescent-pommeled hilt would certainly not be used for anything more than stabbing. It is worth recording that among this large collection are two swords made of iron! Not unnaturally, they are from Anatolia. For it was from here that the knowledge of iron spread to other lands of the Bible some 1,200 years later. Also of interest is the fact that the earliest object made of iron was the sword. And for hundreds of years there were exhaustive experiments with hard metals to fashion blades that would be longer and tougher. The iron sword of Dorak (145, left), for example, was very long, 75 centimeters. But on the whole, these swords of iron are exceptional among the finds of the Bronze Age in general and the third millennium in particular, and were discovered again only at the end of the Bronze Age, in the 14th century.

In the second half of the third millennium, the earliest types of the sickle sword make their début. These were the curved swords used for striking. They are clearly depicted on relics from the Accadian period and they are perhaps the weapons shown on some of the monuments from the Sumerian period. This conclusion is based on the identification of the object held by the warrior at the left of the relief from Telloh (136), in the right hand of King Eannatum (135, lower register), and by the soldier from Mari (137). There is a school of thought which holds that these objects are not swords but hurling-clubs, like boomerangs. It is not easy to be definite on the point. But I incline to the view that all three are in fact sickle swords. The curved sword made its appearance at the same time as the crescented cutting axe, and in many ways they may both be regarded as seeking to achieve the same aim. But while the axe comprised two components—the handle and the blade—with the concomitant problem of securing them firmly together, the sickle sword was an attempt to solve it by fashioning both hilt and blade from the same bar of metal. The serious development of this weapon began at the beginning of the Middle Bronze Age, and we shall therefore be considering it in a later chapter.

The most ancient monuments in our possession, belonging to the end of the fourth millennium, show that the spear, of good technical standard, was already in wide use at that time. It had a long staff tipped with a leaf-shaped blade which had a protuberant spine. This was the weapon of the warrior-hunter as depicted on the Egyptian Hunters' Slate Palette (118 and 119, top) and on the black granite stele from Warka (118). It was in common use throughout the whole of the third millennium, and of all the weapons of this period, it was the most effective for both chariot and infantry charges. It was the basic weapon of the Sumerian (132–133, 134). The Sumerian phalanx (see pages 49–50) was also basically equipped with the long spear, which was shoulder-sloped on the march (134, bottom) and carried horizontally during the assault (132–133, 134–135, top). Indeed its importance here may be gauged by the fact that a literal description of the illustrations on Sumerian monuments would read like an account of the role of the spear in the classic phalanx.

Not all the spearheads during the third millennium were leaf-shaped. Interesting examples of another kind are the three spearheads discovered at Tell el-Hesi in Palestine—together with a crescent axe—one of which is shown on page 149. The blade is long, spined, and triangular, and has two barbs at its base, to the right and left. The length of the blade, 22 centimeters, is a clear indication that this was a spear and not a javelin. On the other hand, its barbs—which made extraction difficult by the wounded enemy—suggest that in the battle charge, this weapon was also used for hurling. In 1962, a group of similar weapons was found in Israel between Haifa and Tel Aviv.

The spearhead had a tang, ending in a hook, which was fitted into the wood. This problem of attaching blade to wood was solved in other ways during the second half of the third millennium, apart from the less common use of the socket.

The Spear and the Javelin

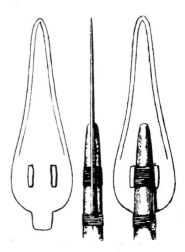

A pierced blade of a spear and reconstructed method of attachment

45

One way, typical and of special interest, was to pierce holes in the blade through which a cord could be threaded. This method was prevalent even at the beginning of the second millennium, having originated in Anatolia in the second half of the third millennium. Several examples of the pierced blade were found by Schliemann in Troy, but the finest were those discovered in the royal tombs of Alaca Hüyük (156). The long leaf-shaped blade ended in a long, slender tang that was bent or hooked to enable it to be fastened more securely to the wood. This improvement was a particular development of the beginning of the Middle Bronze period, and we shall discuss it in greater detail later. This type of blade, so easy to identify, offers an instructive means of tracing ethnic and military ties during this period.

The Sumerian charioteers were bowless. Their compensation was the javelin. Like the Canaanite and Egyptian chariots of a later period which were fitted with arrow quivers, the Sumerian chariots were also equipped with quivers—but theirs were for javelins. This feature stands out clearly in all the monuments in which the chariot is depicted, notably in the vase from Khafajah (128), the relief from Ur (130), the Standard of Ur (132–133), and especially in the chariot of Eannatum (135). Page 134 shows a javelin-blade found at Ur.

LONG-RANGE WEAPONS

The Bow The bow is depicted on many monuments belonging to the end of the fourth millennium covering the Late Pre-Dynastic period in Egypt and the Proto-Literate period in Mesopotamia. The illustrations show a radical difference in the shape of the bow in the two countries. In Egypt it was decidedly double-convex in shape. The Mesopotamian bow was a single-arc weapon.

In Egypt the bow appears in the hands of some of the warrior-hunters in the Hunters' Slate Palette (119, top) and also as an inscribed sign on a cylinder seal from the same period (118). The bow was not composite. For the ends of its arms incline toward the string and not outward. Moreover, it is not easy to imagine that the people of so early a period could have produced a composite bow of the double-convex form, the height of perfection of the composite type. On the other hand, the double-convex form shows that they had already discovered this device for bringing the weapon under greater tension.

The two arcs were sharply convex; their outer ends were close to the ends of the string; and the grip was very wide. These features led several scholars to suggest that the arms of this bow were made of animal horns, bound to a short bar—the grip in fact—at their roots. It is true that a very small number of bows with bodies made of horn have been found in Egypt. But these are only votive models, and offer no justification for the inference that the functional bows were made of horn and not wood. Besides, a horn bow would not be pliable. The best assumption is that if animal horns were used at all, they were attached to the ends of the wooden arms to give them a sharper curve. This would not reduce the pliability of the wood, but would make it more convex.

46

The hunter's bow from Mesopotamia's Warka stele (118), on the other hand, was an almost semicircular single-arc weapon whose ends after meeting the string, curve conspicuously upward. This, too, is a simple and not a composite bow, despite the tendency of its arms to straighten themselves near the ends. The thickness of its body suggests that the power of this bow was achieved by the use of a particularly hard and thick wood, or perhaps by the lamination of several strips of wood, turning it in fact into a reinforced bow. To prevent the string from slipping off the body, the ends of the arms were curved, perhaps with the help of animal horn.

The arrows as depicted both in the Hunters' Slate Palette and on the Warka stele were fork-headed and were no doubt made of flint, like the arrowheads found in archaeological excavations. This kind of arrow was used not only for hunting but also for fighting, as is evident from an Egyptian fragment of a palette depicting the body of a Semite pierced by a fork-headed arrow (119).

The bow, as we have observed, was not used by the Sumerian army. But its use by the armies of other lands of the Bible during this period, and later also in Mesopotamia, is evident from several monuments. One of the most enlightening is the siege and battle scene from Deshashe in Egypt (146), from which we learn the type of bow used by the Semites defending themselves inside the fortified city and also fighting outside it. This bow is definitely double-convex, and is not composite. The Egyptian bow does not appear on the parts of this monument which have been preserved. But since their enemies are depicted with their bodies full of arrows, the assumption is clear that the Egyptians, too, used bows in addition to their cutting axes. Moreover, the posture of the Egyptian soldier to the left of the ladder on page 146 is obviously that of an archer aiming his bow at the top of the wall. In fact, there are some fragments of reliefs from this period which show clearly the shape of the Egyptain bow, which was rather similar (146, bottom left).

Most important of all the monuments showing the development of the bow in general and in the third millennium in particular is the celebrated victory monument of the Accadian king Naram-Sin. Here we have the very first representation of the composite bow in the history of ancient weapons. And it is a singularly well-developed instrument. The King (150, left) is equipped with a battleaxe, and carries a bow in his left hand and an arrow in his right. The bow, which is depicted with detailed accuracy, bears the two characteristic features of the composite weapon; it is small—about 90 centimeters from end to end (an estimate based on its relationship to the size of the figure holding it); and its arms tend to recurve near the ends and then become straight.

The composite bow is shown on another monument, from the Accadian period (151, left), this time in action. Unfortunately only part of this stele is preserved, but it is possible to notice that though the bow is under maximum tension, its arms still curve outward slightly. The fact that the deified king is represented with the bow indicates the Accadian pride in this weapon. And it is perhaps this bow, more than any other weapon, which explains the interesting historic phenomenon whereby the Accadians were able to conquer and gain dominion over Mesopotamia and to penetrate distant regions right up to the

47

Mediterranean. It is indeed no exaggeration to suggest that the invention of the composite bow with its comparatively long range was as revolutionary, in its day, and brought comparable results, as the discovery of gunpowder thousands of years later.

PERSONAL PROTECTION

The difference between the technical achievements of the warriors of Mesopotamia and those of the Egyptian soldiers is one of the notable features of any review of the means of warfare in the third millennium. The difference was not only in the achievements themselves but notably in their character, with Mesopotamia registering advanced developments in the means of mobility and firepower. Firepower in Mesopotamia was now a most efficient piercing axe and the composite bow. This indicates that conditions in the land made them necessary, and that the means of personal protection were first developed there to such a degree as to be proof against such weapons as the simple bow, the mace, the cutting axe, and the stabbing sword. During this very period, while Mesopotamia was making great progress in the fashioning of means of protection, they were, apart from the shield, almost completely absent in Egypt.

The Shield

Hieroglyphic sign for "to fight"

The personal shield was no doubt in use from a very early period. It already appears on a wall painting from the Late Pre-Dynastic period (117, bottom right) where, in the duel, the soldier on the left is shown bearing a rather large shield, made of animal hide stretched on a wooden frame. Several of the warrior-hunters on the Egyptian Hunters' Slate Palette are carrying objects which some scholars believe to be oval shields (118, bottom).

It was certainly in use during the Early Kingdom, where its shape was apparently rectangular, if we are to judge by the hieroglyphic signs for "to fight." This design shows hands holding a mace and a medium-size shield. At all events, by the end of the third millennium, the top of the shield begins to be rounded and end in a point, as we shall explain in the next chapter. But of special interest is the fact that in the battle picture from Deshashe (146) the shield does not appear at all.

Very different is the story in Mesopotamia. Our most important source here, as for many other implements of war, is the celebrated Stele of Vultures from Telloh (134–135). In the top panel, we find for the first time a phalanx of six rows (see below) of heavily armed soldiers, who carry a large rectangular shield which covers them from neck to ankle. The material of which it was made cannot be determined. But from its size and shape it is presumed to have been of wood and covered with hide. The hide may have been studded with metal disks for strengthening. The six circles which appear on the shields symbolize the six soldiers—one in each row—(similar to the six spears), and this suggests that each shield had a metal disk on its breast. The Egyptian shields during the period of the New Kingdom were similarly strengthened.

48

The shield was not the sole means to protect the body of the Sumerian soldier. From the inlaid shell panel from the temple of Ishtar at Mari (138–139), and particularly from the Standard of Ur (132–133), we learn that the Sumerian troops wore a sleeveless cape which fastened at the neck. It is clear that this cape was a form of armor, particularly as it was studded with small circular pieces of metal, a kind of early experiment in the production of a coat of mail. This cape of mail was apparently designed against an enemy armed only with a non-composite bow whose arrows were unable to penetrate it. But it is probable that it was proof also against the javelin and spear.

Armor

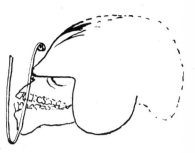

The means of protection with which the Sumerian warrior is most definitely associated is the metal helmet. This is very well depicted in the Standard of Ur, the Stele of Vultures, and the inlaid panels from Mari (138–139). It was slightly pointed and covered both the ears and back of the neck. This type of helmet, with slight changes, was also found in the excavations at Ur, covering the skulls of buried bodies. Such helmets were also worn by the kings, and had a recess in the rear for the hair and plaits. Belonging to this type is the ceremonial gold helmet from Ur. And it is also shown on the conch plaque from Mari (137) and the Stele of Vultures (134–135). The Accadian soldiers wore helmets similar to the Sumerian, as we see from the monuments of Naram-Sin (150) and from the fragment of the Accadian stele shown on page 151.

The Helmet

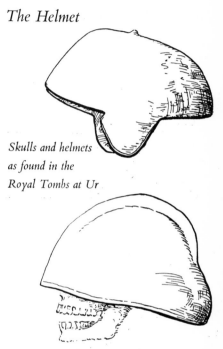

Skulls and helmets as found in the Royal Tombs at Ur

The coexistence of piercing axes and highly developed helmets is most interesting. It is an excellent illustration of the reciprocal reaction between firepower and defense.

METHODS OF WARFARE

The illustrations of warfare in open terrain during the period under review are sparse. But what there is, is rich in content and detail, unmatched by any ancient monument earlier than the period of the New Kingdom in Egypt. The two most important monuments of our period are of course the Standard of Ur and the Stele of Vultures, which have already served as references in our study of individual weapons. Both these monuments reveal that in open battle infantry and chariots functioned in close harmony.

Battle in Open Terrain

The structure of the infantry unit during the action phase of charging the enemy is remarkable for its methodical and disciplined organization, and primarily for its use of the deep phalanx. The soldiers advanced under the protection of rectangular shields, their spears thrust forward at the horizontal.

What was the structure of the phalanx? The answer is problematic, for it depends on our understanding of the schematic conventions of the Sumerian artist in the Stele of Vultures. If we take his design to represent a side view of the phalanx on the march, then what we have is a military unit moving forward in a column of six files with eleven men in each file (some are depicted on the narrow

49

side of the stele which is not shown)—possibly ten men and an officer or NCO. In such a case, the formation would present itself for battle by a right or left turn order, which would offer a phalanx front six ranks deep. This conclusion is also supported by the assumption that the artist in fact sought to show the front presented by a unit, but depicted the warriors in a side view. It is reasonable to conclude that this was the intention. For if not, the phalanx would be charging with a narrow front of six soldiers to a depth of eleven ranks, a structure which would not enable the unit fully to exploit its firepower.

The phalanx assuredly went into action in the immediate wake of the chariot charge or simultaneously. Since the armament of the chariot, as we have seen earlier, was largely medium- or short-range, it may be presumed that soon after the chariots had confused, scattered, and trampeled the enemy by storming through their ranks and used their javelins to wound and kill, the phalanx would follow up the charge from the flanks or the center and finish the battle with their piercing axes and spears. This integrated functioning of chariots and infantry organized in a deep phalanx was possible largely on level ground. And indeed it is on such terrain that we first find them in operation.

Had the Sumerians been able to add to this battle formation a long-range archery unit operating from the rear and the flanks, they would certainly be entitled to the credit of having achieved near perfection in the art of battle in open terrain in the first half of the third millennium in Mesopotamia. But this decisive addition was the contribution of their successors, the Accadians, and indeed it was the integration of the archers which broke up the skillful patterns of the earlier battle machine.

Against all this, how primitive is the form of battle, particularly the duel, shown in the representation of open battle in the monument from Deshashe (146) to the left of the siege scene!

Only more than 1,000 years later do we find a monument depicting a battle scene in which chariots, phalanx of infantry armed with spears and swords, and long-range archers operate together in full coordination. This was a portrayal of one of the most important battles in early history, the battle between the Egyptians and the Hittites.

Battle on Fortified Cities

After a gap of almost 4,000 years, there is evidence of the establishment of fortified cities in all the lands of the Bible at the end of the fourth and particularly at the beginning of the third millennium. This feature signalizes without doubt the beginning of the historic periods and the emergence of powerful kings who succeeded in bringing extensive regions under their domination. It is also a marked indication of the reciprocal commercial contacts between the different peoples at the time, and, no less important, of their military contact.

There was a combination of compelling forces which led to the construction of powerful fortifications for the defense of cities at the beginning of this period. These were, in the main, the concentration of wealth in the cities, partly from agriculture and partly from commerce; expansionist aims of a well-organized people of one land and their encroachment upon spheres of influence of other

kingdoms; and the presence of wandering tribes, large and strong, who drew their livelihood not only from their cattle but from predatory incursions into the cultivated fields of the settled population.

The existence of central authority, anxious to safeguard his lines of communication both to advance his own offensives and to blunt the attacking power of his enemies, led to the siting of fortified cities and fortresses, beginning with this period, not only in accordance with the economic and military needs of the individual cities but with overall strategic considerations. Fortified cities and fortresses were built to command important highways, centers of water, and frontiers. Central direction led to more standardized planning of all fortifications. And the aggressive designs of powerful empires upon distant regions made it essential to construct fortifications able to withstand attack not only from immediate neighbors but also, and for the most part, from nations farther away.

Remains of strong fortifications belonging to the beginning of the third millennium have been found in almost all the large city mounds of antiquity which have been excavated. But since these relics were naturally at the lowest and deepest levels of the tells, only small and narrow sections of the fortifications were accessible to the archaeologists. As a result, we have specific knowledge of the materials with which they were built, the thickness of the walls, and other technical details. But we have on the whole no such specific data on their plan. This gives particular importance to the designs of fortified cities which appear on several monuments from the Late Pre-Dynastic and the Ist Dynasty in Egypt. Unlike the artists of later periods, from the Middle Kingdom up to the Assyrian period, who generally present their cities in elevation, the early Egyptian artists depict their cities in plan, giving as it were a bird's-eye view.

The one that sheds most light on our subject is certainly the celebrated Palette of King Narmer (122, 124), who was probably the founder of the first united dynasty of Egypt. The King himself appears on the palette in two scenes, once wearing the crown of Upper Egypt and once wearing the crown of Lower Egypt.

This palette, which also bears the first clear signs of the beginnings of Egyptian writing, contains scenes whose meaning has been the subject of much controversy. (A description of each side of the palette accompanies the plates in this book.) The assumption of most scholars has been that the palette is dedicated solely to the unification of Upper and Lower Egypt under the rule of Narmer, and its scenes therefore were assumed to be illustrations of his victories in various parts of the country. The entwined serpent necks of the two animals, shown in the middle panel on page 122, are thus interpreted as symbolizing the subjugation and unification of the two parts of Egypt. But none of this discussion sheds light on the problem which concerns us, and that is, what was the character of the fortified cities which Narmer destroyed or whose citizens he conquered?

At the bottom center panel on page 122 the King is depicted in the guise of a bull battering a strongly fortified city with his horns. The city is oval-shaped, its wall studded by several square bastions. The counterpart scene on the reverse (124) of the palette shows, in the bottom panel, two enemies whose identity is symbolized by the artist's plan of the cities to which they belong or their characteristic dwellings. Above the enemy on the left is the plan of a square city, studded on all sides by numerous bastions. This type of bastion-strengthened fortified city is similar to many which appear on other ancient palettes, such as the palette on page 123, or the one which is shown in the drawing on page 51.

These illustrations, on their own, do not contradict the theory that all scenes from the Narmer Palette record battles which took place inside Egypt; for we know that during this period, Egypt boasted fortified cities. But how then can one explain the special form of structure which appears above the enemy on the right in the scene of the two enemies? It comprises two separate elements: (a) a semi-circular structure, and (b) two very long walls leading out from it like the arms of a fan, with a 30-degree angle between them. These walls have neither bastions nor battlements. And the artist seems to have wished to stress their difference from the wall round the semicircular structure which is marked by several thin lines. Now this structure has no parallel in Egypt. Nor have Egyptologists been able to identify it as a hieroglyphic or a pictograph from among the known signs in Egypt. On the other hand, it seems to me, there is a striking similarity between it and structures east of the Jordan and in the Wadi Arava south of the Dead Sea, close to the celebrated King's Way which passed through this region and which linked Egypt with Trans-Jordan, Syria, and Mesopotamia, paralleling the sea route west of the Jordan. In this eastern region, a large number of stone structures were found which, because of their shape, were called by modern archaeologists "kites." These kite-shaped desert enclosures (124) are identical in form with the structure depicted in the Narmer Palette, and they too consist of two distinct parts—the semicircular enclosure and the two long walls running off it, often indeed, as long as 400 meters, and without bastions or towers. On the other hand, the enclosure itself did have "nests" and turrets at the points where they were joined by the two walls which showed unmistakably that it was intended as a defense fortification.

How did it function?

Opinions vary. But the prevailing view was that these kite enclosures were established by wandering shepherd tribes, who tended their flocks near by. When danger threatened, they quickly corralled their flocks between the two long walls and drove them through the semicircular fortified enclosure, from whose turrets they were able to maintain effective defense. This view has received endorsement recently with the discovery in Trans-Jordan of a *graffito* from the Safaitic period, which clearly shows horned animals being driven into the enclosure (124). From this *graffito* we learn that these structures were also in use in later periods.

If the above thesis is correct, then the Narmer Palette and the archaeological finds in Trans-Jordan offer us very rare examples of a form of fortification built not for the defense of a city but of hunters, nomads, and shepherds. It also means that the Narmer Palette depicts not only the King's victories inside but also outside Egypt. To come back to our scene of the two enemies, the kite structure on the right thus represents the King's domination, or struggle to dominate, or perhaps only the aim of dominating, the King's Way in the east. It may be then presumed that the enemy figure on the left with his fortified city signifies the domination, or desire to dominate, the area west of the Jordan. Moreover, the possibility cannot be excluded that the oval-shaped fortified city with its bastions together with the serpent-necked animals which appear on the palette represent not the record of a victory in Egypt but the expression of an expansionist aim or perhaps a closer association with Mesopotamia and her cities. For during this period, animals with their serpent necks entwined was a widely used symbol in Mesopotamia. And in Mesopotamia in this period there existed strong fortified cities like Warka.

The theory that Narmer invasion forces reached Palestine was strengthened very recently when a potsherd was found in one of the southern Palestinian cities, Tell el-Manshieh, on which the name of Pharaoh Narmer was incised (see figure on this page). Incidentally, at this tell the remains of a very well-built brick wall were revealed, including rectangular bastions belonging to the same period.

Even more impressive are the fortifications of the same period recently discovered at Tell el-Far'ah (northern Palestine, Biblical Tirzah?). Here was found not only a city wall with square bastions, but also a magnificent city gate—unique for Palestine—flanked by two protruding towers with empty spaces inside them. These spaces were, I believe, intended for ladders or wooden staircases, to enable the defenders to climb up to the upper parts of the towers. The gate, with its protruding towers is not unlike the gates of Troy, discussed on page 57.

We can see, therefore, that already from the beginning of the Egyptian Dynastic periods, the cities of Palestine were endangered by military attack from Egypt and perhaps also from other nations to the north. This is certainly one of the principal reasons why almost every tell excavation in Palestine lays bare relics of powerful fortifications from the Early Bronze ages, which are equivalent to the Early Dynastic periods in Egypt.

We have mentioned that so far archaeological excavations have failed to uncover very large sections of these fortifications because of technical difficulties associated with the process of excavating. But the small sections which have been uncovered in such ancient cities as Megiddo, Beth-yerah, Gezer, Jericho, and Ai, and now also Tell el-Manshieh, enable us to follow their method of construction.

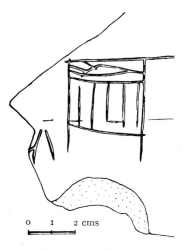

0   1   2 cms

Narmer's name incised on a potsherd found recently in the northern Negev, in the southern part of Israel

53

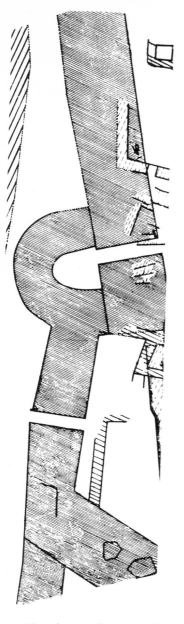

The fortifications were built of brick or stone, depending on the materials available near by, and often with a combination of both—bricks upon a foundation layer of stone. The walls were very thick, a thickness indeed of several meters, which was far greater than was required if the purpose was simply to prevent their being breached by the primitive methods available at the time. The real purpose of the thickness was to enable the walls to be built high enough to prevent the enemy from scaling them with ladders. The construction of these thick high walls of brick or undressed stone required special care and special methods to make them proof against collapse by earthquake or even by local breach. They were therefore often built in vertical sections, one flush against the other, without being bonded, so that the destruction of one section would not bring down others with it. The bastions and towers, whose military role has already been described, also served the technical function of bolstering the walls.

Much of importance can be learned of the history of fortifications and methods of attack upon them during the third millennium from the siege scene on the monument of Deshashe (146), which has already served us to illustrate the axe and the bow. This monument, from the second half of the third millennium, is one of the few belonging to the period of the Old Kingdom in Egypt which deals with military subjects. And it is the only monument extant from this period which depicts a fortified city under attack.

The city on the right is oval in plan, and its principal interest lies in the semi-circular bastions which protrude markedly from its walls. Judging from the portraits of its inhabitants, this would seem to be a Palestinian city. And, indeed, relics of semicircular bastions belonging to this period have been found at archaeological digs in Palestine as well as in Mesopotamia. A very fine specimen was discovered in one of the walls of Jericho from the third millennium. It was 2·5 meters in diameter and was clearly capable also of supporting without difficulty a balcony from which the defenders could direct vertical fire upon the attackers below. Similar semicircular bastions were also found on the walls of the city of Ai belonging to the Early Bronze Age (see figure to the left on this page).

It was possible to exploit such bastions to the full only when the defenders were equipped with effective bows. And, as we have observed in an earlier chapter, the field of fire commanded by the semicircular bastion was well suited to this weapon. The Deshashe siege scene shows quite clearly that the defenders were indeed armed with the double-convex bow, albeit not of the composite type.

Plan of a part of the Early Bronze fortifications at Ai, showing a semi-circular bastion

Plan of a recently discovered fortified city gate, from Tell el-Far'ah (Biblical Tirzah?) of the first half of the third millennium B.C. To the proposed reconstruction prepared by the excavator, Roland de Vaux, I added a series of staircases within the towers

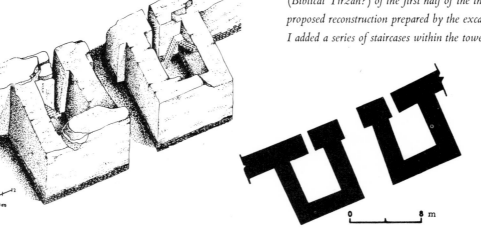

0   8 m

The combination of a well-designed bastion and an effective bow was born of the need to find some defense against an enemy that did not limit his attempted assault to scaling the wall but sought also to breach it. Again, the Deshashe monument provides not only the earliest illustration of the semicircular bastion, whose development in the beginning of the second millennium we shall discuss later, but also of combined attack upon a wall both by scaling and by breaching the gate. While ladders against the wall are being climbed under covering fire from archers, a technique we shall come across in the later periods, other attackers, in an interesting action, are shown trying to breach the left corner of the wall. This is precisely the corner where the bastions are built very close together, and was probably the site of the gate—always the weak spot in the fortifications and always the focus of attempts to break through. The breach was not yet effected by the battering-ram —the earliest example of this implement, and a very primitive example it is, appears only at the beginning of the second millennium—but with the help of spears or long poles which were thrust into the wall by the soldiers. Their commander is shown at their side, directing their operation or perhaps the tempo of their actions. Indeed some of the "spear" blades recently found between Tel Aviv and Haifa—which were already mentioned—may have been, to judge by their immense size, blades of such long poles.

A more primitive method of tearing down a wall is presented in the second Egyptian monument belonging to the next century, the wall painting which appears on page 147. Here the soldiers are shown battering at a wall with axes while standing on a ladder. This method was effective against walls built of brick or mud and even continued to be used in the first millennium when the advanced types of battering-ram were already available to the attacker.

The most remarkable development revealed in this wall painting is the nature of the scaling-ladder. It rests on two solid wheels. This is the only example we have in an ancient monument of a mobile assault ladder which we know to have been in use in the lands of the Bible. The wheels were not designed to facilitate movement of the ladder from one part of the wall to another. This could be accomplished either by being carried or by the provision of several ladders. It seems reasonably certain that they played a part in the breaching operation, enabling the ladder to be pushed gradually closer and closer to the wall while it was being battered. At the beginning of the operation, the top of the ladder would be against the wall and its base at some distance, forming an acute angle with the ground. As the breaching work progressed, it would be pushed forward, the angle at the base widening until the whole ladder was close to the wall. The method of keeping it stable is well illustrated in the scene. To the right of the ladder, a soldier is seen sticking a bar into the ground to prevent the wheels from rolling. The soldier on the left holds the ladder to stop it from falling while his comrades batter away with their axes.

This study on the fortifications of the third millennium would be incomplete without a detailed mention of the celebrated Trojan fortifications in northwest Turkey. Thanks to the most recent excavations in Anatolia, in 1958–1959, we now have definite proof that even during the Chalcolithic period, at the end of the fifth

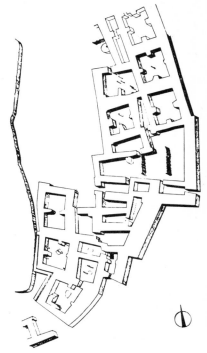

The fort of Hacilar in Asia Minor

55

and during the fourth millennium, there were settlements surrounded by walls which may be described as reasonably fortified citadels. Places like Mersin, Beycesultan, and Hacilar can shed important light on the history of fortifications in this early period. Especially worthy of mention is the interesting citadel of Hacilar which was excavated in 1958, belonging to the last period of settlement on this site of many strata. From the knowledge now in our possession, the archaeologist I. Mellaart was quite right when he declared that "So far, Hacilar is unique in the Near East." (The fortifications of Jericho are very much earlier, while those of Mersin belong to the latter part of the period under review.)

We have not enough to go on as yet to reconstruct the plan of the Hacilar fortifications beyond indicating that the walls were 2 meters thick, are built of brick, and enclosed a number of chambers. But despite their importance in the history of settlement and fortifications in the fifth and fourth millennia, these walls and citadels cannot be compared even faintly to the magnificent fortifications of Troy in the third millennium. Since the excavations of Schliemann and Dörpfeld, more archaeological digs have been carried out at this site in the last few years by Blegen. And we now are in a position, for the first time, to understand the plan of the fortifications and to be able to date them, both relatively and absolutely.

The excavations brought to light several series of fortifications of different periods and an even greater number of buildings of different phases and strata inside the city. We shall confine ourselves in this study to an outline of the principal phases in the plans of the fortifications. We can say right away that these are not the fortifications of a densely populated city but of a large citadel. The diameter of the earliest citadels was not more than 80 meters, and even the large citadel during the third millennium, at its peak construction in Stratum IIc, had a diameter not more than 120 meters. The wall of Troy I in its middle phase is already distinctive in that it broadens toward the base, forming a kind of glacis. Its lines are flush and unmarked by any sign of bastions. Its gates are still quite primitive—a narrow passageway between two towers.

There is a further improvement in the first fortification of Stratum II. The gate is still a narrow opening between two towers, though these have now been considerably extended on the outside, giving them the appearance of two lengthened walls. But the main wall of the citadel, at least in one section, now

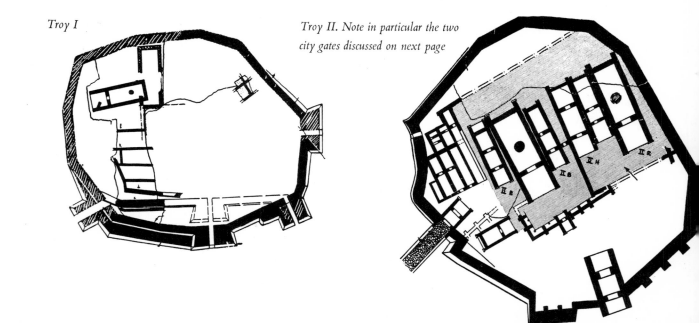

Troy I

Troy II. Note in particular the two city gates discussed on next page

56

comprises a series of very strong bastions built on a sloping base. The bastions are 10 meters apart, 3 meters thick, and project 2 meters from the wall. The wall itself is built of bricks upon a limestone foundation. The foundation in some places is as high as 8 meters from ground level, and its slope is not very steep. Later, when larger stones were used for building, the slope became much steeper.

The most interesting change of all appears in a later phase of citadel II, and reaches its highest stage of development in the celebrated phase IIc, when the city fortifications were at their peak during the third millennium. This was the change in the forms of the gate (see illustration) which was converted into a self-contained structure with inner pilasters. In front of the entrance is an open square protected by a wall on the right and on the left. From the square one reached the gate itself, which was built just inside the city. Its roof was supported by four pilasters, two on either side. In many important particulars this gate is like the gates of the Middle Bronze period in Palestine and Syria, as we shall see later, and it is the most ancient example of this type.

All the phases of the fortifications of Troy I and II belong to the third millennium, ranging from the beginning to the end of that period. We are not yet in a position to associate with any precision this type of fortification with those in other lands of the Bible. But they show that also in Anatolia, as in the other Biblical lands, significant achievements were registered in the construction of fortifications in the third millennium.

CONCLUSIONS

This millennium was a period of extraordinary military activity which brought in its wake innovations and developments in basic branches in the art of warfare. They were to have an important impact on warfare in the second and first millennia, notably in two major fields: battle in open terrain, with chariots and the infantry phalanx; and powerful fortifications and the early attempts to breach them. The composite bow, which began to appear in the second half of the third millennium, continued to be perfected, and proved decisive in many battles both in open terrain and in siege. This acute military activity came to an end in the last centuries of the millennium. All lands of the Bible seemed to go into decline some earlier, some later. The Accadian empire in Mesopotamia collapsed. Catastrophic fire consumed the proud fortifications of the second citadel of Troy with its bastions, towers, and walls. The Old Kingdom in Egypt tottered and fell. And the fortresses of Early Bronze Palestine and Syria were destroyed. This was a "decline and fall" period for all lands of the Bible. Kingdoms and Powers with traditions based on a high material culture seemed to vanish from the map of the Middle East. Wandering tribes came sweeping in with all the winds from heaven and covered these kingdoms, which seemed to crumble at the very height of their prosperity and power. Empires vanished. But not their inhabitants.

After a prolonged period of somber bleakness, the faintly glowing embers of earlier traditions were sparked by the combustive fuel of new cultures into bright flame which lit up a new age, termed by archaeologists as the Middle Bronze period.

57

IV

THE PERIOD OF THE PATRIARCHS

2100–1570 B.C.

The 500-year span between the end of the third millennium and the middle of the second is probably the most significant in the general history of the lands of the Bible. It is a period of special importance in the development of systems of warfare, fortifications, and armaments. Mass wanderings of tribes and peoples, military and commercial contacts between different parts of the Middle East, and changes in the political and ethnic structures of many countries brought the entire region into touch with achievements of the third millennium which had hitherto been confined to a few countries alone. During this period, the art of warfare advanced to new levels, notably by the introduction of the horse and light chariot and by the perfection of the battering-ram, which changed the character of campaigns in open terrain and against fortified cities respectively.

This process is, of course, not suddenly apparent at the beginning of the second millennium. Nor was its development uniform in all lands of the Bible. Not that our knowledge of military events in these lands throughout the entire period under review is uniform and complete. There are differences both in the quantity and quality of our information on the different countries and at different times. This is due simply to the variable nature of the archaeological source material on which our knowledge is based. In some countries and at some periods, it is rich and abundant. In other lands and at other times it is poor. We know, for example, a good deal about Egypt at the time of the Middle Kingdom from the wealth of wall paintings and relics of fortifications from that period (see description, pages 158–161). But in other lands of the Bible during this time archaeological finds shed much light on the different types of weapons in use, but there are no illustrated monuments, and so we cannot reconstruct them in battle array. On the other hand, in the second part of the period under review, the Hyksos period in Egypt and Palestine (see page 176), there are neither drawings nor engravings from Egypt on a military subject. But there is an abundance of archaeological finds from which we learn much about types of weapons and fortifications. And there is a wealth of written documents, notably from Mari on the Euphrates, which enable us to reconstruct the prevailing methods of warfare, communications, intelligence services, and army structure. It is also possible, from the details provided by the available archaeological sources, to gain an insight into other branches of warfare on which no such sources have, as yet, been discovered.

WEAPONS *Short- and Medium-range*

The Axe

Among the weapons used for short-range and hand-to-hand fighting, the axe underwent the most interesting development. It is particularly instructive to trace the development of the flat, multi-tanged cutting axe whose beginnings we have followed in Mesopotamia, Syria, and Palestine in the second half of the previous millennium. Interestingly enough, this axe, effective largely against an enemy not equipped with helmets, became obsolete in the country of its invention, yet continued to be widely used and even perfected·in the land of its adoption—Egypt. This was due, no doubt, to two factors: it conformed to the tradition of Egyptian axes, which were socketless; and it suited the pattern of warfare in Egypt during the first half of this period when the fighting was without armor, the warriors protecting themselves with a large body-shield (see page 155).

The Egyptian epsilon axe was really a union of the short blade with the wide edge, which was already in use in Egypt, and the triple-tang device of the Mesopotamian, Syrian, and Palestinian axe. In the latter type, the three tangs are wedged into the haft and made secure by binding; in the Egyptian axe, the tangs have holes through which they are fastened to the haft either by small nails or with cord, or by a combination of both, similar to their earlier method of attaching blade to haft. Some typical examples of this axe are shown on pages 154 and 155. At least one (154, right) shows that on occasion the haft itself was made of metal. These relics, and the meticulous illustrations on the monuments, complement each other admirably.

Quite different was the development during the very same time in Syria, Palestine, and the neighboring region. And here, too, the weapon that emerged showed the twin influence of tradition and necessity. The tradition in these lands was the socket type; the necessity was occasioned by the appearance of helmets and armor, against which the cutting axe was ineffective. This led to the invention of a completely new type of axe—a piercing weapon with a socket.

It developed out of the epsilon and the anchor axes and is commonly referred to as the eye axe (168–171) because of the prominence of its two holes, which look like hollow eyes. These are really a carry over of the spaces between the two inner curves of the epsilon tang—but they are now bounded at the rear by the socket. The eye axe was a difficult weapon to produce. Some splendid examples of ceremonial axes of this type, made of gold, were found at Byblos and are shown on pages 170 and 171.

The eye axe was brought to Egypt by the Semites when they started to

An epsilon axe from Mesopotamia

A Semite warrior as depicted on a wall painting in Beni-hasan. Note the eye axe

59

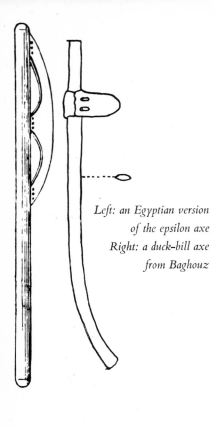

Left: an Egyptian version
of the epsilon axe
Right: a duck-bill axe
from Baghouz

Two types of the Middle Bronze II
narrow socketed axes

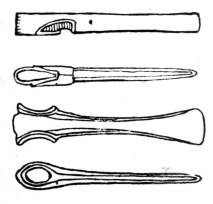

infiltrate and establish themselves there and even serve in the army. But it did not gain acceptance, no doubt because the tradition of the tang type was too entrenched. There are, however, some Egyptian examples (168, right; 169, top) of the tang axe being given an eye form. The illustration at the top of page 169 shows the purely decorative influence of the "eyes," for they are artificially carved on a semicircular blade of the socketless type.

The Syrian and Palestinian eye axe was further developed to make it a more effective piercing instrument by lengthening the blade and narrowing the edge. The hollows have become smaller and less prominent, and the whole blade assumed the appearance of a duck's bill (167, right). This, in fact, is what it is called today. The haft was usually curved to prevent it from slipping out of the hand, for the weapon required to be swung with much force. This is seen in the celebrated Beni-hasan wall painting of the caravan of Semites going down to Egypt, like the Israelites. The warrior on the extreme left on page 166 bears in his right hand an object which looks like an axe of this type. In Baghouz, Syria, a cemetery was discovered belonging to this period which contained graves of warriors who had been buried with their weapons. These included duck-bill axes. Page 166, right, shows such an axe with a curved handle, which had been set at the head of a warrior laid out on a bed at burial.

In the 18th century, the duck-bill axe had already given way to a new type which was designed solely for piercing and penetration. This development was certainly prompted by advances in the development of armor. It demanded a very long blade with a narrow thin edge (174), almost like a chisel. This was a socket axe, the prototype of which we have already come across during the Accadian period in Mesopotamia, and which is illustrated on the Naram-Sin monument (150, left). These weapons were so widely used during this period that there is hardly a warrior's grave in Palestine and Syria in which they are not to be found (see page 166).

In Egypt during this time, there is evidence of an axe with a long and narrow blade more suited to piercing than the earlier cutting axes. But it is still a tang axe and its edge is wide.

Each stage in the development of the axe during this period, and its transformation from the epsilon tang type to the narrow-edged long-bladed socket type, reflect the untiring efforts of armies to perfect their weapons and enhance their effectiveness against the armor of their adversaries.

The Sword

Efforts to design an axe that would more effectively fulfill its function, which resulted in the advanced piercing axe, were also characteristic of the development of the sword. This led to the emergence of a well-made sickle sword, which first appeared in the second half of the third millennium. It was a striking, as distinct from a thrusting, weapon, and was, as we have seen, really a kind of cutting axe whose blade and handle were fashioned out of one bar of metal. Several fine examples of this type of sword, found at Byblos in Mesopotamia and at Shechem in Palestine (172), show that it was quite common during this period. This sword was easy to handle, even by charioteers at the height of a charge.

The distinctive feature of all these swords during the first half of the second millennium is the shortness of the blade in relation to its hilt. The hilt was roughly twice the length of the blade, giving the weapon an axe-like quality. This relationship undergoes a change in the sickle swords of the second half of this millennium, when the blade is as long as its hilt, and at times even longer. It was during this period that this weapon can be said to have become a proper sword.

In addition to the curved or sickle swords, the Middle Bronze Age also produced a series of short straight swords, somewhat like daggers. They were designed no doubt for defense in hand-to-hand combat. Unlike the straight narrow sword of the early part of the Middle Bronze period, the blades become broader during Middle Bronze II, taking on the shape of a pointed leaf. They were designed primarily for stabbing, and the blade was therefore strengthened by a central spine (sometimes more than one) or ribs. Examples of the spined or ribbed sword, both from Egypt and Palestine, are shown on pages 174 and 175.

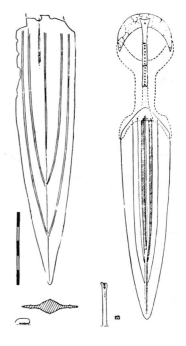

A Middle Bronze I straight two-edged sword

The Spear and the Javelin

At the end of the third millennium, the armorers were still grappling with the problem of finding an effective method of attaching the spearhead and javelin-head to the wooden staff, and had come up with nothing better than the tang. This also marked the type of spear and javelin in use at the beginning of the second millennium, and not until a later stage in the first half of the second millennium was the socket type to be developed and more commonly used.

At the beginning of this period, then, the attachment both in the spear and javelin was by means of a tang which was voluted or curved at the rear. Both instruments were designed to pierce. In action, with the power of the thrust, the wooden staffs were liable to split. With a bent or voluted tang, this danger was checked.

The drawing on page 157 shows the method of attaching these socketless blades to the staff. The top of the staff would be split down the center and the tang inserted, its volute turned outward, and then the entire upper portion of the staff, with the tang wedged in, was tightly bound with stout cord. This method was typical of the spears from Cyprus; of the "eye" or double-pierced blade of the 18th-century spear of Annitas, the Early Hittite king, found in Kültepe in Anatolia (156, far right), which shows that this type of blade was in wide use at this time; and of a similar spear from Megiddo belonging to the same period. The most interesting of the spears and javelins with a voluted tang are those found in Palestine at the beginning of the Middle Bronze period. Their technical standard is quite high.

These weapons belonged mainly to the semi-nomadic warriors who suddenly started pouring into Palestine. Such javelins have been found in many graves, together with the straight sword, but so far no city ruins have been unearthed which can be definitely associated with soldiers who bore arms with a voluted tang. Since this device is characteristic of the military culture primarily of the northern areas of the lands of the Bible at this period, it may be presumed that the nomads trekked to Palestine from these regions at the time of the great wanderings which marked the end of the third millennium. It is conceivable, therefore, that Abraham's journeying to Canaan was part of this great trek, and that the weapons

Hyksos daggers (Middle Bronze II)

used by his household were this type of javelin and spear, as well as the straight and narrow sword.

Another characteristic of the spear and javelin at the beginning of the Middle Bronze period is its metal butt at the base of the staff. We have mentioned that the blades of this weapon were found in many graves. Found with them were metal tips, also voluted (156, second from right). They were assuredly not used as a form of blade. They almost certainly served as the butt of the javelin or spear, enabling the weapon to be stuck in the ground when not in use. Under certain circumstances, they could also be used to strike the enemy, as we see from the Biblical story in II Samuel 2: 23 which describes the slaying of Asahel by Abner: "Howbeit, he refused to turn aside: wherefore Abner, with the hinder end of the spear, smote him under the fifth rib. . . ."

The tang attachment, as we have seen, had serious disadvantages, the most important of which was the danger of splitting the staff in action. Efforts continued to devise an improved method, and by the later part of the first half of the second millennium a socket-type head for spear and javelin, of quite advanced standard, becomes the universal type.

The Egyptian wall paintings on pages 166–167, 169 endorse the point that the spear and the javelin, together with the axe and, as we shall see later, the bow, were the most important weapons for the warrior of the first half of the second millennium.

LONG-RANGE WEAPONS

The Bow   The bow, however, remained the primary war weapon of the Middle Bronze period, despite the high advances in the development of short- and medium-range weapons. This is evident from the many illustrated monuments of the period. We also know much of the character of these weapons from actual bows found in Egypt.

In Mesopotamia the composite bow was, as we have seen, widely used as early as the Accadian period. But in the early centuries of the second millennium its use

Two archers as depicted on a wall painting in Beni-hasan. Note the archer on the left who strings the bow

Archers as depicted on a wall painting in Beni-hasan. Note the piles of arrows, and the archer who uses his leg for bracing the bow

was sparse. This was due no doubt to its complicated manufacture, which was beyond the capacities of the semi-nomadic tribes of Syria and Palestine. And in conservative Egypt, too, its development was slow. Armor was not yet in general use by Egypt's immediate enemies to the south and west, and so the stimulus was lacking for so advanced and expensive a long-range weapon as the composite bow. But we have evidence of such a weapon, of an advanced type, at the beginning of the period of the New Kingdom in the 16th century. This means that it must have been introduced into service at the end of the previous period, during the later centuries of the Middle Bronze period, the Hyksos period.

As we say, there is no clear positive proof of the wide use of the composite bow during the first half of the second millennium. But there is much evidence of the wide use of the simple bow during this period. It was a double-convex weapon. There is reason to suppose that in many cases it was also reinforced.

A fine example of this type appears in the wall painting from Beni-hasan (166–167). The bow borne by the soldier on the extreme left is very pronouncedly double-convex and has a particularly thick grip. Some scholars hold this to be a composite bow, but the inward curve of the arms clearly discounts this view. Nevertheless, though simple, it was a well-made weapon.

Double-convex bows are also borne by several of the soldiers storming the fortifications in other scenes from the Beni-hasan painting (158–159). The monument shown on page 162, also depicts a double-convex bow, although the curves are somewhat shallow.

Conclusive proof that these bows were not composite is given by the weapons themselves, a number of which were discovered in Egyptian tombs (163, bottom). They are made from a single, strong, and sizable piece of wood, and measure up to between 1·5 and 1·7 meters. There is also a painting (165, bottom) showing a workshop for the manufacture of bows. The double-convex bows here are shown without their strings. If they were composite, their arms would surely curve outwards, toward the back. They do not.

In addition to the double-convex simple bow, the ordinary large single-arc bow was also in common use. This can be seen from the wooden model of Nubian archers (163), from actual relics of bows found in ancient tombs, and from the Egyptian wall paintings shown on pages 160 and 161. Though a simple bow, its penetrating force was considerable if the enemy was without armor. This we know from the arrow-riddled bodies of warriors from this period which were found in Egypt. In one case the arrow had gone right through the body from back to chest and protruded for a distance of some 20 centimeters.

63

In order not to strain the pliability of the bow, the string was usually not fitted until shortly before battle. It was then done by slipping one looped end over one end of the bow, the bow held upright with that end on the ground, and then bent to meet the other loop of the string either by the weight of the body (158, top left, and figure on page 62) or by kneeling and pulling it down. This is also described by Sinuhe when he tells of his bracing the bow before starting to practice on the eve of battle.

The quiver was already known in this period. Its Semitic name, *ashpah*, is indeed found in Egyptian documents, which shows that it was introduced into that country from Syria and Palestine. Yet the wall paintings from the period of the Middle Kingdom show that the Egyptians used to carry their arrows mainly not in quivers but in bundles which were laid at the foot of the bow (158, top left, and also figure on page 63).

The bow was used not only in open battle but also—and probably in the main—by both attackers and defenders in the battle on fortified cities, as is shown in the scenes on pages 158–159. Remains of fortifications from this period, as we shall see later, show the provisions of well-designed firing embrasures for the archers defending the wall. The attacking archers were not equipped with shields, they were screened by the shields of the axe- and spear-bearers.

There is no substantiation from ancient monuments or relics, but it may be assumed that the composite bow began to be widely used during the later part of this period, particularly in Syria, Palestine, and Mesopotamia. This supposition is based on the fact that at the beginning of the following period it appears in a very advanced form. And we know that it was in common use in these lands in the preceding period.

The Sling   The slingmen were used in support of the archers, as they were in later periods. They were particularly useful in an attack on a fortified city, since they could direct high-angle fire up a steep slope. They are depicted in the wall paintings shown on page 159, top right.

PERSONAL PROTECTION

The Shield   Since the helmet and armor did not make their bold appearance in Egypt until the end of the Middle Bronze period—the beginning of the New Kingdom —the warrior during the preceding period, that is the Middle Kingdom, had to be protected only by the shield. And it is understandable therefore that this should be a large shield, capable of giving complete cover to the whole of the bare body of the fighter, particularly one equipped with short-range weapons for hand-to-hand combat. A good example of such a shield is shown in the wall painting on page 155, left, which depicts a soldier armed with a cutting axe and bearing a shield which matches his height. It is wide at the base, narrowing toward the head, which is rounded. Though made of wood and covered with hide, it must have been heavy and surely impaired mobility. This perhaps explains the appearance of another type of shield at this time which was smaller and lighter. It was of medium size, and though there were slight variations in shape, its standard form was wide at the base with a pointed or rounded head (158).

We have no concrete information on the type of shield in vogue in Egypt during the latter part of Middle Bronze II, nor in the other countries of the Bible. But in these lands the shields were probably smaller than the Egyptian, for we know that their people had already developed some form of armor and did not need the shield for complete body protection. It is also reasonable to assume that the shape of their shields was rectangular, for the Sumerian shields during the previous period were rectangular and so were the shields of the Asiatic peoples during the Late Bronze period. The round shield, designed mainly to protect the uncovered face, did not come into use until the end of the 14th century, having apparently been introduced by the "Sea Peoples."

Thus we see that this period, too, reflects the interrelationship between weapons and armor—or its absence—in the lands of the Bible, and the time-old struggle between mobility and security.

Ancient relics, archaeological excavations, and written sources from the first half of the second millennium shed more detailed light on the fortifications of the period and the patterns of battle on a fortified city than on any other branch of warfare. The study of these subjects can therefore be most instructive to our general understanding of the art of warfare of this period. It also serves as a significant preface to our consideration of fortifications in the period which follows, since their development sprung from the achievements gained earlier. *Fortifications*

It is well to begin with a description of the Egyptian fortifications of the Middle Kingdom as shown on wall paintings and as revealed by archaeological excavation. A good jumping-off point are the fortresses or fortified cities depicted on some of the wall paintings of Beni-hasan (158–159). These types of structure contain almost all the elements required of a complete system of fortifications: high walls with battlements to facilitate defensive fire, and balconies for the defenders to harass the enemy's flanks and direct vertical fire on troops approaching the wall. The lower part of the wall, strengthened by a sloped bank or glacis, is shown very clearly. These fortresses or fortified cities sometimes have two gates, sometimes only one. The illustration of the gate in the painting is a simple outline, offering no details of its structure. All we can see is that it was rectangular in shape with horizontal lintels. On the other hand, the methods and patterns of defense of the troops on the wall and the methods of attack by the assaulting troops are depicted very well.

But the most illuminating insight into the character of strongholds at the time of the XIIth Dynasty, in the 20th and 19th centuries, is provided by the fortifications of Buhen in Nubia—Sudan of today—on the west bank of the Nile, near Wadi Halfa. These fortifications, which were thoroughly excavated only as recently as 1957 by Emery, are the most complete example of a fortress of this period among the many found along the trade routes and the strategical areas of Nubia. These well-preserved structures, with the help of the wall paintings mentioned above, enable us to reconstruct the plan and appearance of the fortress (160–161).

65

The fortress is almost square, measuring 170 by 180 meters. The fortifications comprise four basic elements: the main (inner) wall, the outer or advance wall, the moat, and the very well-fortified gate structure.

The main wall was built of bricks and was about 5 meters thick. It is considered to have been 10 meters high. The gate was in the center of the western side of the wall. Throughout its entire length the wall was "blistered" at intervals of 5 meters with protruding square bastions, each 2 meters wide. Each corner of the fortress was marked by a large tower, which protruded from the face of the wall even more conspicuously than the bastions.

An impressive feature of the Buhen fortifications is the siting and the form of the low outer wall, which served also as a kind of revetment to the near wall of the moat immediately beneath it. This low wall was also of brick, and along its face a series of semicircular bastions 3 meters wide had been built at intervals of 10 meters. In the wall and bastions there were two rows of firing embrasures, one above the other, with loopholes arranged in groups of three, centering on each shooting embrasure. This is an example of excellent exploitation of the purpose of the semicircular bastion to give a wide-angled field of fire. For each embrasure enabled fire to be applied downward onto the attackers in the moat in three directions: straight down, a little to the left, a little to the right. These bastions, like others in Nubia, such as Aniba, Ikkur, and Kuban, are in the tradition of the curved bastions whose origins we first came across in the middle of the third millennium in Palestine, Egypt, and Mesopotamia.

At the foot of the outer wall there was a dry moat 8·5 meters wide and more than 6 meters deep. To make it even more difficult to cross, an additional low wall had been built on its farther bank, and its outer face strengthened by an earth glacis.

The entire gate complex is ingenious in plan and formidable in structure. The opening in the outer wall and the wall on the further lip of the moat were in line with the double-doored gateway in the western side of the main wall. Two large towers were built on either side of the entranceways, 15 meters in length, stretching from the main gateway to the moat and even beyond. For they protruded even from the wall on the distant bank of the moat, and formed a well-fortified gate complex from which fire could be directed across the moat to the right and left. According to the archaeologists who carried out the excavations, there were indications that originally there had been a wooden drawbridge across the moat which could be withdrawn in time of need by means of rollers.

Some impression of the effectiveness of these fortifications may be gained by recalling that for assault troops to reach their objective, they had to penetrate the first low wall, then cross the moat, then fight their way through the outer wall with its semicircular bastions, and then get through the main wall—all under a hail of arrows. It is quite clear that this would have been nearly impossible except at the points of the gate. And indeed the excavations revealed that there had been great fires at the site of the gate. It is equally clear that no such formidable fortifications would have been necessary if the enemy were not yet in possession of the battering-ram. And evidence that the battering-ram was already in use is provided by the wall paintings of Beni-hasan. We shall deal with this at greater length when we come to study the method of attack on these fortifications and on those of Palestine and Mesopotamia and in the Middle Bronze II period.

One of the characteristic features of the fortifications of Palestine and Syria in this period, beginning, that is, from the 18th century, is the large glacis or steeply sloped bank by which they were surrounded. Since this has been the subject of much controversy among scholars, it is perhaps worth going into some detail as to its nature. It will be recalled that when the people of the Middle Bronze II period came to build new cities on a tell, which had been the site of settlement for some 1,500 years, they found a pretty high mound with steeply sloping sides formed by layers of debris from earlier cities. The Hyksos glacis was in fact built not at the peak of the tell but against its slopes. In other words, it covered and encircled the lower part of the tell which was below the walls of the new city. At the beginning of this period, the glacis was built in a special way, colorfully termed the "sandwich" method. It was constructed of repeated layers of beaten earth, clay, gravel, and limestone. The face of the glacis was covered with thin layers of plaster, and made very smooth. In some cases, as for example at Tell el-Jerishe near Tel Aviv, the glacis was an even more complex structure, being greatly strengthened by the addition of bricks to the layers of limestone. The city walls, built mostly of brick, were constructed at the top of the glacis. During the latter part of this period—although in some cases even earlier—the beaten earth and indeed the whole sandwich system gave way to the glacis constructed entirely of stone, turning it into a battered wall, a wall in fact which covered the foot of the tell. Several fine examples of this type were found, notably in Jericho, Hazor (179), and Shechem. At the foot of the glacis a moat was dug or hewn out of the rock. Many were very wide and deep. At Tell el-'Ajjul, for example, in southern Palestine, the moat was 15 meters wide and 10 meters deep.

In addition to such tell cities whose slopes were strengthened by glacis, a new type of city makes its appearance during the Middle Bronze II period. It, too, has a glacis, of either the sandwich or stone form. But it is quite different from the earlier cities. These new cities were very large and were not built upon an existing tell, but either very close to it, as a kind of extension, or without any relationship whatsoever to a tell. The size of such cities—like Hazor in Israel which covered an area of 1,000 by 7,000 meters, or Qatna in Syria whose area was 1,000 by 1,000 meters—clearly indicates that the earlier tell city was too small and the inhabitants had therefore to build a new one outside the tell area, usually on the adjacent unfortified level ground. Since this new area lacked the natural defensive qualities of a tell city, they had to construct artificial devices for protection. This they did in a remarkable manner, which reflected ingenuity and daring in their engineering. They built walls as well as steeply sloped banks in the following way.

They wanted their wall to be as high as the wall at the top of the tell city. This meant a construction anywhere between 20 to 40 meters high, which was hardly possible. So they solved the problem by digging a moat, utilizing the excavated earth to form a rampart and constructing the wall upon it. This, then, gave the wall the required height. Archaeological digs have laid bare such walls built on

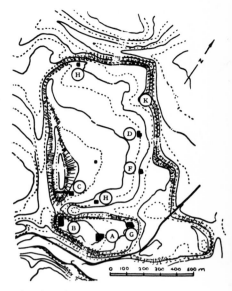

The plan of Hazor. Below: the bottle-shaped upper city. Above: the huge rectangular lower city. At left: the earthen rampart and fosse. Areas of excavations marked with letters

67

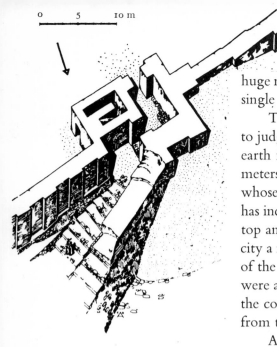

Megiddo city gate of Stratum 13.

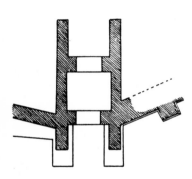

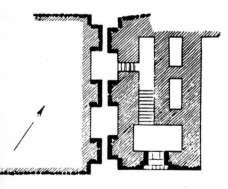

huge mounds of beaten earth. The idea was at once simple and ingenious. And the single operation of excavating the moat served a double purpose.

The project must have kept thousands of laborers on the job for several years, to judge by the scale of the fortifications of Hazor: the western rampart of beaten earth is 700 meters in length. At its widest point, the base of the rampart is 90 meters broad and 15 meters high. The moat to its immediate west (178), from whose scooped out earth this rampart was formed, reaches a depth of 15 meters. It has inclined sides, like the cross-section of a basin, and is 80 meters wide across the top and 40 meters wide at its base. This, therefore, gives the side of the fortified city a man-made steep slope 30 meters in height—15 meters being the sloping side of the moat and 15 meters the height of the mound. Structures on a similar scale were also found at Qatna and new cities of the same type elsewhere. Incidentally, the considerable width of the moat kept enemy archers that much farther away from the mound, and weakened the effectiveness of their weapons.

Archaeological excavations of the Middle Bronze II period also provide us with much information on the plan of the city gate. At the beginning of this period the gate is still angled, like the letter L, so that anyone who entered had to go through a turning. An enemy fighting his way through would thus have to turn and leave one side exposed to the fire of the defenders. A typical example of such a gate was found at Stratum 13 of the Megiddo excavations (see figure on this page). The path leading to the gate was stepped. And this together with the turning in the gate would have made it difficult for a chariot to maneuver. It may therefore be presumed that at this time, chariots were not yet in use, not even by the rulers of the city.

This gate belongs to the middle of the 18th century, shortly before the introduction of the new type of glacis on fortifications. With the innovation of this glacis, we find a change in the type of gate now built in all the cities in Palestine and Syria during Middle Bronze II. Instead of the angled gate, the entrance is now straight and direct. But to give them greater protection, they are built in depth, the length of the passageway reaching from 15 to 20 meters. These gates (see figures on pages 68–69) all have six inner pilasters, three on each side, which narrowed the entrance at these three points. We do not know whether there was only one set of doors—which is most likely, between the twin pilasters nearest the external face of the wall—or additional doors between the other sets of pilasters. The Trojan gates from the middle of the third millennium are perhaps the earliest example of this type, although they have only four pilasters.

The gates found at several archaeological excavations in Syria and Palestine are protected by two large towers, one on either side. They were almost certainly multi-storied, as is evidenced by the stairways found inside.

An extremely strong gate of this type was also found in the northeast corner of the lower city of Hazor, belonging to the 18th century (Areak).

This relic at Hazor also provides a good illustration of the integration of the approach path to the gate within the overall system of fortifications of the city. The gate itself was built on the high ground of the city site, and was some 25 meters above the surrounding countryside. A direct approach path from below to so high

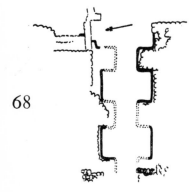

City gates. Troy, Alalakh, and Qatna

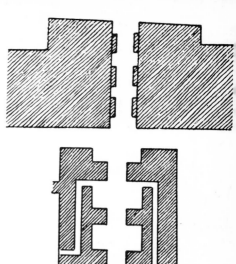

a point would have been too steep. And so an oblique path with an embankment was laid across the slope, of gentle gradient, which reached the gate from the right—from the point of view of the person facing the city—so that the right, or exposed, side of an enemy would be at the mercy of the city's defenders. Immediately in front of the gateway, the path ended in a leveled piece of ground wide enough to allow a chariot to turn and enter the gate from the right. The path, its embankment, and the leveled space in front of the gate were protected by a thick revetment wall built of large basalt boulders which formed a kind of defensive glacis for the entire slope (179, top). The degree of thought, planning, resources, and sheer physical labor that went into the construction of the path and the revetment wall are an indication of the high importance attached to this solution to the problem of entry into the city. There is no doubt that the change from the stepped approach and the angled gateway to the sloped path and the direct entranceway coincided with the introduction of the chariot to wider use in the 18th century—a feature on which we shall have more to say later.

METHODS OF WARFARE

The large cities built either as an extension of or apart from a city on a tell were heavily populated. A city like Qatna, for example, could hold some 40,000 inhabitants, and Hazor could hold close to 30,000. Clearly, only with the help of so considerable a population could such cities defend their walls, whose perimeter reached 4 kilometers at Qatna and 3 kilometers at Hazor.

The appearance of this new type of fortification, with its glacis, the new gate structure offering entry to chariots, and the large lower cities looking like huge camps, is explicable only in terms of a revolutionary change in the methods of warfare which demanded appropriate counter-measures. Since this occurred at the same time as the introduction of the horse-drawn chariot, and because of the character of the new gate and the camp-like form of the lower city, it was widely believed until quite recently that the powerful glacis was designed as a means of protection against attack by chariots.

No elaborate explanation is required to dismiss this theory as groundless. For apart from the difficulty of conceiving that chariots could carry out a charge up such steep slopes, we know that at no time was the chariot ever used to breach a fortification. And it is fallacious to compare it, as some do, with the modern tank. The chariot, for breaching purposes, could never be more formidable than the foreheads of the horses by which it was drawn. And, in any case, an upright wall would surely be more effective than a glacis in stopping a charging column of galloping horses.

There can be no question that the strengthening of the lower portion of the wall, and particularly the smooth, beaten-earth slopes of the tells, were certainly designed to prevent enemy attempts to tear down and destroy the wall and the slopes beneath it and enter the city through the breach. This explanation would long have been generally accepted if it were not for the widespread, though

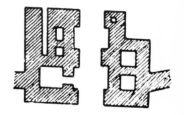

City gates. Top to bottom: Gezer, Sichem, and Beth-shemesh

Battle on Fortified Cities

69

erroneous, belief that the battering-ram did not make its appearance on the battle-field until the Assyrian period in the 10th century—that is, nearly 1,000 years later. But the evidence both of illustrated monuments and written documents shows that quite well-developed battering-rams were already being used in the first half of the second millennium. We can go even further and say that, from the siege scene of Deshashe dating back to the 25th century, and from the character of the powerful third-millennium Trojan fortifications, for example, with their glacis and bastions, it is reasonable to assume that a primitive type of battering-ram was in use as far back as this early period.

At all events, we have clear proof that it was in use in the first half of the second millennium. The earliest illustrations of battering-rams known to us so far are those which appear on the wall paintings of Beni-hasan dating back to the 20th century (158–159). To the right of the fortress we see a mobile structure, rather like a hut with a slightly pointed arched roof, which could be moved with the help of two parallel crossbars. It served as cover for two or three soldiers whose hands grasp a very long beam with a sharp tip, probably made of metal. The point of the beam is aimed at the top of the fortress wall, to the balconies and battlements, for the lower portion of the wall is already protected by a low glacis. The fortifica-tions of Buhen, referred to earlier, complement the details of the Beni-hasan paintings to give a complete picture.

These battering-rams, though they seem primitive, were no doubt effective under the prevailing conditions. Otherwise, it is hardly likely that they would be depicted in these siege scenes as the principal weapon of an army attacking a fortress. Moreover, the excavations at Buhen show that its magnificent fortifica-tions were destroyed as a result of breaching by a more developed battering-ram, and being set on fire, during the Hyksos period in the 17th century.

On improvements to the battering-ram in the 18th century we learn from the many written documents of Mari on the Euphrates. The Mari letters make several mentions of the battering-ram, made largely of wood, and of its effectiveness. Ishme-Dagan, for example, writes as follows:

"Thus saith Ishme-Dagan, thy brother! 'After I conquered [the names of three cities], I turned and laid siege to Hurara. I set against it the siege towers and batter-ing-rams and in seven days I vanquished it. Be pleased!'"

The power of the battering-ram must have been great, for in another letter, Ishme-Dagan reports that he conquered another city in a single day. It was also possible to move this heavy implement over long distances and even to surmount natural barriers. For another letter talks of transporting it by wagon and boat.

More detailed evidence of how the battering-ram was operated is contained in a Hittite document from Boghazköy which describes the siege of a city named Urshu at the end of Middle Bronze II. The text reads:

"They broke the battering-ram. The King waxed wroth and his face was grim: 'They constantly bring me evil tidings. . . . Make a battering-ram in the Hurrian manner! and let it be brought into place. Make a "mountain" and let it [also] be set in its place. Hew a great battering-ram from the mountains of Hazzu

70

and let it be brought into place. Begin to heap up earth. . . .' The King was angered and said: 'Watch the roads; observe who enters the city and who leaves the city. No one is to go out from the city to the enemy. . . .' They answered: 'We watch. Eighty chariots and eight armies surround the city.'"

This document sheds light on several details concerning the action of the battering-ram and its manufacture. The "mountain" is nothing other than the mound or ramp of earth which had to be laid up to the wall, to fill in part of the moat, over which the battering-ram could be moved into position, as we shall see very clearly from the illustrated Assyrian monuments from the first millennium. The description also completes the picture of the besieging units. The chariots, of course, were there not for storming the city but to seal off the approach roads against allied help to the besieged.

The purpose of the siege towers referred to in the Mari documents, as in the later period, was to enable the attacking archers to give covering fire from a greater height to the men operating the battering-ram, and to neutralize the weapons of the defenders upon the battlements. The importance of this covering fire by archers is endorsed in the Beni-hasan paintings, but here the mobile tower had not yet been introduced and the bows are fired from the standing or kneeling position from the ground.

All the evidence, it seems to me, clearly supports the view that the tremendous resources and labor invested in the fortifications of the Middle Bronze period were designed primarily to prevent breaching by the battering-ram. This was the major purpose of the moat, the outer or advanced wall, and the glacis, which protected the steep slope and lower portion of the wall. The gate, on the other hand, was given its new form to enable the city's own chariots to enter and leave, without, at the same time, making it easier to breach by the enemy. We see, therefore, that already in the first half of the second millennium, the foundations were laid for the extraordinarily advanced methods of attack on and defense of a fortified city which reached their apogee in the first millennium.

The absence of paintings or reliefs on the monuments belonging to most of the Middle Bronze II period, unlike the periods which preceded and followed it, leaves us without any detailed illustration of the methods of open battle at this time. Fortunately, however, we can fill the gaps by drawing on the written documents of the period which have much to say on vital aspects of our subject.

In a 20th-century B.C. document from the period of the Middle Kingdom, we find the earliest detailed written description of a unique form of battle—the duel.

Battle in Open Terrain: The Duel

Duels as depicted on a wall painting in Beni-hasan

Warriors depicted on a wall painting in Beni-hasan

This, let us recall, covers the period of the Beni-hasan wall paintings with their battle and siege scenes. The duel was a contest between two warrior-heroes, as representatives of two contending forces. Its outcome, under prearranged agreement between both sides, determined the issue between the two forces. This system, which obtained even in later periods such as the Mycenaean in Greece, found its most dramatic expression in the duel between David and Goliath, and between the warriors of the House of Saul and the House of David as we shall see later. A description no less colorful, and amazingly similar to the David-Goliath epic, is found in a document known as "The Story of Sinuhe the Egyptian." Sinuhe, a Chamberlain in the royal court of the XIIth Dynasty, had chosen voluntary exile and went to live with the Semitic tribes in northern Palestine and Syria. His hosts were hospitable and he spent a very happy time among them. But he finally returned to his country at the invitation of the Egyptian court. During his stay with the Semitic tribes, an encounter took place which Sinuhe describes in the following way:

Two Canaanite warriors on an 18th-century B.C. vase, recently found at Tell el-Far'ah (northern Palestine)

"A mighty man of Retenu [i.e., Syria and Palestine] that he might challenge me in my own camp. He was a hero without his peer, and he had repelled all of it [i.e., he had beaten everyone of the land of Retenu]. He said that he would fight me, he intended to despoil me, and he planned to plunder my cattle, on the advice of his tribe. That prince [the host of Sinuhe] discussed it with me and I said: 'I do not know him. Certainly I am no confederate of his, so that I move freely in his encampment. Is it the case that I have ever opened his door or overthrown his fences? Rather, it is hostility because he sees me carrying out thy commissions. I am really like a stray bull in the midst of another herd, and a bull of these cattle attacks him. . . .' During the night I strung my bow and shot my arrows [in practice]. I gave free play to my sword and polished my weapons. When day broke, Retenu was come. It had whipped up its tribes and collected the countries of a good half of it. It had thought only of his fight. Then he came to me as I was waiting, for I had placed myself near him. Every heart burnt for me. They said: 'Is there another strong man who could fight against him?' Then he took his shield, his battleaxe, and his armful of javelins. Now after I had let his weapons issue forth, I made his arrows pass by me uselessly, one close to another. He charged me, and I shot him, my arrows sticking in his neck. He cried out and fell on his nose. I felled him with his own battleaxe and raised my cry of victory over his back, while every Asiatic roared. I gave praise to Montu, while his adherents were mourning for him. Then I carried off his goods and plundered his cattle. What he had planned to do to me I did to him. I took what was in his tent and stripped his encampment."

This lively and detailed account can be completed by the Deshashe siege scenes which depict (146) dueling warriors near the fortress. Though they are not duels in the basic sense with which we are concerned they show the characteristic fighting pattern which was followed by the representative duel. Incidentally, Sinuhe's adversary seemed to have used the eye axe which, as we have observed earlier, was apparently in wide use in this period.

With all the importance of the duel, it does not mean, of course, that the major campaigns between national armies were settled in this way. The wooden model of spear-carrying Nubian archers from Egypt (163), belonging to the Middle Kingdom, shows that armies of this period were already organized in units which marched in disciplined order. The written records also contain much detail on the size of armies and the units taking part in battle, which indicate that there was open combat on a large scale. Thus we find several references in the Mari documents from the 18th century to militia units of 10,000 warriors. Mostly, of course, the units referred to are smaller, containing 3,000, 2,000, 1,000, 600, and 100 men. Also mentioned is the 300-man unit, used mainly as an assault unit, comprising three companies of 100 men each. It appears from the documents that the basic unit, the section, was probably composed of 10 men. This is also borne out by Sinuhe's reference to the palace guard: "When the day had broken, very early, they came and summoned me 10 men coming and 10 men going to usher me to the palace."

Standard Combat

If this period is poor in documents and monuments which show the movement of armies and their maneuvers on the battlefield, there is detailed written information on the intelligence and communications services without which it would not have been possible effectively to plan and execute large-scale military operations. We draw again on the Mari documents on an account of the quite well-developed communications system. It was based on signaling, and the signals were given by torches or firebrands according to a prearranged code. The following two letters explain the system:

"To my lord: Thus Nannum, thy servant. Yesterday I departed from Mari, and spent the night at Zuruban. All the Benjamites raised fire signals. From Samanum to Ilum-Muluk, from Ilum-Muluk to Mishlan, all the cities of the Benjamites of Terqa district raised fire signals in response, and so far I have not ascertained the meaning of those signals. Now I shall determine the meaning and I shall write to my lord whether it is thus or not."

Communications and Intelligence

This letter shows that the signals were flashed in accordance with a code, and that the writer of the letter recognized them as a system of transmitting information. This practice was in wide use as the second letter indicates:

"When I had made ready the city of Himush over against him and he saw that

73

the land was hastening to my aid, he raised a fire signal, and all the cities of the land of Ursum on the other side acknowledged."

From other letters we learn that this method of signaling was used for calls for immediate help by those under attack. There is no specific information on the means of communication between units during an attack, but it was probably carried out by special runners, by semaphore, or by trumpet-calls as in a later period.

The intelligence services were also well developed. This can be well imagined, for it would have been impossible to plan and carry out long-range operations and handle large formations in different conditions of terrain without advance intelligence. And again the documents of Mari illuminate the systems of intelligence in use during this period. From one of these letters we learn of the practice of dispatching powerful reconnaissance units for the express purpose of capturing prisoners for interrogation. Here is the letter:

"Hammurabi spoke to me as follows: 'A heavily armed force had gone to raid the enemy column, but there was no suitable base to be found, so that force had returned empty-handed and the column of the enemy is proceeding in good order without panic. Now let a light armed force go to raid the enemy column and capture informers [literally, "men of tongue"].'"

These "men of tongue" were, according to other letters, a most important means of intelligence. The documents also show that battle intelligence was based on fast and detailed reports from commanders to their superior officers. The commanders of Mari indicate whether they are transmitting direct or only hearsay information, and they record in detail the movements of the enemy: He has reached the river. He has not yet crossed. He is now organizing for battle. The following formula is typical: "On the sixth day of the month . . . 6,000 soldiers of so and so reached such and such a place. Their rumored aim is to conquer such and such a city. . . ."

The administrative services also operated at a high level of efficiency. This can be seen from the receipts and the detailed lists of equipment and supplies found in the Mari archives. We have seen earlier how the engineering and transport services of the army managed to move siege towers and battering-rams over long distances by wagon and boat. These operations predate by at least 200 years the action of Thutmose III who transported boats on ox-drawn carts. Before the discovery of the Mari documents, the operation of Thutmose III at the beginning of the 15th century was considered one of the most daring engineering feats of the period.

There must also have been some sort of medical service, judging from the reports of the Mari commanders who frequently refer to the health of their men, and send "strength" reports like "No dead; no sick."

The Chariot   Our knowledge of the chariot during this period comes almost exclusively from written documents. This does not imply that its function at this time was of secondary importance. On the contrary, there is much reason to believe that beginning from the 18th century the horse-drawn chariot was one of the most important instruments of battle in open terrain. But its fate in the first two centuries of the second millennium is not at all clear. We know of its existence from the Assyrian documents, but the general picture is blurred. It is certain that during the 20th and 19th centuries, the chariot was not yet in use in Egypt and it is doubtful if it was used in the region of Palestine and Syria. In the many wall paintings from the XIIth Dynasty, which have been referred to in earlier chapters and which often deal with military subjects, the chariot does not appear at all, neither among the Egyptian warriors nor among the Semites. There is no doubt that, had it been in use, it would have been depicted on these monuments.

On the other hand, the documents from Mari of the 18th century speak of horse-drawn chariots. That they were brought into common use from now on is certainly to be inferred from the new gate structure in fortifications designed to take chariots, which we have already discussed. But we also have concrete evidence in the skeletons of horses found at excavations and in the chariot horses' bits also found in strata belonging to the Middle Bronze II period. A fine example is the bit with spoked cheek-pieces found at Tell el-'Ajjul in Palestine which appears on page 180. Incidentally, these bits show the great advance in the chariots of this period over the chariots of the third millennium. For they enabled the driver to maintain full control over his fast horses and to guide them at the gallop even on sharp turns and in other maneuvers.

Additional important evidence of the use of the chariot in this period is the mention of the "horses of Hyksos" in a document from the time of Pharaoh Kamose, the last king of the XVIIth Dynasty, at the beginning of the 16th century. The Hyksos were the Asiatic tribes who ruled Egypt in the 17th century, and Kamose, by fighting against the "horses of Hyksos," paved the way for their final expulsion from Egypt. It is clear from this that the Hyksos were using chariots before their encounter with Kamose, that is, already in the 17th century.

Our final piece of evidence comes from the period immediately following, the period of the New Kingdom. At its very beginning, as we shall see later, Canaanite chariots make their appearance for the first time in Egypt. The standard of their development indicates clearly that they must have been in prolonged use before this time. The sum total of all this evidence does not amount to a sharply etched picture, but it is enough to show with certainty that the might of armies in the Asiatic lands of the Bible in the second half of the Middle Bronze period was based on the light horse-drawn chariot with spoked wheels.

It is equally evident that the art of warfare reached its highest standard in the first half of the second millennium. This was true of combat in open terrain, with the chariot and the composite bow as the principal battle instruments; of the structure of fortifications, with their glacis and moats; and of attack on a fortified city, in which the battering-ram held a prized place. In no later period, until the invention of gunpowder, did the armies of the world succeed in introducing on to the battlefield new methods or new weapons of war. But they did succeed in perfecting them, as we shall see in the following chapters.

75

V

THE PERIOD OF THE SOJOURN IN EGYPT, THE EXODUS, MOSES, AND JOSHUA

1570–1200 B.C.

The period of the New Kingdom in Egypt, or the Late Bronze period, to use the language of archaeology of Palestine and Syria, is the period which saw the renaissance of Egypt and its development into a mighty Power that struck terror in the entire region right up to the frontiers of the Hittite kingdom. This is also the period in which the great Hittite Empire became a formidable military force, the only one indeed able to stand up to the Egyptians. This is the period which covered the Exodus of the Israelites from Egypt under the leadership of Moses, and the conquest of Canaan under Joshua. And, in its final phase, this was the period which saw the beginnings of the collapse of the two mighty empires, Egyptian and Hittite, and the rise of the "Sea Peoples," who gained domination of the coastal region at about the same time as the Israelite tribes were securing control of the eastern area.

These momentous historic events would have vanished into oblivion if it were not for the rich legacy of written documents and illustrated monuments in which they are recorded, and which illuminate the social, cultural, and military context in which they were set. The number of wall paintings, reliefs, and other archaeological finds from this important period, which provide direct information on its military problems, is greater than those which have been preserved from the previous period and from many of the later periods.

But this information, however valuable, would be incomplete without the written documents. These are of extraordinary importance, particularly for the subject of our study. In addition to the Bible itself, there is much material of significance in the thousands of documents discovered in the archives of Nuzi, Boghazköy, Ugarit, and Tell el-Amarna, from the 15th to the 13th centuries B.C., coinciding with the period under review. The diversity of the documents is also of great value in completing the gaps in our knowledge. They include chronicles, peace treaties, administrative records, and exchanges of correspondence between the various kings and rulers. The military events referred to earlier find their echo in these documents either directly or indirectly.

And this period, too, left behind in documents and illustrated monuments, the earliest detailed descriptions of warfare in the lands of the Bible: the battle of Thutmose III near Megiddo; the celebrated battle between Rameses II and the King of the Hittites near Kadesh on the Orontes; and Joshua's battle of conquest. These documents and monuments enable us to follow the military features of the period with an authenticity and detail which was impossible before. They show that many of the weapons and methods of warfare and fortifications were the heritage of the previous period. But they also show considerable advances in military fields.

We shall begin our study as usual with the basic elements of warfare, mobility, firepower, and security. And we shall follow with a description and analysis of several of the celebrated battles of the period in which we shall see these elements in operation.

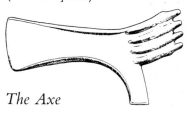

An axe from Chagar-Bazar
(*18th century* B.C.)

WEAPONS *Short- and Medium-range*

The Axe

In this, as in the previous period, we again come across the two earlier and conflicting traditions: the Egyptians continue with conservative consistency to stick exclusively to the tang-type axe, while the other lands of the Bible continue to use, in addition, the socket-type weapon.

At the beginning of the period, particularly from the 16th to the 15th century, the Egyptian axes follow the earlier Hyksos pattern. They are piercing axes with a long, narrow blade, and wide edge. The finest examples of such weapons, which can be dated absolutely, are presented on pages 180 and 181. They belong to the end of the XVIIth and the beginning of the XVIIIth Dynasties, at the very outset of the New Kingdom. The axe on page 180 bears the name of Kamose, the Pharaoh who started the expulsion of the Hyksos from Egypt. The axe on page 181 is the ceremonial axe of his mother, Queen Ahhotep, who received it as a present from her second son, Ahmose, the founder of the XVIIIth Dynasty, who completed the Hyksos expulsion started by his brother Kamose. Both axes are similar in shape, with a long and narrow blade which curves to a wide edge and a wide rear. The rear portion has two lugs by which the blade, whose back is inserted into the wooden haft, is tightly bound to strengthen the join. The edge is very sharp and convex, which makes it an excellent piercing weapon.

This axe was used throughout the period of the New Kingdom, though its shape underwent slight changes. Beginning from the 15th century, its blade becomes shorter and its edge narrower until eventually the edge becomes the narrowest part of the blade. The beginning of this development is well illustrated in the axe (184) which bears the name of Thutmose III, whose dates are

The axe of the warrior from Boghazköy
(*page 222*)

1490–1436 B.C., and, in the axes depicted in the relief from Deir el-Bahri belonging to the same period (185). The end development can be seen in the axes in the hands of Tutankhamun's infantrymen as depicted on the painted lid of a wooden chest found in his tomb at Thebes, belonging to the middle of the 14th century (214–215), and those borne by the soldiers of Rameses II as illuminated in the relief from the temple of Karnak (228), belonging to the middle of the 13th century.

In other lands of the Bible, we come across a tang-type axe reminiscent of the earlier period. This weapon (184, top) differs from the Egyptian type in that its rear portion is much longer, forming a deep tang. And the lugs here are positioned between the tang and the blade.

But the most interesting and indeed the most beautiful group of axes from the other lands of the Bible in this period are of the socket type. Two representative examples are shown on page 222. The portion of the blade to the rear of the socket is fashioned into ornamental lugs, or prongs, in the shape of fingers of a hand, or an animal's mane. This had a functional and not only a decorative purpose, for the prongs gave the rear part of the axehead an operational value. The 18th-century axes from Kültepe in Anatolia and from Chagar-Bazar in northwestern Mesopotamia (see figure on page 77), which have something akin to lugs at the rear of the socket, are no doubt the prototypes of those shown on page 222 which are typical of the axes of the Late Bronze period.

The Sword

The pattern in the development of the sword during this period has the same central design as in the previous period but there are several interesting and characteristic changes. The curved or sickle sword of the Middle Bronze period was, as we have seen, little more than a cutting axe, and it therefore had a comparatively long hilt and short blade. But with the total disappearance of the cutting axe in the Late Bronze period as a result of the widespread use of the helmet and armor, the warrior was left without a cutting weapon for use in chariot fighting or against an unarmored enemy. This explains the change in the curved sword during this period and the revolutionary difference in the relationship of blade and hilt. The blade is now long, equal in length to the hilt, and sometimes longer. There are many examples of this type of curved sword, both among the archaeological finds and in the graphic representations on the reliefs of the period. From these illustrated monuments in particular do we learn how widespread was the use of the sword from Anatolia to Egypt. The 13th-century rock carving from Yazilikaya near Boghazköy in Anatolia (205) depicts warrior-gods marching in column (see figure on page 79) bearing the curved sword with the long blade on their shoulder. This apparently was how the sword was carried on the march, as depicted also on the late-13th-century ivory carving from Megiddo (206). The four swords shown on page 207 complete our knowledge of its detailed form and shape. The first specimen was found at Gezer in Palestine in the tomb of a nobleman, belonging to the first half of the 14th century. (The sword shown on page 209 (left) from the same period, was discovered at Ugarit; 209 (center) is from the tomb of Tutankhamun and was found together with another sword of similar type. They were certainly not Egyptian, but probably reached the Pharaoh as a

The warrior-gods from Yazilikaya, with sickle swords (page 205)

gift or as booty.) The sickle sword on page 207 (left) bears the name of the Assyrian king, Adad-Nirari (1310–1280 B.C.), and therefore is of extreme importance for dating some other specimens. In shape it is transitional between those of the 14th century and those of the 12th and 11th centuries.

In the period of the New Kingdom, the Egyptians, too, began to use the sword very widely. They no doubt learned the art of its manufacture from the people of Canaan, as they did with the chariot and the composite bow, as we shall see later. The Egyptians called this sword *khopesh* after their term for the foreleg of an animal. In their swords, the blade was somewhat longer than the hilt and was quite wide. This is further evidence that it reached Egypt during the period of the New Kingdom, for at this time this type of sword was already established among the Canaanites. Not only was the *khopesh* sword in common use with the Egyptian army of this period, as is shown by such monuments as the relief at the temple of Karnak (228, left), but it became the symbol of Pharaonic authority. The relief showing Rameses III smiting his Canaanite enemies (350) depicts him brandishing this type of sword. In earlier periods, the Pharaoh is shown wielding a mace.

The fact that the long-bladed curved sword, a smiting weapon, was so widely used at this time, explains the Biblical phrase so frequently applied to Joshua's actions of conquest, which started in this very period—"he smote with the edge of the sword." This expression could not be used for the action of the short, straight narrow sword, which was a thrusting or stabbing weapon, but for the operation of the curved sword, with whose edge one smote the enemy.

Side by side with the smiting sword, which was the most convenient weapon for the charge of the phalanx in hand-to-hand combat (228), much progress was made during this period in the development of the straight sword. At the beginning of the period, it is still a kind of dagger, with a narrow blade (208–209), similar to the dagger-swords of the Middle Bronze period. But starting from the 13th century, the long straight blade begins to be more popular under the influence of the Sea Peoples.

The Sea Peoples, some of whom were mercenaries serving in the royal Egyptian armies of the XIXth Dynasty, were armed with very long swords of the same type as those used by the Egyptian soldiers, particularly when scaling ladders in an assault on fortifications where a smiting weapon would have been ineffective (228, the warrior on the right-hand ladder). A sword of this type belonging to the end of the 13th century, bearing the name of Pharaoh Merneptah, was discovered at Ugarit (209, left). Its blade was 60 centimeters, and its hilt added another

79

14 centimeters to the length of the sword. Another group of four swords, probably slightly earlier, were also found at Ugarit in the house of the high priest.

The Spear   The spear was a basic weapon of the infantry. Several illustrated monuments clearly depict special spear units, carrying spear and shield (216–217, 230). They formed, together with the sword- and axe-bearers, the main power of the phalanx in assault (238).

The socketed spearhead was leaf-shaped and strengthened by a protuberant spine. A good example is shown in the relief from Shihan in Trans-Jordan (223, top). Some scholars ascribe this relief to the end of the third millennium, but from the shape of the warrior's helmet and his curled locks it clearly belongs to the latter half of the second millennium. The top part of this relief is broken, and this gives the impression that the warrior is holding a short-handled weapon. But it is certainly a heavy spear with a long staff. Even the way in which it is held with both hands shows that the action was spear-thrusting and not javelin-hurling as has been suggested.

The spear was also used effectively by defenders on the ramparts to stab attacking troops ascending ladders (229). And it had an interesting function in the chariot units. Egyptian chariots were not equipped with the spear. But it was frequently to be found in the chariots of the neighboring armies, where it was kept in a special pipe-like socket, at the rear of the vehicle. This spear was the weapon of the driver, and it was no doubt used under certain battle conditions when the charioteer was pressed into service as an infantryman. This difference between the Egyptian and the Asiatic chariot units is strongly in evidence in the chariots of the Hittite King in the Battle of Kadesh. The chariots of the Hittites and their allies were manned by two warriors in addition to the driver. The warriors were armed with a shield and a long spear (239). The spear in this case assuredly served as the principal weapon in the charge into the enemy ranks. This tradition is followed by the chariot units of the first millennium in Syria and Assyria. Their standard equipment always includes a spear, which is kept at the rear of the vehicle and serves as the weapon of the driver.

As against this, beginning with the XIXth Dynasty, the Egyptian chariots are equipped with short javelins which are carried in a special quiver (240).

LONG-RANGE WEAPONS

The Bow   The illustrated monuments and written documents carry the clear implication that the composite bow was the decisive weapon in all the big armies of the lands of the Bible during this period. Its effectiveness to the chariot units and the infantry as well as for the defense of ramparts made it a most sought after weapon, and special workshops were established for its manufacture. It was, however, a difficult weapon to make, and not every warrior was equipped with it. The armies of small kingdoms and the fighting men of small tribes, unlike the regular forces of rich empires, could not produce this type of weapon in mass quantities. An

80

additional difficulty was that not every type of wood, horns, and tendons were suitable for the manufacture of an effective composite bow. An interesting document, which itemizes the types of materials required to produce this instrument, is found in the Ugarit texts. Aqhat promises Anat to supply her with the necessary materials:

> "Let me vow *īqbm* [birch tree?] from Lebanon
> Let me vow tendons from wild bulls
> Let me vow horns from wild goats
> Sinews from the locks of bulls."

The shape of the composite bow is well illustrated in many monuments. Two basic types are in evidence: the triangular bow and the recurved bow. Both are carried by Semites bearing votive offerings as depicted on a wall painting of the 15th century (195). The triangular bow is a shallow isosceles, with a wide-angled peak of about 120 degrees and the angles formed by the string and the ends of the arms each 30 degrees. Some good illustrations of this bow are to be seen in the Thutmose IV chariot reliefs, both in the hands of Pharaoh himself and in those of his enemies (193) and in the wall paintings on pages 195 and 199.

The recurved composite bow is easily recognized by the tendency of its arms to curve away from the string near its ends when it is not drawn, and even when it is, as the bow of Rameses II well shows (240–241). The composite bow was liable to be damaged by changes of weather, among other reasons, and so, like the violin, it was frequently kept in a special case. Such bow cases were fitted to the side of the chariot and the bow remained there when not in use. These cases, too, offer additional testimony to the extensive use of the triangular composite bow. A detail from the wall painting of the tomb of Kenamon (199) shows one of these cases being carried by an arms-bearer. It is the same shape as the bow, a shallow isosceles triangle. A similar case is depicted in the relief from Deir el-Bahri (185). Several illustrations, notably the wall painting from the tomb of Nebamon (210), show that it was easy to open—from the top—to allow the bow to be quickly withdrawn and put into operation. Other cases appear on pages 192, 196, 215, and 216.

The arrows usually had a body made of reed. This was an ideal substance, strong, pliant, easy to shape and to receive the arrowhead and tail-feathers. Many arrows of reed were found in Egypt in a good state of preservation. This material is also mentioned in the Ugarit text referred to earlier. Following his undertaking to Anat, which we have quoted, to send her materials for the bow, Aqhat goes on to promise special reeds from a place noted for the excellence of its specimens. The common use of the reed for this purpose also finds substantiation in the word for arrow in Nuzi. It is "reed."

The arrowhead for battle was generally of bronze. In this period it was rather thick in the middle and had a spine, either protuberant or flat. This is explicable by the prevalent use at this time of the coat of mail which could be penetrated only by a spined or ribbed arrowhead. Much effort went into fashioning the thick portion of the head, between its rear part and the beginning of its tang. This thickening prevented the arrowhead from being pushed into its reed body and splitting it on impact with the target. This was, of course, essential for combat against armor. The aim of more effective penetration of armor also found expression in the manufacture of an iron arrowhead, but it was very rare. One was found in Egypt, belonging to the beginning of the 14th century, the period of Amenhotep III.

The arrows were generally carried in a quiver. It was long and cylindrical and made of leather (198, center). To make it easier for the archer to carry, it had a shoulder strap (198, right). Although quivers were fitted to chariots, some charioteers also carried additional quivers on their shoulders (186, 187, 214–215, 216–217). Each quiver held between twenty-five and thirty arrows. This we know specifically from the Nuzi documents of the 15th century. In one document, listing military equipment, we find the following: "5 leather quivers, 30 arrows in each"; ". . . Total 7 leather quivers, 178 arrows placed in them."

The operation of the composite bow required strenuous training. The archer had to develop his muscles, acquire the correct stance, learn to hold the arrow correctly while drawing the bow. For this purpose special practice ranges were established. The instructors would stand behind the trainees and correct their position and aim. Training would begin on the simple bow (201, bottom right) and lead up to the composite weapon (201, bottom left). The left forearm—the bow arm—was bound with a special leather guard to protect it from the snap of the string on release (192, 199, 215, and 240). The range targets were rectangular boards of wood fixed to a bar. For testing a particularly strong bow with great power of penetration, a target board of crude copper was used. Here is a contemporary boasting report of practice firing by Pharaoh Thutmose III which shows his strength and skill:

"He shot an ingot of copper, every shaft being split like a reed. Then His Majesty put a sample there in the House of Amon, being a target of worked copper of three fingers in thickness, with his arrow therein. When it had passed through it, he made three palms come out of the back of it [i.e., about 25 centimeters of the arrow protruding from the back of the target]."

The system of training on the ranges and the siting of the targets is described in the report on the prowess of another Pharaoh, Amenhotep II, son of Thutmose III. This shows that stress was laid in the training of chariot archers on firing with the horses at full gallop. This is also depicted on illustrated monuments such as 200:

"He [the king] entered into his northern garden and found that there had been set up for him four targets of Asiatic copper of one palm in their thickness, with twenty cubits between one post and its fellow. Then His Majesty appeared in a chariot like Montu [the god of war] in his power. He grasped his bow and gripped four arrows [see page 200] at the same time. So he rode northward, shooting at them like Montu in his regalia. His arrows had come out of the back thereof while he was attacking another post. It was really a deed which had never been

82

done nor heard of by report: shooting at a target or copper an arrow which came out of it and dropped to the ground. . . ."

The archers were long-range warriors and fought at times with the slingmen. In the Egyptian monuments from the New Kingdom, the sling appears only at the beginning of the XXth Dynasty. We shall have more to say about the function of the bow in battle when we discuss tactics and methods of warfare.

PERSONAL PROTECTION

The Shield

The shield underwent considerable changes during the period of the New Kingdom in Egypt—the Late Bronze period in the other lands of the Bible—for armor and the helmet were already in wide use. This prompted far-reaching modifications in the shape and size of the shield. It became smaller and smaller as the coat of mail and the helmet became more and more effective.

A typical Egyptian shield of the New Kingdom

But there were differences in the types of shield used in Egypt, Palestine, Syria, and Anatolia and the shields of the Sea Peoples of the Egyptian armies during the XIXth Dynasty in the 13th century. The Egyptian shield throughout the period of the New Kingdom is comparatively small. Its top is rounded and is slightly wider than its base, which is straight. This suggests that it was designed primarily to protect the face and the upper part of the body. This shape remains virtually unchanged, with only minor modifications throughout the New Kingdom.

The shields were made of wood and covered with leather (202–203). In the 13th century, the top part of the shield protecting the face is strengthened with a metal disk. The loop or strap could be lengthened to enable the shield to be carried on the back. This was very practical in operations against a fortified city (228), both in scaling the ladders and breaching the gate.

The light circular shield was used in the Egyptian army exclusively by the Sea Peoples (229). These troops were well armored; their basic weapons were the long sword and spear. This shield was particularly well suited to hand-to-hand combat, and did not encumber movement.

The Canaanite, Palestinian, and Syrian shields may have followed the tradition of the old Sumerian pattern, which was conceivably popular in this region. We have no actual shields found at excavations. But we know the type of shields used by the Palestinian and Syrian warriors for they are represented on illustrated Egyptian monuments. The most important for our purposes is the relief on the chariot of Thutmose IV from the 15th century (192–193). The shields here are rectangular, and are apparently no larger than 60 by 30 centimeters. It is possible that they were slightly convex. There are two types. One is made of plaited reeds (192) and the other of wood covered with leather studded with numerous metal tacks and disks, both for added protection and for decoration (193, 199, top right). There are somewhat similar illustrations of Semitic shields on the painted side panel of the chest from the tomb of Tutankhamun from the 14th century (216–217) as

83

against the round-topped shields of the warriors in the Egyptian army with whom they are seen locked in battle.

The Canaanite shields depicted in the reliefs of Seti I (231) and Rameses II (where the Canaanites are fighting together with the Hittites) are also oblong. But we find a radical change beginning with the 13th century when both the round and the rectangular shields appear on the battlefield. We find the round shield in the hands not only of a warrior from the city of Ashkelon (228) but also of the fighters depicted in the Megiddo reliefs. In the Megiddo illustrations, some are shown equipped with a sickle sword and carrying a round shield on their back (206–207), some carry an axe and a round shield (242), and some a spear and a similar shield (243). There is no doubt that this shield was introduced into the Canaanite armies under the influence of the Sea Peoples who made their appearance in this part of the world precisely at this time.

The Hittite shield was quite different from all the others, and is well illustrated in the Rameses relief of the Battle of Kadesh (see figure on page 88). It is shaped like a rough figure 8, round and wide at the top and bottom and narrow at the waist, broadly following the lines of the human body. The Hittite chariots were used for short-range combat, and this perhaps explains the form of their shield. For it gave protection to the whole body, yet was reasonably light by virtue of its narrowness at the center.

Armor

The coat of mail is the outcome of the advancement of the bow and the chariot to extensive use. The charioteer and the archer were the only warriors who required both hands to operate their battle instruments, and so lacked the means of protecting their body with a shield. At the beginning, the archer, even wielding the simple bow, was in large measure protected by distance, since he was out of range of enemy missiles. But with the development and wider use of the composite bow, this military advantage was neutralized. It was of course possible to solve the problem for the archer and the charioteer by means of the special shield-bearer. And this method was indeed adopted in later periods. For the chariot it meant the addition of a third man—driver, archer, plus bearer—which put a heavy strain on the light vehicle. Despite this, the system was prevalent among the Hittites. But the search for the ideal solution persisted. It was found in the coat of mail, with its metal scales, hard, reasonably light, and flexible. It was expensive, and not all armies could afford it. Even large armies could not afford to armor all the men in every unit. They laid down priorities. Top of the priority list were the archers and the charioteers.

As the bow and the chariot became more and more common in the Late Bronze period, so did the coat of mail. Thutmose III records, for example, that in the Battle of Megiddo he took more than 200 coats of mail as war booty. An instructive illustration of the use of this type of armor by the Canaanite chariot drivers is to be found in the Thutmose IV chariot relief (192, 196, top). Here we see how the driver wore his scaled armor. It covered his body and the top part of his arms almost to the elbow. His neck, too, is protected by a leather collar stiffened by pieces of metal.

The Egyptian artist also points up the weak spots of the coat of mail by showing an arrow stuck in to the driver at the armpit, at the join of the sleeve to the body of the coat. (Compare this with I Kings 22: 34: "And a certain man drew a bow at a venture, and smote the king of Israel between the joints and [of] the armor....") This relief also shows in detail the shape of the scales. They are largely rectangular, with the bottom edge fashioned into a point, and they have a protuberant spine down the center. A well-preserved part of an earlier coat of mail, found at Nuzi (196, bottom), has a row of scales in one section which are rounded at one side. From this relic we learn that the scales were not of even size. They varied according to their position on the coat. The smallest ones were 64 millimeters long and 36 millimeters wide; the intermediate were 101 by 45 millimeters; and the largest, 118 by 63 millimeters. Their average thickness was 2 millimeters.

By comparison, the scales of the coats of mail found at Thebes in the palace of Amenhotep III (197, bottom) come to a point at the bottom and are 115 millimeters in length. Armor with precisely this type of scale is excellently illustrated in complete form in the wall painting from the tomb of Kenamon in the reign of Amenhotep II (197, top).

These large scales must have been very heavy, and in time improvements were effected and the scales made smaller. A coat with small scales was worn by Rameses II at the Battle of Kadesh (240–241).

Since the ancient artists often depicted the scales simply in painting, which wears off in time, their apparent absence from many reliefs was interpreted by some as indicating that the coat of mail was not widely used. But the Battle of Kadesh wall painting (237), whose colors were apparently well preserved when the copy was made, shows that even the Hittite charioteers wore similarly scaled armored clothing.

The coat of mail in the Kenamon wall painting has about 450 large scales. The armor of Thutmose IV's enemies (196, top) had a similar number—or slightly less. Details on the number of scales per coat are given in the equipment lists from the Nuzi archives. Large and small scales are itemized separately. The text of one tablet deals, for example, with four coats of mail. One is listed as having 400 large scales and 280 small scales—680 in all. Another has a total of 1,035 scales. The coats were thus of different sizes and different quality. The bigger and better the coat, the larger the number of small scales.

The method of attaching the scales to the garment of leather or cloth is also well seen in the armor found in Nuzi, Egypt, Palestine, and Syria. The scales were sewn on to the garment with strong thread which passed through tiny holes punctured in each scale—usually three at the top, two at the bottom, and two at one side. But the number and position of the holes varied from one type of armor to another. And they were also suited to the part of the body the scale was to cover.

These details serve to underline the two weaknesses of the coat of mail: its weight and its complicated manufacture.

The helmet, too, was in extensive use by warriors in the Late Bronze period. *The Helmet* Those worn by some of the enemy chariot drivers in the Thutmose IV chariot relief (192–193) are slightly pointed and cover the ears and the forehead up to the eyebrows. This metal headgear must have become very hot in battle, and so it was covered by some insulating material, which was also decorative. Some helmets, for example, had long feathers stuck to the crown, their points meeting at the top, their broad portions fanned and covering the metal. Some were overlaid with a cloth-piece, or cloth strips. And some had a tassel attached to the crown and knotted at the back like a plait. Such a helmet, albeit with well-defined ear-shields, is worn by the warrior carved in the relief on the gate jamb at Boghazköy (222, top). Egyptian warriors also wore helmets, especially in assault. These, like their coats of mail, were quite expensive, and it is presumably because of their value that helmets are often depicted in Egyptian wall paintings in the hands of Semites bearing gifts. The piercing axe, a universal weapon in this period, was primarily designed against this metal helmet.

As the means of security reached the point where they matched the means of firepower, mobility became the decisive factor in battle. And so as armor and the helmet on the one hand and the composite bow on the other both achieved high standards of development, the chariot assumed a more significant place on the battlefield.

MOBILITY

The Chariot   The chariot reached Egypt from Canaan. This is also borne out by the fact that Egyptian terms for the chariot and horses are borrowed from the Canaanite. Moreover, the Egyptian chariot in the first half of the XVIIIth Dynasty is exactly like the Canaanite chariot. This is seen in wall paintings which often depict Canaanites bearing chariots as votive gifts to the Egyptian royal court.

Our sources of information on the chariot in the Late Bronze period are rich and varied. They comprise wall paintings, reliefs, remains of actual chariots, and literary descriptions, from which it is possible to reconstruct, down to the last detail, the shape of the chariot, its measurements, the materials from which it was made, its crew, horses, armament, and the way it was used in battle.

Chariots in the 16th and 15th centuries were light. They had two wheels, each of four spokes. The body had a wooden frame partly covered with leather or some other light material, and was harnessed to two horses. In order to understand the changes in development of the chariot during this period, it is well to give detailed study to this Canaanite-Egyptian type at the beginning of the period. A good example for our study is the chariot found in Egypt and now in the Florence Museum, from the Early XVIIIth Dynasty in the 15th century (191). It was apparently made in Canaan and brought to Egypt either as war booty or as a gift.

This chariot has three main elements: the body, the wheels, and the pole and yoke. The body has a wooden frame. From a side view the body looks like a quadrant, one radius forming the upright front, the other radius forming the horizontal base with its rear resting on the axle, and the arc forming the back. Its base is 1 meter wide and $\frac{1}{2}$ meter deep. It is 75 centimeters high in front—which

86

would cover about halfway up to the thighs of the charioteer. The leather covering has not been preserved, but from wall paintings of the period, we see that the whole of the front and the bottom part of the sides of the body were so covered. The axle-rod is 6 centimeters thick at the center and its length between the wheels is 1·23 meters—23 centimeters longer than the width of the body, so that the clearance of each wheel from the side of the body was 11·5 centimeters. The total length of the axle-rod is 1·53 meters, for it extended beyond each wheel by 15 centimeters. Making the axle-rod so much longer than the width of the body gave the chariot greater stability on sharp turns. The wheels had four spokes whose thickness near the center reached 4 centimeters.

The chariot pole is 2·5 meters long, its hind end attached to the rear bar of the body frame and running under the body, giving additional strength to an otherwise frail structure. It is 6·7 centimeters at its thickest point. As it emerges from the underside of the body, it is attached to the top part of the vehicle's front by leather thongs. All wall paintings of chariots seem to make a point of showing this (186, 187, 189). The yoke is shaped like a double-convex bow and is attached to the forward end of the pole by nails. The yoke in all its detail is portrayed with minute accuracy also on the Canaanite chariot depicted on the wall painting from the tomb of Rekhmire in Thebes showing Canaanites bearing gifts (189). The Florence chariot reveals how much thought and effort went into the making of a chariot and how each part required its own special wood. The pole, for example, was made of elm, the tires of pine; the binding of the spokes and other parts of the body was done with strips of birch. Everything was planned to make the vehicle light, flexible, and strong. And, indeed, several illustrated monuments depict gift-bearers carrying a chariot on their back—which shows that it must have been very light.

Throughout most of the 15th century the Egyptian chariot is still almost identical with the Canaanite, and the axle-rod, though well to the rear, is not yet flush with the rear of the body (190). But starting with the reign of Thutmose IV, at the end of the 15th century, the Egyptian chariot begins to shake off its Canaanite influence and undergo considerable change.

Thutmose IV chariot's body bears reliefs on both sides (192–193). From these reliefs we see clearly that the chariot is now heavier and its wheels have not four but eight spokes. This sudden doubling of spokes was apparently an experiment which was not successful. For with the reign of Amenhotep III, we find the Egyptian chariot fitted with six-spoke wheels (190, 210, 211, 212, 213, 215, 216, 232, 235, 240). So widespread and meticulous is the delineation of the number of wheel spokes on chariots depicted on Egyptian monuments that they can be used as a criterion for determining whether the monument is earlier or later than 1400 B.C.

Excellent examples from which we learn the trend of chariot measurements in the second half of the 14th century are those of Tutankhamun. The vehicle is 1·25 meters high and 1·02 meters wide. The axle-rod from wheel to wheel is 1·75 meters. The width of the body was thus four-sevenths of the length of the rod, and this must have given it great stability on turns. The diameter of the wheels is

87

The Hittite chariots in the Battle of Kadesh (for the inaccuracy of this drawing see page 239, bottom, where the wheels have six spokes and not eight)

92 centimeters and the length of the pole is 2·56 meters. The pole, as with Canaanite and other Egyptian chariots, runs under the body and gives it additional support. This chariot is depicted in action in the splendid paintings on the wooden chest found in the tomb of Tutankhamun (214–215, 216–217).

The Egyptian chariot in the 13th century remains virtually unchanged, having apparently reached peak quality in the 14th. This is evident from the superb relief showing Rameses II charging through the Hittite army, his bow at the draw (240–241). The single difference seems to be that in this century, the side of the vehicle is fitted with a special quiver for hurling javelins (240) in addition to the bow case and arrow quiver. We can identify the type of these javelins, of which we shall have more to say when we come to the chapter on Goliath.

In Canaan itself the chariot, which made its impact on the Egyptian vehicle, developed in much the same way as the Egyptian. But from the XVIIIth Dynasty, when Egypt gained dominion over Canaan, the Canaanites ceased to be their own masters in the manufacture of chariots, and a certain decline set it. However, the influence now seems to be in the reverse direction, with Canaanite chariots, beginning with the 14th century, following the Egyptian pattern. They become heavier and their wheels have six spokes. On the other hand, since they apparently did not succeed in developing a light enough body, the axle-rod is positioned under the center and not at the rear edge of the body, so as not to put too heavy a strain on the horses (206–207). As a result, the chariot lost a good part of its maneuverability on the fast turn. This difference between the Canaanite and Egyptian chariots is well underlined in the Tutankhamun painting (216–217).

The Hittite chariot is known to us only from the Rameses II reliefs portraying the Battle of Kadesh. It is difficult to be specific about it, for the Hittite forces were a coalition of several peoples. The reliefs show a number of chariots whose axle-rod passes under the center of the body; others show a much taller case. But in some cases (as in 239), there is no apparent distinction between the Hittite and Egyptian chariots. Both have the rod at the rear edge of the body base. It is of course impossible to determine the measure of accuracy of the Egyptian artists in this case. For differences are shown in the various shapes of Hittite chariot portrayed on other reliefs in various temples. At all events, it would seem that the Hittite chariot did have the axle-rod under the center and not the rear, for we know that it carried a crew of three, which would have made it too heavy for a rear axle.

In action, the Egyptian, Canaanite, and Hittite chariots were harnessed to two horses. But the proportion of horses to chariots captured in battle, which we see quite often from the written records, was three to one. This suggests that the full complement was three horses per chariot, two committed and one in reserve, unharnessed. In a later period, in the 9th century, the third horse was also occasionally harnessed to the vehicle, as we shall see later. The horse was often protected in battle by special armor which covered its back.

The delicate and precise structure of the chariot demanded special workshops for its manufacture. From Egyptian wall paintings (202) we see the process, which seems to follow the assembly-line pattern. One group makes the rim, another the spokes, another assembles the wheel. Other groups are concerned with the wooden parts of the vehicle, some making the body, others the pole, others the axle-rod. Some are seen fitting the leather and the accessories, like quivers and bow cases.

One of the big problems was maintenance. The chariot had to be kept in good condition on the march, in battle, and afterward. Wheels and other parts of the vehicle would break. They had to be changed, strengthened, or repaired. To meet this need, special repair workshops were established, even along specific routes, and equipment stores for spare parts were put up at appropriate places. Thus we read in one of the letters sent to the Governor of Ta'anach in the 15th century (according to Albright's translation):

"I was ambushed in Gurra; so give me this day two chariot wheels and an axle and two. . . . And when the making of the axle has been completed, send it to me. . . ."

Several important documents which relate to the subject of maintenance were found in the royal archives of Ugarit. They record the number of chariots brought into the workshops for repair, and the state of their condition. One, for example, says that eight chariots were brought in to the King's palace, complete with their wheels, poles, and harness. But "two chariots are without quivers." The document goes on to say that three pairs of wheels and one pole were taken for repair to the "chief artificer," namely, to the person in charge of the workshops.

A rather amusing and interesting chronicle of the experiences of an Egyptian courier driving his chariot in the land of Canaan appears in one of the Egyptian papyri. He starts with an account of how the knaves of Jaffa sabotaged his vehicle while he was asleep:

"A coward steals thy bow, thy dagger, and thy quiver. Thy reins are cut in the darkness. Thy horse is gone and starts a runaway over the slippery ground, as the road stretches out before him. He smashes thy chariot. . . . Thy weapons have fallen to the ground. . . ."

After this comes a description of the chariot-repair workshop in Jaffa:

"Thou art introduced into the armory, and workshops surround thee. Craftsmen and leather workers are close by thee, and they do all that thou hast desired. They take care of thy chariot, so that it ceases to be loose. Thy pole is newly trimmed, its attachments are applied. They put bindings on thy collar-piece. . . . They fix up thy yoke. . . . Thou goest forth quickly to fight, to accomplish deeds of heroism."

89

There were of course also mobile workshops for the repair of weapons and chariots on the march and in battle. One such workshop is depicted in the relief showing the camp of Rameses II at the Battle of Kadesh (236–237). At the side of the camp (236, top panel) we see the artificer repairing a chariot pole, assisted by two apprentices.

We mentioned earlier that different parts of the chariot were made of different wood—each suited to the function of the part. The woods had therefore to be brought from different places, and the written documents specify geographic regions (like the area of Beth-shan) in Palestine and Syria which were known for the quality of tree that was just right for a particular part.

Incidentally, chariots were not the only wheeled vehicles used by the armies of this period. They also had transport vehicles to carry equipment and supplies for the fighting men. From the reliefs of the Battle of Kadesh, we see that both the Hittite and the Egyptian armies had quite a number of such wagons hitched to draft animals. The Hittite wagons were four-wheelers and were certainly heavier than the two-wheeled Egyptian types (236–237, center). They look like large boilers with a rounded lid. Supplies were also carried by pack asses.

METHODS OF ASSAULT ON FORTIFIED CITIES

The Fortifications   Most of the cities of the Late Bronze period were established on the city sites of the previous period. Where the fortifications of the earlier settlements were completely destroyed, new fortifications were built. Where they had been only partially demolished, they were repaired and renovated. Where they had remained undamaged, they were taken over for use in this later period. This is the case, I believe, with the celebrated wall of Jericho, with its stone glacis, referred to earlier —the very "walls of Jericho" mentioned in the Biblical description of the conquest by Joshua. For although its bottom part is certainly Middle Bronze, it was so solid that if the wall had been damaged in the 16th century—that is, at the end of Middle Bronze II—only the upper part would have been affected, the part built of brick, and this was probably renovated in the Late Bronze period. It would be idle to go on searching for another wall from the time of Joshua, or to seek to ascribe its absence to erosion. This, I believe, is the wall of Joshua's Jericho.

We find evidence in other cities of this period in Palestine, Egypt, and Syria that earlier fortifications continued in use, either as they were or with partial reconstruction. Occasionally some serious change was introduced. In Hazor, for example, the earlier wall of the large lower city remained. Its gates were rebuilt on the same site and after the same pattern as the original. The change they may have made is the construction in some places of stone walls or isolated towers on top of the earth ramparts which protected the city from the west and north. In Megiddo, too, the four-chambered city gate, built at the end of the Middle Bronze period, remained standing.

Where the earlier fortifications had been ruined, or where their design no longer met the needs of the new Late Bronze city, new fortifications were built.

An instructive example of the impressive fortifications of this Late Bronze period in Palestine is the well-preserved "outer wall" of Gezer. It encompasses the entire area of the tell and is built of huge stone boulders. It is 4 meters thick and in some places it has remained standing to a height of $3\frac{1}{2}$ meters. It has several rectangular bastions, which protrude both from the inner and exterior surfaces of the wall. They are more than 10 meters long and their corners are strengthened by quarried stone. Some were built at the same time as the wall, others were added later.

The fortress of Buhen, whose design in the Middle Bronze period was described in detail earlier, also had its character changed in this later period, and it now has walls with square bastions.

But the finest example of Late Bronze city fortifications are undoubtedly those of Hattussas, capital of the Hittites in Anatolia, now called Boghazköy. Here one can readily discern the innovations of the Late Bronze period, for this city was built anew in stages at the time of the Hittite Empire over an incomparably greater area than its predecessor. Its system of fortifications is therefore original, and is clearly characteristic of the period. It is one of the largest cities of this time whose fortifications are well preserved. It also offers an insight into the engineering skills of the period. For it is built on hilly ground, with different sections at different levels, and the fortifications had to be suited to the prevailing topographic conditions. They show all the features of a perfect system.

The city at this period comprised three basic elements: (a) The acropolis or citadel, known in Turkish as Büyük Kale—"the great citadel"—built on a hill above the west bank of a deep ravine. Its measurements are 150 by 250 meters. (b) The lower city, lying northwest of the citadel, between two ravines, measuring about 1,000 by 500 meters. (c) The large upper city, built to the south of the citadel and lower city on ground which rises steadily southward. It is 1,400 by 1,100 meters. The overall length of the city complex, lower and upper, from north to south reaches 2,000 meters.

To understand the essential character of the Hattussas fortifications it must be remembered that the three components of the city were not built at the same time. The citadel is the earliest, and was built largely in the first half of the second millennium. The lower city fortifications belong mainly to the 15th century. The large upper city was built at the beginning of the 14th century or later, and shows the vast expansion of this settlement at a time when the Hittite Empire was in full blossom. It also shows the mighty efforts of the Hittite king, Suppiluliumas, to include within the overall fortifications the commanding high ground to the south of the lower city. The features of the terrain, the hills and the river-beds, necessitated the construction of this new wall whose perimeter approximated to 4 kilometers! Add to this the 2 kilometers of outer wall round the lower city and the citadel, and we have a total of 6 kilometers of wall which had to be defended by the 14th–13th-century inhabitants of Hattussas.

The part of the lower city wall which has remained is mostly the southern section. It is built on a high earth rampart and is a double wall, of the casemate type, its outer "skin" being 3 meters thick, the inner skin 2·7 meters, and the space between 2·1 meters, giving the wall an effective thickness of some 8 meters.

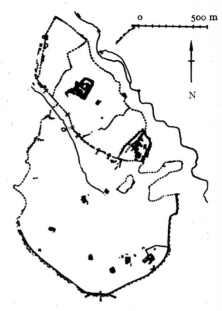

Plan of Boghazköy—Hattussas—the capital of the Hittites. Central right: the citadel. Top left: the lower city. Below: the upper city

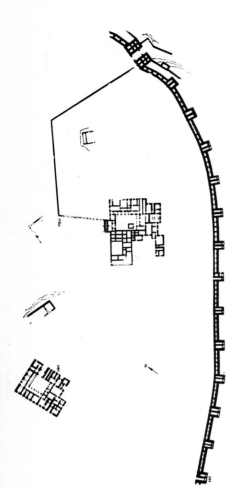

*The King's Gate of Boghazköy with
the city wall and temples*

Rectangular bastions or towers had been built on the outer surface of the wall, some small, containing one chamber, and some large, up to 15 meters wide, containing two chambers.

At the foot of the rampart, six posterns had been built leading in to the lower city. Their length was the width of the rampart at its base—some 50 meters. Ceiling and walls were of stone, which had then in turn been covered with earth. With the construction of the upper city in the later period, these posterns served as useful throughways to it from the lower city and saved the inhabitants the need to use the more distant main gates. But since they had been built before the upper city, their main function must have been part of the fortification design of the lower city. The suggestion has been made that they were conceived as *hidden* corridors through which a counterattack could be launched against an attacking force. But this is hardly acceptable, for the tunnel exits could very well be seen by the enemy. It is most probable that they were indeed used for action against an assaulting group, but not to hide their movement. Rather was it to enable the defenders to make sorties at the moment when the enemy were beginning to *collapse*, or to enable them to engage the enemy in open battle outside the city walls while receiving strong covering fire from their comrades on the formidable towers on both sides of each postern gate.

These posterns were of course additional weak spots in the system of fortifications. But their considerable length, their narrowness, and the protection afforded by the flanking towers made the task of penetration by a hostile outside force excessively difficult.

Posterns are a typical feature of the fortifications in Anatolia. One was discovered in Alaca Hüyük, belonging to the Middle Bronze period, 50 meters long. Here, too, its additional purpose was to afford passage to the inhabitants in and out of the city at times of emergency when the gates were closed. It was sited between the two city gates which were 700 meters apart. A superb postern was discovered at Ugarit, belonging to the Late Bronze period and certainly built on the pattern of the Hittite tunnels. At Boghazköy itself, a very large postern was found in the fortifications of the upper city.

These fortifications of the upper 14th–13th-century city are the most powerful of the entire complex. And though similar to those of the lower city, their plan and the quality of their construction are more advanced. Here, too (225, bottom), they are built on a very high and wide rampart. They comprise two walls: the main wall, and, at a distance of 8·5 meters, an outer wall. This outer wall is also built on a rampart, and is 1 meter thick. It is strengthened by rectangular bastions, built at a distance of 30 meters from each other and set exactly between the towers on the main wall. This main wall, like the wall of the lower city, is a double-casemate structure, its outer skin 1·6 meters thick, its inner skin 1·4 meters, and the space between them 1·25 meters, giving it an overall thickness of more than 4 meters. Its formidable quality, apart from the outer wall, derived from the considerable number of towers (not bastions) built into it. They were 8 meters wide and protruded outward some 5·5 meters. Its lower section, too, was filled with earth and stones between the skins. And it was upon this flat surface that the upper wall

The King's Gate of Boghazköy from the outside

structure of brick was built, most probably with casemates. The casemates were too narrow to serve as storehouses or dwelling-chambers. They were used as passageways for the troops at the low embrasures which were cut into them, as illustrated on the wall reliefs (see figure on this page). Through these embrasures, the defenders could engage those of the enemy who had succeeded in breaching the outer wall and had reached the area which was "dead ground" to the soldiers on top of the main wall.

The top of the rampart, particularly in the region of the gates, was covered with large polygonal stones. Most impressive were the two main city gates themselves—the southeastern King's Gate (224) and the southwestern Lions' Gate (225, top). Both were similar in plan. They formed a "gate citadel" between the main and outer walls which comprised two long towers, and entrance to the city was through the passage between the towers. This passage had two gateways, a double door at each, an outer one near the outer wall and an inner one near the main wall. The jambs of each gateway were huge vaulted stone pillars. The outer doors apparently opened inward and the inner doors outward. The gate was reached by an oblique sloping path or ramp which exposed hostile users to fire from the towers and bastions of the main and outer walls. In front of the gate was a leveled open "square."

The Lions' Gate gets its name from the lion carved in high relief on each of

West Gate of Boghazköy (section)

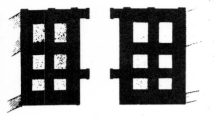

Plan of the gates of Boghazköy.
Above: The King's Gate
Below: The Lions' Gate

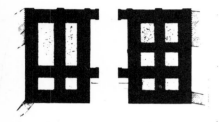

The postern at Yerkapu, Boghazköy.
A view through the postern. A section
through the postern and the walls

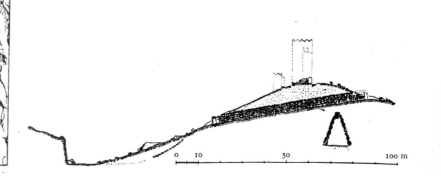

the two jambs of its outer gateway—"the keepers of the gate." The King's Gate is so called today because of the figure of the warrior or deity, which was carved on the inner left jamb—from the point of view of someone inside looking out. This relief (222, top) is now in the Hittite Museum in Ankara and is therefore not seen in the photograph on page 224.

Far the most interesting feature of the southern wall is the fortification arrangements in the middle of the area between the Lions' Gate and the King's Gate. This is known today as Yerkapu—the Earth Gate (225, bottom).

In the main wall between these two city gates is a small opening for the use of pedestrians called the Sphinx Gate, because of the figures of a sphinx which decorated its jambs. The rampart at this point is quite high—about 11 meters. To gain access to the Sphinx Gate from outside, two rows of steps were cut in the rampart some distance to its right and to its left. At the top of each stairway, a small wicket gate had been cut in the outer wall which gave entry to the space between the main and outer walls through which the Sphinx Gate could be reached.

At the foot of the rampart in front of the Sphinx Gate and midway between the two stairways, a postern had been constructed into the rampart leading right through into the city. Its length was 80 meters—the width of the rampart at this section—reaching, at its other end, a point 11 meters immediately beneath the Sphinx Gate. This was the Earth Postern, or Gate, and its purpose is believed to have been both to save the inhabitants from the steep climb up the rampart, and, in attack, to enable sorties to be carried out against the enemy in certain conditions of battle. This postern apparently had doors at both ends which could be closed during siege.

To complete the picture of the Boghazköy fortifications, it should be added that the lower city also had a number of inner defensive walls which created a kind of citadel within a citadel. It is possible that these inner walls were the boundaries of earlier cities and became "inner" only with the growth and expansion of the settlement. But in the city's final phase, they certainly added strength to the system of fortifications. The upper city, too, was strengthened by several independent citadels, built on rock cliffs, which formed a chain of fortifications within the city itself.

Nowhere, neither in Boghazköy nor in any other city in Syria, Palestine, or Egypt, has there been any discovery of the upper parts of fortifications. To find out what they looked like, we must have recourse to the illustrated monuments of the period. Fortunately there are many Egyptian reliefs which depict cities which were attacked or conquered by the pharaohs of the XIXth Dynasty. Incidentally, Seti I and Rameses II fought much in Canaan. In these battles, many cities certainly suffered destruction, an occurrence which is substantiated by archaeological excavations. As a result, the fortifications of cities of the 13th century were greatly weakened. Where a city had been captured, no new fortifications were constructed. The earlier ones were either repaired, often in a slapdash manner, or remained untouched, in ruin. This may explain why the tribes of Israel, under the leadership of Joshua, were able to conquer some of these cities.

The pharaohs never conquered Hattussas. And so there is no Egyptian relief which illustrates its fortifications. But reliefs showing other cities tell us much about the upper structures of their fortifications and are also instructive, by inference, about cities like Hattussas.

Most of the reliefs depict the captured cities in the standard form, presenting them as two-story structures (228, 230, 232). In the main, the intention is assuredly to show an elevation view of the high inner citadel, or acropolis, and the main wall. Sometimes the artist manages to depict also the outer wall (229), as in the Hattussas fortifications.

The reliefs suggest that the gates in Canaan were not vaulted, as in Hattussas, but were rectangular. One can discern, in some of the reliefs, the embrasures and windows in the wall (229). This testifies to an upper structure of casemates. The balconies on the towers and bastions, whose vital function we have discussed earlier, are shown with the utmost clarity in all the reliefs. And this is also true of the battlements on the outer wall, the main wall, and the buildings of the acropolis.

A special type of fortification of this period were the *migdols*. These were small citadels built to guard such important military objectives as wells and communications. They, too, appear on some reliefs. A migdol of this type was discovered in 1960 in Israel, not far from Ashdod. It is square in plan, with rectangular bastions, and has two stories—just as depicted in the reliefs (see figure on page 97).

A word about the fortified temples inside the city. These are the places to which the citizens would flee after their wall had been breached, as described in the Bible in the story of the tower of Shechem during the period of the Judges (which we deal with later). The principal strength of these temple fortifications lay in the thickness of their walls, the two towers at the entrance, and certainly the roof with its balconies and battlements.

In the planning of fortifications, one of the toughest problems that demanded solution was the guarantee of a regular supply of water in time of siege. In the period under review, ingenious devices were introduced to meet this need, staggering in the scale and quality of their skilled engineering. The most interesting and formidable of all that have come to light so far are those discovered at Megiddo. The well which supplied water to the city was in a natural cave at the

Water Supply under Siege

95

Left: The "fallen gates"
of a destroyed city as
depicted on Egyptian relief
of Rameses II

Right: The submission
of a Syrian city as depicted
on Egyptian relief of
Rameses II

western foot of the tell—outside the boundaries of the city fortifications. The sole methods of securing water from this source during siege were to pump it from the well into the city, or to devise some approach system which would give the inhabitants access without having to venture beyond the walls. The stratagem conceived by the planners of the Megiddo fortifications was at once simple and a stroke of genius. Within the city compound, at a point not far from the well, they sunk a vertical shaft to the same depth as the well—30 meters. The first 8 meters were fairly easy going, for they were digging through the dust and ashes of earlier ruined settlements. But the next 22 meters had to be cut through solid rock. From the base of this shaft, they cut a horizontal tunnel right through to the well—a distance of 67 meters. The tunnel had an average height of 3·5 meters. The floor of the tunnel was engineered with a slight gradient sloping down toward the city, so that there was a gravity flow of water from the well into the city. On completion of the engineering job, the well was sealed from the outside by a thick wall. The labor involved in this excavation and tunneling project must have been enormous. But it was vital for the defense of the city.

On occasion, these stratagems were apparently not unknown to the enemy. And so from time to time, as the archaeological diggings show, the outside wall sealing the well was breached or torn down, and another wall built in its place later with the repair of the fortifications. These installations were until very recently ascribed to the Late Bronze period. But our excavations at Megiddo in 1960 showed that the whole enterprise should actually be attributed to the reigns of Solomon or Ahab in the Israelite period. On the other hand, installations similar in basic patterns to that of Megiddo, but of inferior standard, were also discovered in other Palestinian cities which belong to the Late Bronze period.

Attack and Defense

The conquest of fortified cities posed a grim problem in this period, too, for the attacking army. Of the five methods of capturing a fortified city mentioned in our Introduction, we can, with the help of illustrated monuments and written documents, follow the use of only a few of them. One of the most remarkable features of the many detailed Egyptian reliefs and of the written documents of this period is that in not one of them is there a single sign of or reference to the battering-ram. Some scholars, it is true, have sought to recognize battering-rams in the four cover-tents depicted in the relief portraying the conquest of Deper (229). But the details of the relief do not support this thesis. If these tents were indeed intended as battering-rams, the artist would surely have given prominence to the most important element of this weapon—the metal-headed beam. And this does not appear at all. It is far more probable that these tents represent the camp of Pharaoh and his sons, set up near the city, as in the relief showing the Battle of Kadesh (236-237).

The absence of the battering-ram in the Egyptian armies of the New Kingdom, when it was already in use in Canaan and Anatolia in the first half of the second millennium, and indeed also in Egypt, may have several explanations: the considerable distance between the military bases in Egypt and the battlegrounds in Canaan, which no doubt proved a tough administrative and technical obstacle for the movement of this heavy instrument; the conservatism of the ancient Egyptians; and, more particularly, the firmness of the fortifications at the end of the previous and the beginning of this period. These fortifications were built especially to withstand the battering-ram. And they succeeded in blunting its effectiveness, for it was not as yet a perfect instrument. This is a good example of one aspect of the chain reaction produced by offensive and defensive devices. Proficient counter-measures, as we can see, render obsolete, at least temporarily, the weapon or a particular model of the weapon against which they were devised.

The most usual method of attack on a city was penetration *above* the walls, using scaling-ladders. This system is well illustrated in the reliefs (228, 229). Under heavy covering fire from the archers, the assault troops would rush to scale the walls and try to reach the top. The Egyptian shield, with the shoulder-strap attached to its inner surface, was particularly suited to this task. For the attacking soldier could hang it over his back (228), and this left his hands free for the climb and the fighting.

A second method, which paralleled the first, was penetration through the city gates. The assault troops would storm the gate, their backs protected by shields, and, armed with axes (228), they would try and tear down the bolts and hinges.

Both operations demand much courage. And thus does one of the proud soldiers of Thutmose III deliver himself:

"His Majesty sent forth every valiant man of his army, to breach the new wall which Kadesh had made. I was the one who breached it, being the first of every valiant man."

Against such forms of attack, the defenders responded with several measures. They posted archers on the wall to give counter-fire to the enemy's bows (229), while other troops armed with spears attacked the assaulting soldiers scaling the ladders. A number of the defenders hurled stones upon the enemy below. Some of the stones were large and heavy, requiring the use of both hands (229, top right). If at the beginning or during the battle some of the defending units fighting outside the wall found themselves compelled to fall back to the city, they were hauled up by their comrades at the top of the wall with rope or with strips made of clothing. This is surely the representation by the artist of the two figures hanging to a rope on the wall in the relief shown on page 229. Endorsement of this

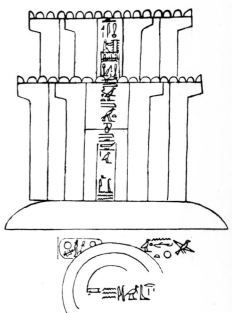

A Migdol guarding a well in the desert between Egypt and Palestine, as depicted on a relief of Seti I

interpretation is to be found in this description of the siege of Megiddo by Thutmose III which talks of the retreat of the enemy after their failure outside the city:

"They abandoned their horses and their chariots of gold and silver, so that someone might draw them up into this town by hoisting on their garments. Now the people had shut this town against them, but they let down garments to hoist them up into this town."

Attack by breaching the gate and scaling the wall involved the assault units in very heavy casualties, and could be undertaken mostly against cities whose fortification system was not of a high standard or whose troops were not the best. Often the invading army resorted to siege or infiltration stratagems.

And indeed we hear at the very beginning of this period of one of the most prolonged sieges carried out at this time. The Egyptian documents record that Pharaoh Ahmose, founder of the XVIIIth Dynasty, in his campaign against the Hyksos armies, laid siege for three consecutive years to Sharuhen, a fortified city in southern Palestine (also mentioned in Joshua 19: 6).

Thutmose III tried to follow up his celebrated success on the battlefield near Megiddo by taking the city by storm. But his soldiers, instead of pursuing the retreating troops who were retiring to entrench themselves behind their city walls, tarried on the field of battle to collect war booty. And when they reached the city, they were repelled. Thutmose was therefore forced to put Megiddo under siege for seven months, as recorded in one of the documents.

The siege operation, though less dangerous than breaching, was nevertheless very difficult and complicated. For the besieging army had to encamp for a long period in the open, set up encampments all round the city, and maintain vigilant defense against sorties and raids by the troops under siege. There is a detailed description in one of the Egyptian documents of how these encampments were established:

"Orders were issued to the commander of the troops to provide for their division and to inform each man of his place. They measured this city, which was corralled with a moat, and enclosed with fresh timbers of all their pleasant trees, while His Majesty himself was in a fortress east of this town being watchful. . . . People were appointed as sentries at the enclosure of His Majesty, and they were told: 'Be steadfast! Be vigilant, be vigilant! . . .'"

In these siege operations, they would cut down the trees in the area, as we see from the above document, with which to build their encampments or forts. This, too, is depicted in the Egyptian reliefs (346). A faithful description of this custom appears in the Bible—Deuteronomy 20: 19-20:

"When thou shalt besiege a city a long time, in making war against it to take it, thou shalt not destroy the trees thereof by forcing an axe against them: for thou mayest eat of them, and thou shalt not cut them down (for the tree of the field is man's life) to employ them in the siege: Only the trees which thou knowest that they be not trees for meat, thou shalt destroy and cut them down; and thou shalt build bulwarks against the city that maketh war with thee, until it be subdued."

We have seen that the conquest of a fortified city was a very difficult operation. It is not therefore to be wondered that side by side with the above methods of warfare, the attacking army continuously sought means of entering the city by cunning and stratagem. For all the solidity and strength of a city's fortifications, they had their weak spots. And since the defenses were all designed to meet attack from the outside, once the enemy had succeeded in penetrating one of the weak points and entering the city, the rest of the fortifications were rendered valueless. There were of course exceptions, as at Boghazköy, which had inner citadels and walls. And this lessened the danger. But, in general, penetration of the fortifications at one point was likely to cause a total collapse of the city's defenses.

There are many stories of celebrated stratagems whereby cities were entered and captured. Many have about them the ring of legend. But their very composition makes it evident that such devices were used. One of the most famous descriptions of a stratagem of this nature is undoubtedly that contained in the story of the Trojan Horse, in the Battle of Troy.

JAFFA. But there is a legendary Egyptian tale, which predates the Trojan battle by several hundred years, which relates, in the style of Ali Baba, how the city of Jaffa was captured by the forces of Thutmose III. The Commander of the besieging army, Thot, notified the Governor of Jaffa that he had decided to surrender and that it was his intention to give himself up, together with his wife and children:

"And he [Thot] had the 200 baskets brought which he had made, and he had 200 soldiers get down into them. And their arms were filled with bonds and fetters, and they were sealed up with seals. And they were given their sandals, as well as their carrying poles and staves. And they had every good soldier carrying them, totaling 500 men. And they were told: 'When you enter the city, you are to let out your companions and lay hold on all the people who are in the city and put them in bonds immediately.' And they went out to tell the charioteer of the Enemy of Jaffa: 'Thus speaks your lord: "Go and tell your mistress [i.e., the wife of the prince of Jaffa]: 'Rejoice, for Seth the god has given us Thot, along with his wife and his children!' See the vanguard of their tribute. You shall tell her about these 200 baskets [which were filled with men with fetters and bonds].""' Then he went ahead of them to bring the good news to his mistress, saying: 'We have captured Thot.' And they opened the locks of the city before the soldiers. And they entered the city and let out their companions. And they laid hold on the city, small and great, and put them in bonds and fetters immediately. So the mighty arm of Pharaoh—life, prosperity, health—captured the city."

JERICHO. The Biblical story of Joshua's conquest of Jericho apparently describes another kind of stratagem whose military implications, however, have been obscure. Its highlights, apart from the collapse of the walls, are to be found in Joshua 6: 3, 16, 20:

"And ye shall compass the city, all ye men of war, and go round about the city once. Thus shalt thou do six days. . . . And it came to pass at the seventh time, when the priests blew with their trumpets, Joshua said unto the people, 'Shout! for the Lord hath given you the city . . .' so that the people went up into the city, every man straight before him, and they took the city."

It seems to me that this stratagem is explicable in the light of a later one which is described in a Roman book of military ruses composed by Frontinus:

"When Domitius Calvinus was besieging Lueria, a town of the Lugerians protected not only by its location and siegeworks but also by the superiority of its defenders, he instituted the practice of marching frequently around the walls with all his forces, and then marching back to camp. When the townspeople had been induced by this routine to believe that the Roman commander did this for the purpose of drill, and consequently took no precautions against his efforts, he transformed this practice of parading into a sudden attack, and gaining possession of the walls, forced the inhabitants to surrender."

AI. A simpler stratagem, and one easier to understand, is that described in the Biblical story of the capture of the city of Ai. Its main purpose was to draw the city's inhabitants away from the fortifications, and then enter. The plan is presented simply and clearly in Joshua 8: 3–8:

". . . and Joshua chose out thirty thousand mighty men of valor, and sent them away by night. And he commanded them, saying, 'Behold, ye shall lie in wait against the city, even behind the city: go not very far from the city, but be ye all ready: And I, and all the people that are with me, will approach unto the city: and it shall come to pass, when they come out against us, as at the first, that we will flee before them, (For they will come out after us,) till we have drawn them from the city; for they will say, "They flee before us, as at the first": therefore we will flee before them. Then ye shall rise up from the ambush and seize upon the city: for the Lord your God will deliver it into your hand. And it shall be, when ye have taken the city, that ye shall set the city on fire. . . .'"

Battle in Open Terrain

Before discussing the organization and services of the army in this period, it may be found useful to describe two of the most celebrated battles that took place at this time, which are depicted and described in detail in the Egyptian monuments.

The Battle of Megiddo

The first is the battle of Thutmose III which led to the capture of Megiddo at the beginning of the 15th century. This is, in fact, the earliest battle in human history of which a detailed account exists. And it is the first of a series of battles fought near Megiddo (244–245), each of which was decisive, each determining the fate of Palestine.

The strategic importance of Megiddo lies in its position commanding the exit from Wadi Ara, the narrow defile which links the coastal plain of Palestine with the Valley of Jezreel through the hills south of the Carmel Mountains. This was the route of the famous Via Maris, the great trunk road which served as the main communications line between Egypt and the important empires of Mesopotamia, Syria, and Anatolia in the north. Whoever controlled Megiddo controlled this communications route, and, consequently, important areas of the Fertile Crescent.

This explains why the King of Kadesh on the Orontes, in the north, moved southward with all his allies to Megiddo in an effort to bar the northward advance of Thutmose III. The defeat of the King of Kadesh in this battle at Megiddo, far as he was from his main bases, apparently served as a "classic lesson" to the later northern kings. For in the second battle, this time at Kadesh, some 200 years later, against Rameses II, the Hittites apparently tried the opposite strategy, seeking to draw the Egyptian forces as far northward as possible so that *they* would be far from *their* bases, and this time *they* would suffer defeat. When we analyze these two battles, we shall do well to bear in mind these two basic and diametrically opposed strategic approaches of the northern kings—offensive strategy and defensive tactics in the Battle of Megiddo, and defensive strategy and offensive tactics in the Battle of Kadesh. These two approaches have in fact always been the two basic doctrines of warfare of the nations up to present times. Their application, when there has been a failure to learn the lessons of the Megiddo and Kadesh battles, has brought defeat in the most decisive campaigns. Perhaps the most interesting recent parallel of the alternate use of these two doctrines occurred in the Second World War, in the series of battles between the Allied Powers and the Germans in the North African Campaign. But we must return to Megiddo.

In the spring of the year 1468 B.C., Thutmose III set out from Egypt at the head of his armies to campaign against the nations of Syria and Canaan who had fortified themselves in the neighborhood of Megiddo under the leadership of the King of Kadesh. Nine days later, he and his forces reached their base in Gaza, having covered some 26 kilometers a day. From here he advanced northward to the city of Yehem in the northern Sharon. He now took counsel to decide how he would advance on Megiddo, for he had the choice of three routes: the direct route through the defile of Aruna (Iron, Wadi Ara); the northern route through Djefti, which would bring him out north of Megiddo; or the southern route, leading to Ta'anach, a few kilometers south of Megiddo. The report of this council of war, as transmitted by the royal scribes and recorded on the walls of the temples, is most instructive, and points to the practice of the army staff conference before the commander made his decision. It is worth quoting.

The Pharaoh first briefs his commanders on the latest intelligence on the enemy, as elucidated from spies; gives them his appreciation of enemy strength; and informs them of the enemy decision to make a stand at Megiddo, or, in his words:

"For he says—so it is reported—I shall wait here at Megiddo [to fight against the Pharaoh]."

The report records that the conference continued with the commanders expressing their objections to an advance on Megiddo by the shortest and most direct route. This is what they say:

"What is it like to go on this road which becomes so narrow? It is reported that the foe is there, waiting on the outside, while they are becoming more numerous. Will not horse have to go after horse, and the army and the people similarly? Will the vanguard of us be fighting while the rear guard is waiting here

101

in Aruna unable to fight? Now two other roads are here. One of the roads—behold it is to the east of us, so that it comes out at Ta'anach. The other—behold, it is to the north side of Djefti, and we will come out to the north of Megiddo. Let our victorious lord proceed on the one of them which is satisfactory to his heart, but do not make us go on that difficult road!"

According to the written record, the Pharaoh decided for prestige reasons to choose precisely the short and difficult route:

"They will say, these enemies whom Re abominates: 'Has His Majesty set out on another road because he has become afraid of us?'—so they will speak."

On the other hand, his decision may well have been based on his appreciation of the intelligence reports. For from the continuation of the written record, it appears that the enemy expected the Egyptian Pharaoh to advance either northward or southward.

The southern flank of the Canaanites was certainly near Ta'anach, and their northern flank was apparently near the exit of the Djefti route. Near Megiddo itself was established the main camp of all the allied kings, with all their following, who had combined to resist Thutmose III. For the city of Megiddo was too small to contain all this vast force.

When Thutmose's vanguard had reached the neighborhood of the exit from Wadi Ara and halted at the Qina brook (between Megiddo and Wadi Ara), his rearguard was still at Aruna. And now he listened to the supplication of his commanders to wait until his rear units have caught up with them:

"Then they said to His Majesty: . . . 'Behold, His Majesty has come forth with his victorious army, and they have filled the valley. Let our victorious lord listen to us this time, and let our lord guard for us the rear of his army and his people. When the rear of the army comes forth for us into the open, then we shall fight against these foreigners, then we shall not trouble our hearts about the rear of an army.'"

This sound advice by his commanders, who were insisting on the concentration of force before the assault, was accepted by the Pharaoh, and he set up camp south of Megiddo, on the banks of the Qina brook. This camp was certainly similar to the provisional camp established two centuries later by Rameses II near Kadesh, as we shall see later. In the evening the army was informed of the plan to launch the attack next morning against the enemy near Megiddo, whose main forces were still some distance away near Ta'anach, in the south, and near the exit of the Djefti route in the north. The announcements declared: "Prepare ye! Make your weapons ready, since one [the Pharaoh] will engage in combat with that wretched enemy in the morning."

This apparently was the customary preparation of an army for battle. As Joshua 1: 10–11 records:

"Then Joshua commanded the officers of the people, saying, 'Pass through the host, and command the people, saying, Prepare you victuals; for within three days ye shall pass over this Jordan, to go in to possess the land. . . .'"

Before the assault, and with his forces assembled, Thutmose divided them into three groups and assigned their areas of operation: the southern flank, between the Qina brook and the exit from Wadi Ara; the northern flank, northwest of Megiddo; and the center, where he himself would be. The assault was launched at dawn against the enemy camps near Megiddo. It ended with the rout of the Canaanites, who started fleeing with their kings toward Megiddo, and, as we noted earlier, they were hauled over the walls into the city by their garments. And now there was an occurrence which is typical of many undisciplined and untrained troops. The Egyptian army, instead of adhering to the principle of maintenance of aim and continuing to destroy the enemy and prevent his escape, fell upon his possessions left behind in the camps, collecting booty. As the royal scribe put it, with unadorned simplicity:

"Now if only His Majesty's army had not given up their hearts to capturing the possessions of the enemy, they would have captured Megiddo at this time."

And so the King of Kadesh and his allies managed to escape. Such is the irony of fate that 200 years later, in the Battle of Kadesh, it was precisely the Egyptian army of Pharaoh Rameses II who were saved from certain annihilation by the same circumstances, when the Hittite chariot force, which had stormed his camp, jumped off their chariots to collect the Egyptian spoils instead of sticking to the job of destroying the army. The capacity of an officer to make his men respect the principle of "maintenance of aim" is indeed one of the supreme tests of command.

Megiddo was eventually captured after a seven-months' siege. The high importance of its conquest is well expressed in the words of the Pharaoh to his army:

"Capture ye effectively, my victorious army! Behold all the foreign countries have been put in this town by the command of Re on this day, inasmuch as every prince of every northern country is shut up within it, for the capturing of Megiddo is the capturing of a thousand towns!"

And now, before summarizing our conclusions on the methods of warfare in this period, let us consider the second celebrated battle that took place some 200 years later between the Pharaoh Rameses II and the coalition armies of Hittites and Canaanites under the leadership of the King of the Hittites. This was the Battle of Kadesh on the Orontes.

The Battle of Kadesh

This battle is so well described and in such detail in Egyptian written documents and so widely illustrated in many reliefs, complete with captions (see figures on pages 104 ff.) that it is possible to reconstruct it in all its minutiae. This is also the only battle in the period in which we have full particulars on the organization and tactical handling of its chariot units.

Since this battle is so well documented, let us begin with a few quotations from the narrative and complement them later by the illustrations in the reliefs.

The March

Rameses II set out from Egypt in the spring with four divisions, moving northward along the coastal route until he arrived south of Kadesh, on the east bank of the River Orontes. He then crossed over to the west bank:

The Battle of Kadesh as depicted in the Ramesseum. All the wheels should have six spokes and not eight, as it was erroneously copied by modern artists here and widely reproduced in many books. Cf. pages 88, 239, 240–241

"His Majesty . . . crossed the ford of the Orontes, with the first division of Amon. . . . His Majesty reached the town of Kadesh. . . . Now the wretched foe belonging to Hatti, with the numerous foreign countries which were with him, was waiting hidden and ready on the northeast of the town of Kadesh, while His Majesty was alone by himself with his retinue. The division of Amon was on the march behind him; the division of Re was crossing the ford in a district south of the town of Shabtuna, at the distance of one *iter* [about 2 kilometers] from the place where His Majesty was; the division of Ptah was on the south of the town of Arnaim; and the division of Seth was marching on the road. His Majesty had formed the first ranks of battle of all the leaders of his army, while they were still on the shore in the land of Amurru."

The Surprise Attack

"Behold, the wretched foe of Hatti was stationed in the midst of his infantry which was with him, and he came not out to fight, for fear of His Majesty. Then he made to go the people of the chariotry, an exceedingly numerous multitude like the sand, being three people to each chariot. Now they had made their combination thus: among every two youths was one man of the wretched foe of Hatti, equipped with all the weapons of battle. Lo, they had stationed them in battle array, concealed northeast of the city of Kadesh. They came forth from the southern side of Kadesh, and they cut through the division of Re in its middle, while they were marching without knowing and without being drawn up for

104

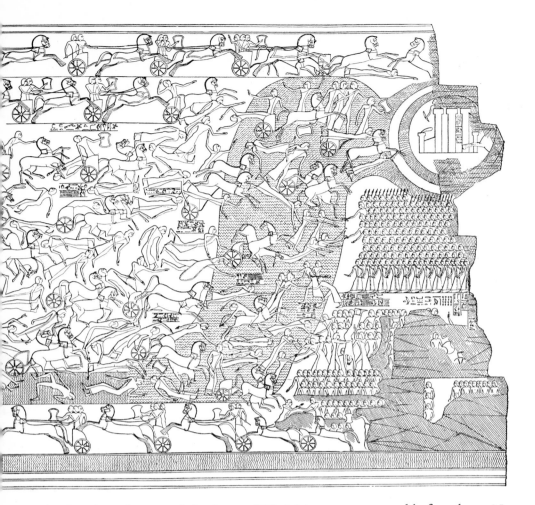

battle. The infantry and chariotry of His Majesty . . . retreated before them. Now His Majesty had halted on the north of the city of Kadesh, on the western bank of the Orontes. Then came one to tell it [i.e., the disaster] to His Majesty."

The Counterattack

"His Majesty . . . shone like his father Montu when he took the adornments of war, as he seized his coat of mail he was like Baal in his hour. . . . His Majesty halted the rout, then he charged into the foe, the vanquished foe of Hatti, being alone by himself and none other with him. When His Majesty went to look behind him he found 2,500 chariotry surrounding him, in his way out, being all the youth of the wretched foe of Hatti, together with its numerous allied countries . . . being three men to a span, acting in unison."

Before starting our analysis of this battle, the first question that springs to mind is how could Rameses II have advanced on Kadesh without paying attention to security, and with the complete assurance that none of the Hittite enemy was in the vicinity until he was suddenly taken by surprise from the south? The document from which the above quotations are taken is silent on the subject. This document is a narrative "poem" on the battle. But a more detailed account appears in the official documents. And these show that Rameses was lulled into a false sense of security by the King of Kadesh who used one of the earliest known ruses to deceive the enemy.

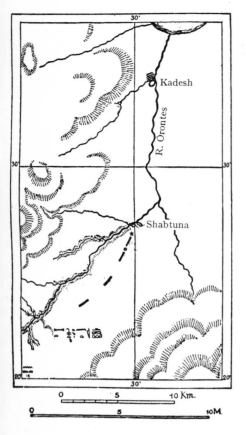

The Battle of Kadesh: The march of the four Egyptian divisions before crossing the Orontes, as reconstructed by Breasted

The mound of Kadesh—Tell Nebi Mind—surrounded by rivers and water canals

To link the following description with the previous, we go back a little in our next quotation and start it just before the story of the deception:

"When His Majesty appeared like the rising of Re, he assumed the adornments of his father Montu. When the king proceeded northward, and His Majesty had arrived at the locality south of the city of Shabtuna, there came two Shasu [Bedouin] to speak to His Majesty as follows: 'Our brethren, who belong to the greatest of the families with the wretched foe of Hatti, have made us come to His Majesty to say: "We will be subjects of Pharaoh . . . and we will flee from the wretched foe of Hatti who is in the land of Aleppo, on the north of Tunip. He fears because of Pharaoh to come northward;"' Now these Shasu spoke these words which they spoke to His Majesty falsely, for the wretched foe of Hatti made them to come to spy where His Majesty was, in order to cause the army of His Majesty not to draw up for fighting him, to battle with the wretched foe of Hatti."

But at the time, Rameses did not perceive that they had come on a mission of deceit. He swallowed their story, and advanced to the neighborhood of Kadesh, fully convinced that the Hittite coalition forces were far to the north, near Aleppo. He set up his camp (depicted in reliefs on pages 236–237—see detailed description in the captions and figures in the text) to the west of Kadesh. And only then did he discover his grim plight, as a result of the capture of two Hittite reconnaissance scouts:

"Then, as His Majesty sat upon a throne of gold, there arrived a scout who was in the following of His Majesty, and he brought two scouts of the wretched foe of Hatti. They were conducted into the presence and His Majesty said to them: 'What are ye?' They said: 'As for us the wretched foe of Hatti has caused that we should come to spy out where His Majesty is.' Said His Majesty to them: 'He! Where is he, the wretched foe of Hatti? Behold, I have heard saying: "He is in the land of Aleppo."' Said they: 'See, the wretched foe of Hatti is stationed together with many countries. . . . They are equipped with infantry and chariotry, bearing their weapons, more numerous are they than the sand of the shore. See, they are standing, drawn up for battle behind Kadesh the deceitful.''

From the reliefs, it is clear that these reconnaissance scouts gave this information only after they had been very severely beaten. This is also noted in the caption beneath the relief:

Rameses camp near Kadesh as depicted at the Ramesseum, to be compared with the same camp as represented in Abu-Simbel (page 108), and Luxor (page 109)

Abu-Simbel (cf. pages 236–237)

"The arrival of the scout of the Pharaoh . . . bringing the two scouts of the wretched foe of Hatti into the presence of Pharaoh. They are beating them, to make them tell where the wretched foe of Hatti is!"

But for Rameses the information had come too late. He was already trapped. At the moment when he was sending word to alert his other divisions near Shabtuna, the Hittite chariots sprung their charge on the marching divisions, as described in the narrative "poem." The bewildered division fled toward Pharaoh's camp, with the Hittites in hot pursuit and eventually encircling the camp. The Pharaoh then launched a desperate counterattack, slightly checking the enemy assaulting units, and striking against other Hittite units on his eastern flank, near Kadesh. And now the Hittite assault charioteers began to plunder and pillage the Egyptian camp. This turned the tide fatally against them. For while they were gathering their booty, they were suddenly attacked by a formation which had been held in reserve and which had now arrived in the nick of time. These were the Na'arun troops, a crack Canaanite unit serving with the Egyptian forces. *Na'arun* means literally "young men." They were picked troops, who had apparently been detailed to protect the distant western flank. Now they fell upon the plundering Hittites and wiped them out.

The Egyptian defeat was thus turned into a local victory, while the Pharaoh pressed his attack against the enemy in the east near Kadesh, driving them toward the river. The Hittite King, with his infantry division numbering some 6,000 men, halted on the other side of the river. But he was now powerless. For all his chariots had been committed and his infantrymen alone were ineffective against the assault of Rameses' chariots. The Hittites accordingly retired to Kadesh and fortified themselves within the city. The battle ended in stalemate. Both sides had been badly mauled, and they satisfied themselves with the signing of a non-aggression pact. This is the most detailed treaty of its kind which has been left to us from this period.

Tactics

The methods of warfare and the principles of strategy and tactics followed by both sides are quite clear. The Hittite King pursued a defensive strategy, and succeeded in drawing the Egyptian Pharaoh deep within his territory so that he could smite his flank at the proper moment in a surprise attack, while he himself was based on Kadesh and the Orontes, which gave him both concealment and a secure shelter.

This battle also offers a splendid example of the use of the chariot unit as a striking force, which carries out an assault up to hand-to-hand combat range. These tactics matched the particular character of the Hittite chariot, which was equipped mainly with the spear, a short-range weapon. The chariot crew of three virtually turned the Hittite chariots into a transported or mounted infantry unit, qualified also to engage in hand-to-hand combat at the end of the charge.

This kind of maneuver could, of course, succeed in operations against an enemy flank which was on the march and without security. But the weakness of the Hittite chariot was immediately evident when the Egyptian chariots, armed with the long-range composite bow, went over to the counterattack. The brilliant maneuver of the Hittite King failed because he had given insufficient thought to the planning of the action he would need to take if his surprise attack failed.

Rameses, on the other hand, failed hopelessly in his strategic judgments. And he managed to extricate himself from utter defeat only because of his keen leadership in battle, recognizing that attack is the best defense. His counter-offensive saved him at the decisive moment.

But it seems that in his eagerness to glorify the personal heroism of Rameses, the royal scribe underrated his strategic ability too heavily. For the sudden fortuitous arrival of the Canaanite Na'arun formation from the west, which saved the day for Rameses, finds, strangely enough, no mention in the general chronicles of the battle. The scribe may have considered that giving credit to the Na'arun unit would derogate from the measure of his Pharaoh's prowess. But to Rameses credit, it may be claimed that when he raced north toward Kadesh without effective

The camp in the Luxor reliefs

security, he must have taken into account the presence of this striking force on his western flank, and he used it not only to secure a strategic flank, but also as a hidden reserve to be rushed into action at a decisive moment.

The Battle of Kadesh offers us an insight into the military patterns of the period, with its imperial armies of high standard, whose commanders are capable of handling large formations of infantry and chariots in accordance with the soundest principles of strategy followed to this day.

Intelligence   The description of the battle near Megiddo and especially the chronicle of the Battle of Kadesh underline the high importance attached by the armies of the lands of the Bible to the intelligence services. Operations like deceptive patrols and the capture of Hittite scouts by Egyptian scouts point to the existence of a well-developed system of intelligence. The questions put by Rameses to the Hittite prisoners also show that the purpose of the interrogation was to secure precise tactical information:

1. What nations does the Hittite armies comprise?
2. What is the composition of the army—infantry, chariots?
3. Their weapons?
4. Their numbers?
5. Their exact location and the measures of their preparedness?

This alertness to intelligence and the use of spies are stressed also in the Biblical stories of Joshua's conquests. Spies were dispatched to Jericho and to Ai before the military operations, and the intelligence they brought back on the spirit and strength of the enemy served as the basis of the attack plan.

As opposed to this tactical intelligence, there is an eloquent example of strategic intelligence in the instructions given by Moses to the twelve spies before their departure for the land of Canaan. The points on which the espionage mission is ordered to gain information are different from those sought by Rameses and Joshua, and have a definite strategic character:

1. "And see the land, what it is. . . ."
2. "And the people that dwelleth therein, whether they be strong or weak, few or many."
3. "And what the land is they dwell in, whether it be good or bad."
4. "And what cities they be that they dwell in, whether in camps, or in strongholds."
5. "And what the land is, whether it be fat or lean, whether there be wood therein, or not."

Ambush
and Night Fighting   The functioning of good intelligence service enabled small forces in particular to undertake ambush as a regular method of warfare. Tactically, the ambush is the most murderous form of battle, which exploits the principle of surprise to its maximum.

Apart from the ambush incidents included in the general battle operations mentioned earlier, we have additional information on the use of the ambush in this period. The Anastasi Papyrus I contains the following interesting question which is put to a military scribe to test his knowledge:

"Behold, the ambuscade is in a ravine 2,000 cubits deep, filled with boulders and pebbles. Thou makest a detour as thou graspest the bow. Thou makest a feint to thy left, that thou mightest make the chiefs to see, but their eyes are good and thy hand falters. Thou perish like a lion, O, good *mahar* [swift military scribe]."

This type of ambush was carried out particularly in rugged areas of rough broken ground, marked by ravines and dry riverbeds, which impeded the maneuverability of the enemy's chariots. There is little doubt that this kind of ambush is what the officers of Thutmose feared when they sought to dissuade him from taking the direct route through the defile of the Aruna stream. The defile and the hazard of ambush while moving through it are dramatically described in the same Anastasi Papyrus:

"The narrow valley is dangerous with Bedouin, hidden under the bushes. Some of them are 4 or 5 cubits from their noses to the heel, and fierce of face. Their hearts are not mild, and they do not listen to wheedling. Thou art alone; there is no scribe with thee, no army behind thee. Thou findest no scout, that he might make thee a way crossing. Thou comest to a decision going forward, although thou knowest not the road. Shuddering seizes thee, the hair of thy head stands up, and thy soul lies in thy hand. Thy path is filled with boulders and with reeds, thorns, brambles, and 'wolf paw.' The ravine is on one side of thee, and the mountain rises on the other. Thou goest on jolting, with thy chariot on its side, afraid to press thy horse hard. If it should be thrown toward the abyss, thy collar-piece would be left uncovered and thy girth would fall. Thou unfasten the yoke in order to repair the collar-piece in the middle of the narrow valley. Thou art not competent in the way to bind it; thou knowest not how to lash it. . . . Thou startest to trot. The sky is opened. Then thou thinkest that the foe is behind thee. . . ."

The darkness of night necessary to the laying of an ambush, was also required by irregular forces operating against a regular army, both to cover their advance and to launch their attack. The book of Joshua describes how at times Joshua would advance all through the night in order to surprise the enemy at dawn. Similarly, one of the documents of Mursilis, the Hittite King, speaks of the special security orders he gave to his forces for his own safety when he was compelled to make a night march. The same document echoes the wrath of the regular armies against night attacks and night ambush by the irregulars:

"They [the irregulars] did not dare to attack me in the daylight, and preferred to fall on me during the night. In the night we will attack him."

The ambush was only a minor action among the operations of regular armies —though it was not so considered by its victims. The chronicles of war and the

Standard Formations

many illustrated monuments show that in the imposing battles in open terrain, large military formations took part, well organized in the phalanx, charging each other in hand-to-hand combat.

The allied army under the Hittite King at Kadesh is estimated at between 16,000 and 17,000 men. In the chariot units were 7,500 men—each of the 2,500 had a crew of three. The rest were infantry, stationed behind Kadesh, who were organized in phalanx battle formation.

The Egyptian army had four divisions, each of 5,000 men. This estimate is supported by the information contained in the Anastasi Papyrus, in another test question put to a military scribe on the subject of supplies to an Egyptian expeditionary force composed of Egyptian troops and various mercenaries:

"Thou art sent on a mission to Djahi at the head of the victorious army, to crush the rebels called Na'arun. The bowmen of the army which is before thee [i.e., the Egyptian army] amount to 1,900, the Sherden 520, the Qeheq 1,600, the Meshwesh 100, and the Negroes 880—total 5,000 in all not counting their officers."

Similarly, the King of Byblos (Gebal) in the Tell el-Amarna letters requests the Pharaoh to send an expeditionary force of 5,000 men and 50 chariots to save his city.

Army Organization

It is not easy to present with accuracy the structure of the smaller units which went to make up the large formations. But from the various monuments and also from the Bible, it can be assumed that they were based on the decimal notation. The smallest unit, the section, apparently comprised 10 men, and the platoon 50 men. We have no clear information on the strength of the company, but we can infer from the Egyptian documents that it consisted of not more than four or five platoons—200 or 250 men. Between the company and the division (really a brigade) there was certainly the battalion whose total strength was not fixed but was composed of several companies, four or five.

At all events, both the written documents and the reliefs clearly indicate that these divisions not only marched together, arranged in a specially organized pattern but that they also fought under the organization of the deep phalanx, made up of straight ranks in close order. A poetic description of an army on the march in close formation appears in one of the documents of Ugarit:

"They march in thousands serried and in myriads massed. After two, two march, after three all of them."

The reliefs of the Battle of Kadesh clearly portray the assault of the Na'arun unit in phalanx formation, with a phalanx of ten ranks, line abreast, and the ten men in each section forming a file, one behind the other, one in each rank. The Hittite infantry behind the city of Kadesh are depicted in the same way. But they are shown before the action, while their phalanx are still organized for the march. So they are depicted as a column, and the ten-man section is converted from a file into a line-abreast rank. From the reliefs, it is easy to gather how the phalanx transformed its pattern of organization for the march into its organization for attack. It can be best explained by a diagram.

On the March

In Attack

112

The allied army under the Hittite King at Kadesh had 2,500 chariots. We have no breakdown of this figure which would enable us to determine the size of the chariot unit of each king. But since we know that this allied force comprised the men of very many kings, we can assume that each unit was not larger than 300 chariots, and many were very much smaller.

The documents of Tell el-Amarna make frequent mention of units of 50 chariots, 30, and even 10. Similarly, we know of 100- and 30-chariot units in Anatolia. The documents of Nuzi mention units of 50 chariots under the command of a "Captain of Fifty." And this is true also of Egypt. All this suggests that the basic unit consisted of 10, and several such units would make up a squadron of 30 or 50 chariots. Presumably the largest tactical unit consisted of 150. These were usually attached to infantry divisions of expeditionary forces.

It may be recorded that in this period, chariot units were still the only mobile formations in the armies of the lands of the Bible, for the cavalry regiment did not make its appearance until the end of the second millennium. In this period, we know of the horseman being used only for isolated communications functions, such as messengers (221). Let us add, as a piquant item, the following extract from a letter by the King of Byblos:

"The messenger of the king of Acco is more heeded than my messenger, because a horse was given to him."

The employment of such large armies and their operation at such distances from their main bases naturally called for ramified military administration. And, indeed, the numerous written documents from Nuzi, Ugarit, Anatolia, and Egypt clearly indicate the existence in this period of well-developed quartermaster and adjutant services which maintained detailed records of the army formations, their equipment, the sums of money paid to them, and so on. We also learn from these records and from the illustrated monuments that detailed lists were prepared of captured booty, categorized according to type.

The problem of supply to expeditionary forces was not easy. And the military scribes and quartermasters underwent special exercises to make them proficient in determining the battle rations required by the various army corps. Here, for example, is a test question on the subject which appears further down in the Anastasi Papyrus I which we quoted earlier in connexion with the 5,000-strong Egyptian expeditionary force:

"There is brought thee a peace offering before thee; bread, cattle, and wine. The number of men is too great for thee. Whereas the provisions are too small for them. . . . Thou receive them, place them in camp. The troops are ready and prepared. Make them quickly into portions, that of each man at his hand. . . . Midday is come, the camp is hot. Time to start! Don't let the troop commander be angry! Much marching is ahead of us. What bread have we at all!? . . . So thou art an experienced scribe, if thou canst approach to give the provisions."

This document, too, shows that an expeditionary force did not bring with it all the supplies it would need, but got much of its food from the produce of the land through which it passed and from supplies and equipment provided by the various enthralled local governors. From the narrative of the Battle of Megiddo by Thutmose III, we learn that a good part of the food for his men and fodder for his beasts came from the local produce. The letters of Tell el-Amarna contain many notifications to the Egyptian Pharaoh from the kings of Canaan, assuring him that they have prepared all the requisite supplies for his expeditionary army, as requested in prior orders by the military scribes.

Those supplies which accompanied an army were carried by pack ass and ox-drawn wagons. The wagons bore the collapsible parts of camps, as at Kadesh, and sometimes even boats needed for ferrying troops across a river, as we see from the document of Thutmose III:

"When my Majesty crossed over to the marches of Asia, I had many ships of cedar built on the mountain of God's land [the Middle East], near the Lady of Byblos. They were placed on chariots with cattle drawing them. They journeyed in front of my Majesty, in order to cross that great river which lies between this foreign country and Naharin."

The military panorama of this lively period of history is one of formidable fortifications encircling the key cities of the Middle East; of large, well-trained armies, equipped with chariots and supply and engineering services, moving between Egypt and Mesopotamia, Anatolia, and Canaan; of ferocious battles waged between mighty empires, involving high tactical skill and ingenious stratagems. These military campaigns eventually drained the energy and resources of most of these kingdoms and led to their downfall. And this opened the way to new nations, like the Tribes of Israel from the east and the Sea Peoples from the west and north, who conquered and settled large areas of Palestine over which the mighty nations of earlier ages had fought for so long.

PLATES
VOLUME ONE

The most ancient fortifications known to man

Recent excavations show that Jericho had Pre-Pottery Neolithic fortifications some 6,000 years before Joshua—including a moat and this huge stone tower, the function of which remains a mystery.

The ivory handle of the flint knife (c. 3000 B.C.) shown here depicts shaven-headed warriors with arc-shaped boats of an Egyptian type and long-haired soldiers with boats having the characteristically Mesopotamian high stern and prow. Facing page: A wall painting from an Egyptian tomb of the same period shows arc-shaped boats similar to those on the knife. The soldiers at the lower right are armed with spears or staffs and carry leather shields.

Above and right: Knife from Gebal el-'Araq, Late Pre-Dynastic. Louvre. Facing page: Wall painting from Hierakonpolis, Late Pre-Dynastic. Cairo Museum.

The first record
of an amphibious battle

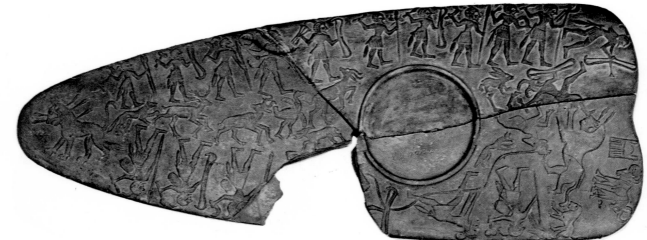

118

The bow. Two types emerge in the fourth millennium— in Mesopotamia, a single-arc form; in Egypt, a double-convex weapon

The Nimrod-like Mesopotamian king (?) depicted on the c. 3000 B.C. commemorative stele on page 118 (upper left) holds an almost semicircular single-arc weapon in the lower hunting scene. In contrast, the Egyptian bow forms on both the cylinder seal (page 118, middle) and the celebrated Hunters' Slate Palette (lower left, and enlarged fragment, upper right) show a double-convex instrument in use at the same time. Hunting figures on the palette also exhibit long spears, maces, boomerangs, double-headed axes, and the fork-headed arrow. Another instance of the last is shown in the fragmentary Egyptian carving at the lower right, in which a fork-headed arrow has pierced a warrior's body.

Page 118: Upper left, granite stele from Warka, Late Proto-Literate. Baghdad Museum. Bottom, Hunters' Slate Palette (including cast of the upper right fragment), Late Pre-Dynastic. British Museum. Middle, cylinder seal from Hierakonpolis, Pre-Dynastic. The Petrie Collection. Page 119, top: Original upper fragment of Hunters' Slate Palette. Louvre. Bottom: Slate fragment from Lower Egypt. Pre-Dynastic. Metropolitan Museum of Art.

119

The mace—
key weapon
for hand-to-hand
fighting until
the appearance
of the helmet

The maceheads shown here, all from the period between 3500 and 2500 B.C., embrace a variety of materials and shapes. The round copper examples (upper left) are from excavations near Beer-sheba. Below them are two Mesopotamian limestone maceheads, both pear-shaped and fluted. The porphyry, disk-shaped example (above) and the magnificent ceremonial macehead of King Scorpion (right) are both Egyptian.

Above left: Maceheads from Tell Abu Matar, Chalcolithic. Department of Antiquities, Archaeological Museum, Jerusalem. Below left: Maceheads from Tell Agrab, Early Dynastic. Museum of the Oriental Institute, Chicago. Above: Egyptian macehead. Pre-Dynastic. British Museum. Right: King Scorpion macehead from Hierakonpolis, Late Pre-Dynastic. Ashmolean Museum, Oxford.

A graphic record of a great Egyptian warrior-king's battles sheds light on the defense of cities

Left: The Slate Palette of King Narmer, first ruler of the united Upper and Lower Egypt. In the top register, the King, wearing the crown of Lower Egypt, and preceded by standard-bearers, surveys the corpses of his enemies. In the bottom register, he is represented as a bull battering at an oval-shaped fortified city, the wall of which is studded with square bastions. The reverse side of the palette is shown on page 124.

Slate Palette of King Narmer from Hierakonpolis, 1st Dynasty (c. 2900 B.C.). Cairo Museum.

Right: King Narmer may also appear in the guise of a bull trampling his enemy on this Bull Slate Palette. Below: Two fortresses or fortified cities enclose symbolic figures that identify them.

Bull Slate Palette from Egypt, Ist Dynasty (c. 2900 B.C.). Louvre.

124

King Narmer subdues Southern Palestine

Left: Here, on the reverse side of the Palette of King Narmer, the King wears the crown of Upper Egypt. Below him, two enemies flee from strongholds that are depicted in miniature—one, a rectangular bastioned city, which may represent settlements west of Jordan; the other, a kite-shaped enclosure, possibly symbolizing territory east of Jordan. The drawings represent Trans-Jordanian kite-shaped enclosures similar to that shown on the palette.

Far left: Palette of King Narmer. Left, above: Plan of a kite-shaped desert enclosure. Below: Stone *graffito* from the Cairn of Hani', Safaitic period. Trans-Jordan.

The mace in action

The famous slate palette on page 124 shows the King striking his enemy with a mace. Its handle is bound with cord, probably to prevent slipping. A similarly bound mace (c. 2900 B.C.) appears in use on an ivory plaque from Abydos (upper right) commemorating the victory of King Wedymu over the Semites, and inscribed "First time of smiting of the East." The middle illustration of a cylinder seal from the same period shows a bound captive being struck with a mace. Two fine Egyptian maceheads (both c. 2900 B.C.), one of breccia rock and the other of alabaster, ornamented with serpents and falcons, appear below.

Right, top to bottom: Plaque from Abydos, Ist Dynasty. British Museum. Ivory cylinder seal from Hierakonpolis, Ist Dynasty. British Museum. Early Dynastic maceheads. British Museum.

This socketed axehead, found in a cave in the Judean desert in Israel between Ei Gedi and Massada in 1961, is part of a discovery that makes revolutionary impact on accepted ideas of the technical level and ethnic character of —and contacts between—the lands of the Bible during this early period. The more than 450 copper objects found belong to the end of the Chalcolithic and the beginning of the Early Bronze periods—c. 3100 B.C.

The axeheads, like this one, reveal the high technical standards that the period achieved. They are certainly not inferior to the Sumerian socketed axes of the first half of the third millennium (see page 137) which, prior to the 1961 Judean discovery, were considered as a standard of perfection for contemporary metal-work.

The exact origin of the objects—which includes many cult instruments—in the Judean find is unknown. The presence among them of socketed piercing axes suggests the mountainous regions to the north and east of Mesopotamia—the area which gave birth to, or was dominant in, the launching of Sumerian culture. On the other hand, both the shape and quantity of the maceheads found indicate close contact with Egypt, Palestine, and Syria.

Since access to the cave in which the cache was located was very difficult, it is presumed that the objects were brought there by local residents who were forced to flee before an invading force. The possibility is that this outside force was an Egyptian army, for at the end of the fourth millennium, and the beginning of the third, the Egyptians began to undertake widespread military action (see page 124) in the southern regions of Palestine and Trans-Jordan and even beyond.

Socketed axehead from Nahal Mishmar (c. 3100 B.C.). Department of Antiquities, Archaeological Museum, Jerusalem.

126

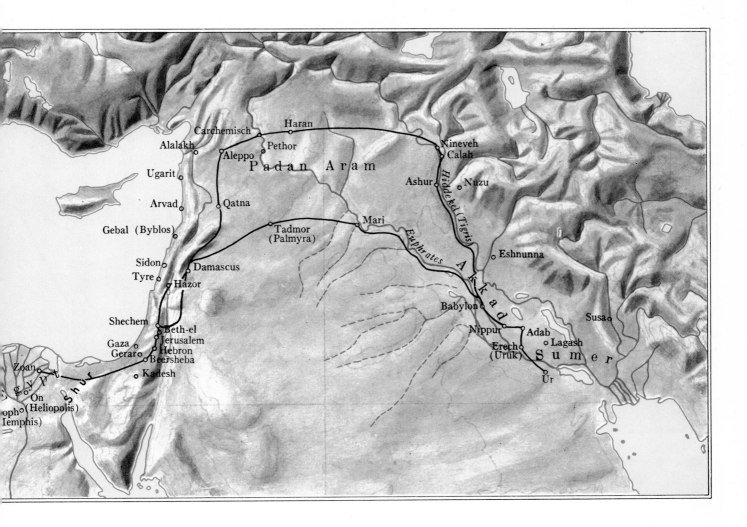

An important cache of weapons and cult objects

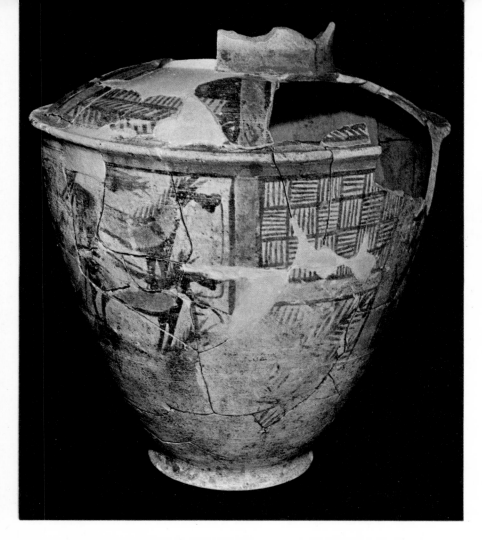

The four-wheeled battle chariot harnessed to four equines, depicted on this Mesopotamian vase, was capable of carrying two men. Despite its early date (c. 2800 B.C.), it incorporates such features as milled (or studded) wheels for improved traction.

Left: Two views of a vase from Khafajah, Early Dynastic II. British Museum. Above: Drawing of the vase panel depicting the chariot.

A lighter, two-wheeled Sumerian chariot from the same period (c. 2800 B.C.), harnessed to four onagers. Although not equipped with arms like the javelin-carrying four-wheeled chariot, these smaller chariots undoubtedly served on the battlefield, at least for communications. This modern model, patterned on an ancient 3-inch copper miniature, reveals characteristic details like the studded three-board wheels and the rein ring, through which passes the single pair of reins attached to an inside animal.

Facing page: Model, in Museum of the Oriental Institute, Chicago, based on copper miniature from Tell Agrab, Early Dynastic II. Baghdad Museum.

Chariots—in widespread use in
Mesopotamia in the first half of
the third millennium B.C.
although unknown in Egypt
until more than 1,000 years later

A fragment of a limestone relief, dated c. 2500 B.C., clearly depicts the three-boarded rimmed structure of the chariot wheel. The pole emerges from the body of this chariot in a high curve, and descends toward the four onagers. The reins pass through the rein ring attached to the pole. This two-wheeled chariot is equipped for battle with quiver of javelins and swords with crescent-shaped pommels.

Left: The crude clay model of a two-wheeled Sumerian chariot, dated c. 2800–2700 B.C., has two holes for the reins carefully pierced in the breast.

Above: Relief from Ur, Early Dynastic III (Ist Dynasty of Ur). University of Pennsylvania Museum. Left: Model from Kish, Early Dynastic. Museum of the Oriental Institute, Chicago.

The Mesopotamian chariot characteristically made use of a rein ring mounted on the pole to keep the reins from snarling. This silver rein right (far right), found in the tomb of Queen Shubad of Ur and dated c. 2500 B.C., is decorated with an onager of electrum, an alloy of silver and gold.

Right: A much later clay cult model of a two-wheeled chariot (c. 2000 B.C.) is essentially the same as the one found at Kish and illustrated on this page.

Far right: Rein ring from Ur, Early Dynastic III. British Museum. Right: Model from Lagash, Neo-Sumerian. Louvre.

The legacy
of chariot illustration
is rich and varied

The Standard of Ur war panel, one of the two most important military documents of the third millennium B.C.

Upper register. The Sumerian King (center), followed by the royal guard and his four-wheeled war chariot, receives a procession of bound captives.

Middle register. A phalanx of Sumerian soldiers, armed with spears and wearing metal helmets and studded capes, charges the enemy.

Lower register. Four four-wheeled chariots in a battle charge, which some authorities interpret as the same chariot in successive stages of motion. The type of chariot shown here has room for two men—driver and warrior—and is equipped with quiver and javelins. The rein ring (most clearly shown at left), although undecorated, is similar to the silver example shown on page 131.

Above: Panel, encrusted with shell, lapis lazuli, and red limestone, Early Dynastic III (c. 2500 B.C.). British Museum. Left: A clay model of a chariot from Kish.

The Sumerian army
fights and subdues its enemies

133

The King of Lagash leads his troops to battle

The other of the two most important military documents of the third millennium B.C.—the Stele of Vultures.

Upper register. Eannatum, King of Lagash (right), leads a heavily armed phalanx of soldiers in a column of six files (indicated by the six tiers of spears and six metal studs on the shields). The troops, wearing metal helmets and heavy rectangular shields, and armed with heavy spears which they hold with both hands, charge over the bodies of their fallen enemies.

Lower register. Eannatum, in a chariot equipped with quiver, light javelins, and a battleaxe, leads charging troops wearing metal helmets —but without shields—and armed with long spears and socketed axes. The King holds a long spear in his left hand, a sickle sword in his right.

Limestone stele from Telloh, Early Dynastic III (c. 2500 B.C.). Louvre. Right: Silver javelin-head from Ur, Early Dynastic III.

134

135

The sword that Eannatum holds in the lower register of the Stele of Vultures (page 135) appears again at the left of this relief, dated c. 2500 B.C., and in the similarly dated conch plaque from Mari on page 137. These three instances argue that the sickle sword had made its début in the Sumerian period. Here the sword-bearer with a shield faces a warrior armed with a spear.

Above: Relief on a circular column base from Lagash, Early Dynastic III. Louvre. Right: Socketed axehead from Khafajah, Early Dynastic III. Museum of the Oriental Institute, Chicago.

Weapons
for hand-to-hand fighting

The socketed axe was one of the Sumerians most remarkable technical achievements. Blades like the copper one shown on page 136 (c. 2500 B.C.) were capable of piercing sturdy metal helmets by virtue of a long, narrow profile and firm anchoring on handles that could be swung with force. The royal axe shown here (also c. 2500 B.C.), a ceremonial object with gold bands around the wooden haft, embodies the salient features. Above: A metal-helmeted warrior (shown on a conch plaque from the same period) carries a socketed axe and a weapon that has been identified as a sickle sword.

Left: Axe from Ur, Early Dynastic III. British Museum. Above: Conch plaque from temple of Ishtar at Mari, Early Dynastic III. Louvre.

137

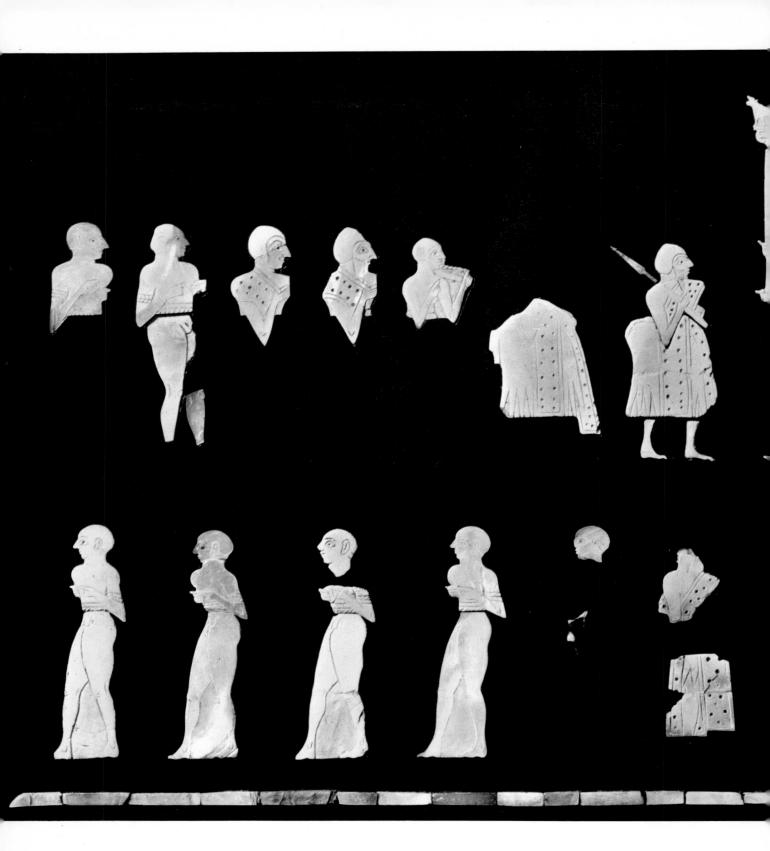

Dignitaries carry socketed axes

This panel, dating from c. 2500 B.C., shows four armed dignitaries at the upper right preceded by a standard-bearer who faces armed and helmeted warriors leading a group of captives. The standard is crowned with a figure of a bull which may represent a rein ring similar to that illustrated on page 131.

Below are shown a group of bound prisoners and a very fragmentary chariot, similar to those of the Standard of Ur (pages 132–133).

Bitumen panel inlaid with mother-of-pearl plaques from temple of Ishtar at Mari, Early Dynastic III. Louvre.

The sword lagged behind the mace and the axe as a decisive weapon of warfare

The swords that appeared in the third millennium were more like daggers—designed mainly for stabbing. Hilts, like the lapis lazuli one shown at left, were secured to the blade with nails, an attachment too weak to permit a downward swing. A crescent hilt, like the one on the iron sword (left, above) definitely limited use to a forward thrust.

Left: Gold sword and gold-decorated openwork sheath from the Royal Cemetery at Ur. The plain back of the sheath has two vertical slits to allow it to be attached to the belt. Early Dynastic III (c. 2500 B.C.). Baghdad Museum. Left, above: Iron sword with gold-covered crescent hilt from the royal tomb at Alaca Hüyük, Anatolia (c. 2500 B.C.). Hittite Museum, Ankara. Right: Gold sword similar to the one at the left of page 140, Early Dynastic III (c. 2500 B.C.). Baghdad Museum. Far right: Copper sword with gold crescent hilt from the Royal Cemetery at Ur, Early Dynastic III (c. 2500 B.C.). Baghdad Museum.

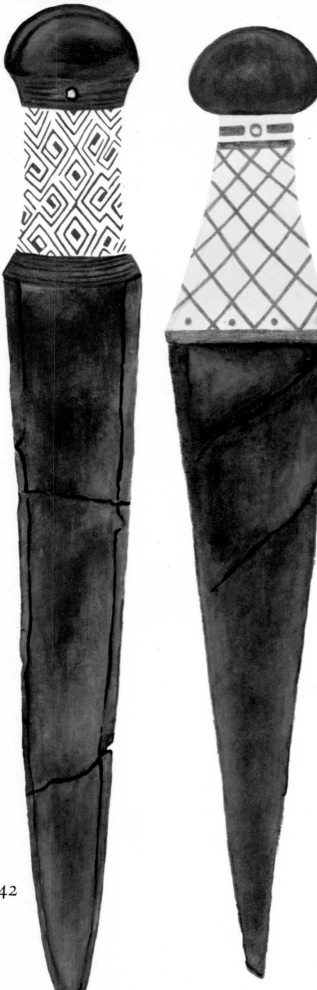

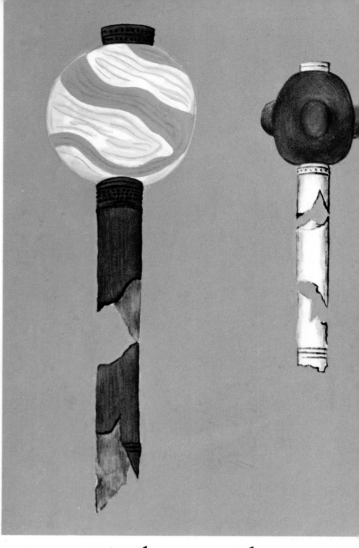

Finely wrought weapons from a royal tomb

These beautiful swords, maces, and axeheads (all dated c. 2500 B.C.) are part of the royal treasure discovered at Dorak in northwestern Anatolia near the Sea of Marmara. Both swords are bronze, the one at far left having an ivory hilt with red fillings; the other having a gold hilt decorated with carnelian studs. The mace (above left) has a pink-veined marble head and a gold sheathing over its wooden handle, while that at the right has an amber head and a silver-cased handle. The ceremonial axeheads on page 143 are made of (top to bottom) nephrite, lapis lazuli, obsidian, and amber. The sockets of all four are bound with gold and silver.

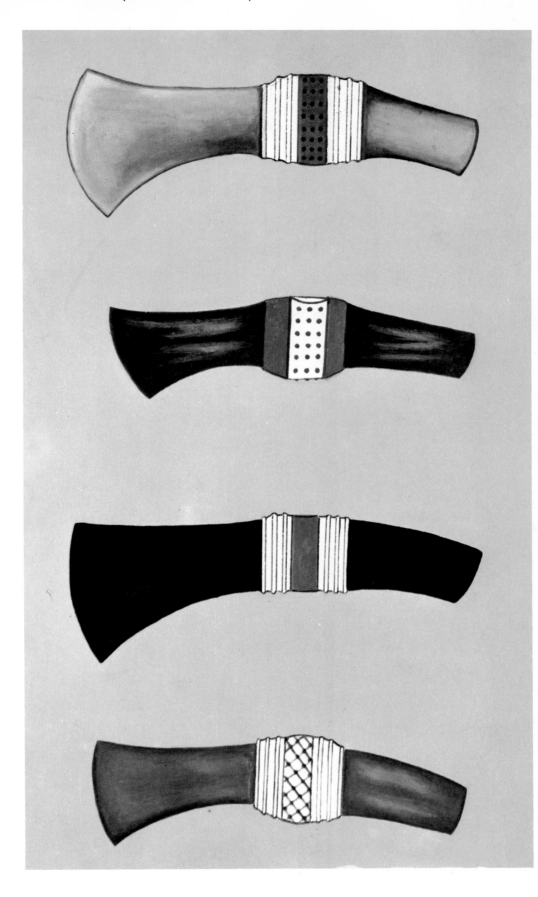

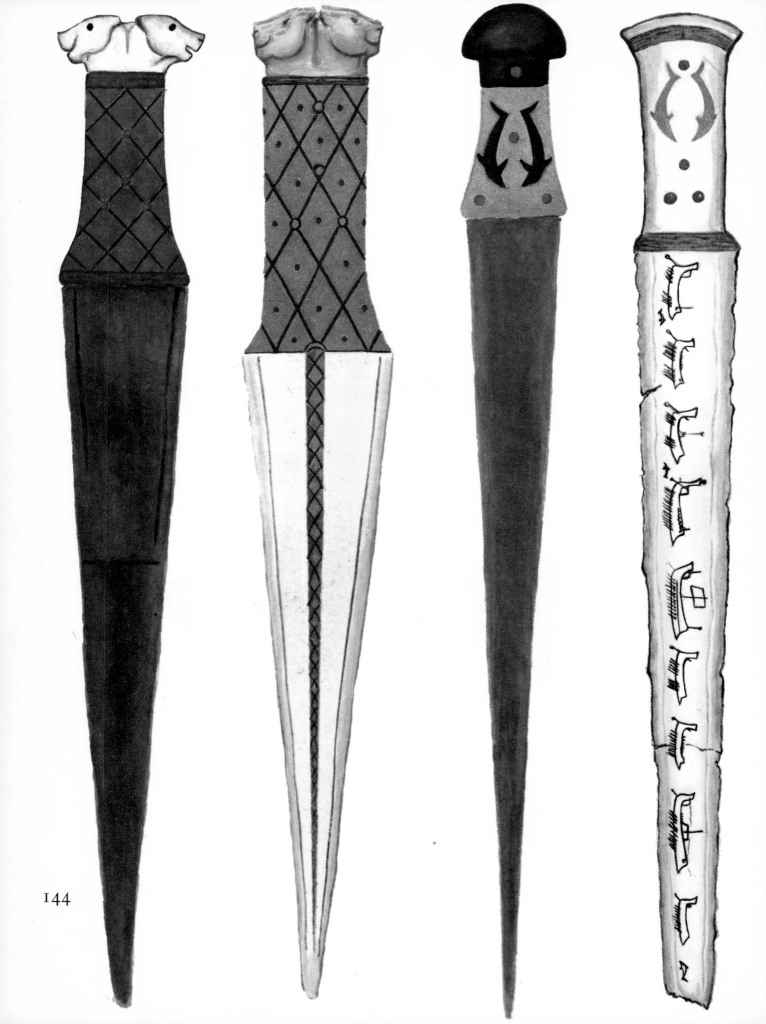

144

The sword was one of the earliest objects made of iron

Anatolian armorers were experimenting with iron blades as early as the third millennium in order to produce a longer and stronger weapon. At left on this page, an iron sword from the royal treasure of Dorak, with obsidian pommel and hilt studded with gold and amber, is 75 cms. long. The bronze sword beside it (also from Dorak) has a stained ivory handle covered with gold and a pommel of rock-crystal.

Four additional swords from Dorak, shown on page 144, incorporate (left to right) a bronze blade and lion-head pommel of rock-crystal with eyes of lapis lazuli; a silver blade and a gold central spine and a lion-head pommel of pale blue stone with nephrite rivets; a bronze blade, gold hilt, and lapis lazuli pommel; and a silver blade decorated with a boat motif, silver hilt decorated with gold dolphins.

This drawing of a limestone relief (above) from the 24th century B.C. shows Egyptian troops armed with shallow axes in open battle with long-haired Semites. At the right, in the earliest known depiction of siege activities, the Egyptians raise a scaling-ladder against the walls of their enemies' fortified city and, below, use battering-poles to breach the gate of the city, which is flanked by semicircular bastions, like the other bastions of the city.

The late-third-millennium shallow axehead (below right), of the same type as those depicted in the siege scene, is pierced with holes for securing it to a haft. The scene of Egyptian archers (below left) was discovered at Lisht in the vicinity of the pyramid of Amenemhet I, the founder of the XIIth Dynasty. Taken by him from earlier buildings, such fragments were used as fill for his own tomb. This piece probably came from structures connected with

the Great Pyramid of Cheops, which have almost entirely disappeared as a result of such despoiling.

Above: Relief in the tomb of Anta, Deshashe, Upper Egypt, Late Vth Dynasty. Below right: Axehead. British Museum. Below left: Relief from the reign of Cheops, IVth Dynasty.

The Egyptian

siege and attack a fortified city

A wall painting from a 23rd-century B.C. tomb shows another Egyptian siege, here involving a unique mobile scaling-ladder. The attacking army uses axes with semicircular heads like the one shown at right.

Above: Wall painting from the tomb of Kaemheset, Saqqarah, VIth Dynasty. Right: Axehead, late third millennium B.C. Metropolitan Museum of Art.

Weapons from
Syria and Israel

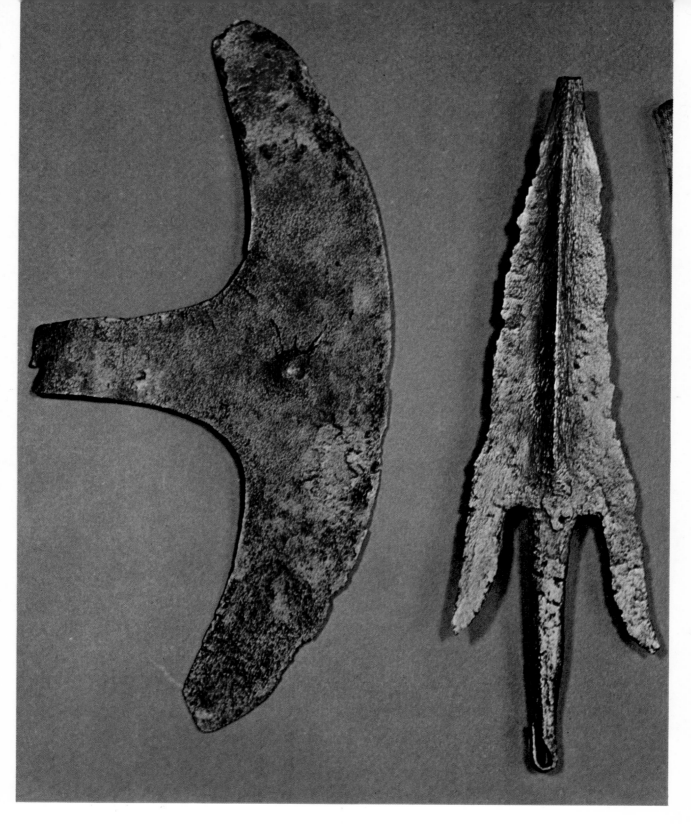

The Syrian socketed axeheads at the left of page 148, all from a tomb at Til Barsip, illustrate the variety of blade shapes in use at the end of the third millennium capable of armor piercing. The axehead at the right of page 148 has animal heads at the rear of the socket. (All examples are now in the Louvre.)

The crescent-shaped tanged cutting axeblade and the unusual barbed spearhead with pronounced midrib (above) are both from the lowest stratum of excavations at Tell el-Hesi, and probably date from the 24th century B.C. (Early Bronze III). (Both axe and spearhead are now in the Institute of Archaeology, London.)

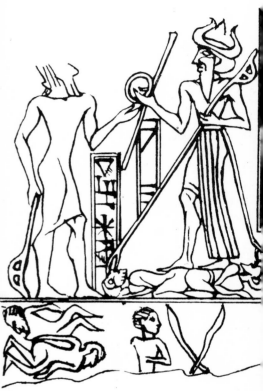

The composite bow may have been the decisive factor in Accadian victory over the Sumerians. In the detail (above) from a commemorative stele found at Susa, the victorious King Naram-Sin, shown trampling his enemies, holds what seems to be the first recorded example of this effective weapon. The King wears a horned helmet—a symbol of deification—and also carries a narrow-bladed axe on his left arm, an arrow in his right hand. Above at right, the c. 2000 B.C. Ilushuilia (the ruler of Eshnuma) shows a similarly victorious and helmeted deity (Tishpak) armed with an epsilon axe.

Above left: Sandstone stele from Susa, 23rd century B.C. Louvre. Right: Impression of a seal from Tell el-Asmar, Neo-Sumerian period. Museum of the Oriental Institute, Chicago.

Facing page, left: A fragment of another Accadian stele shows the composite bow in action. Right, a second Accadian fragment shows bound captives before a soldier armed with a battleaxe.

Facing page, left: Limestone stele fragment from Lagash, period of Sargon or Naram-Sin. Louvre. Right: Diorite stele fragment from Susa, Accadian period. Louvre.

The earliest known
representation of
the composite bow

The age that is probably most significant in the general history of the lands of the Bible is of special importance in the development of systems of warfare

After a period of decline (the First Intermediate period) in the 23rd and 22nd centuries B.C., Egyptian civilization embarked on a glorious era beginning with the XIth Dynasty and known as the period of the Middle Kingdom. This flowering reached its zenith with the XIIth Dynasty (1991–1778 B.C.) under the reigns of kings invariably called either Amenemhet or Senusert. During it, contact between Egypt and Asia flourished and the Egyptian rulers extended their influence as far north as Syria. The magnificent wall paintings decorating the various tombs and edifices of Egypt tell us much of the art of warfare of the period and the characteristics of the armed forces of both Egypt and the Asiatic countries. In Biblical terms, this is the "period of the patriarchs"—embracing the migration of Abraham into Palestine and his contact with Egypt.

A Middle Kingdom ruler—King Senusert III (1879–1841 B.C.)—portrayed as a sphinx.

153

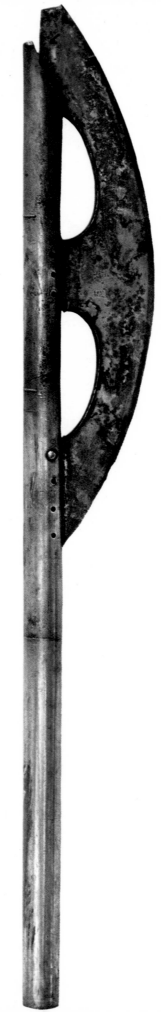

The flat, socketless cutting axe—originating in Mesopotamia, Syria, and Palestine—found popular use in Egypt as an effective weapon against warriors without helmets

On this page, right to left: A bronze-bladed shallow epsilon battleaxe secured to a silver haft; and a separate bronze epsilon blade, showing the piercings through which it was secured to its haft. Both axe and blade, Middle Kingdom (c. 20th century B.C.). British Museum.

Wall paintings and reliefs of the period show exact representations of the weapons on this page. The arms-bearer at above right on page 155 also carries a water-skin and a quiver with arrows. At left, an Egyptian warrior wears no armor, but carries an epsilon axe and a huge shield, as does the soldier depicted in the relief below.

Facing page, right: Detail of painting from the tomb of Senbi in Meir, XIIth Dynasty. Left: Detail of painting from tomb of Tehutitep at El Bersheh. Bottom: A rare depiction on a relief from the XIth Dynasty funerary temple of Mentuhotep II of Deir el-Bahri (cf. 169).

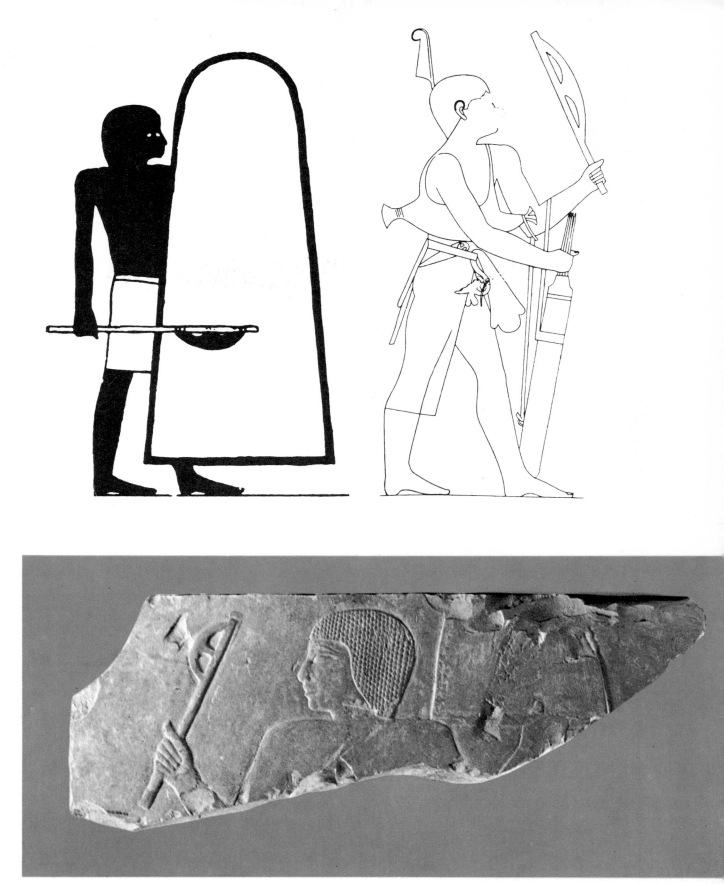

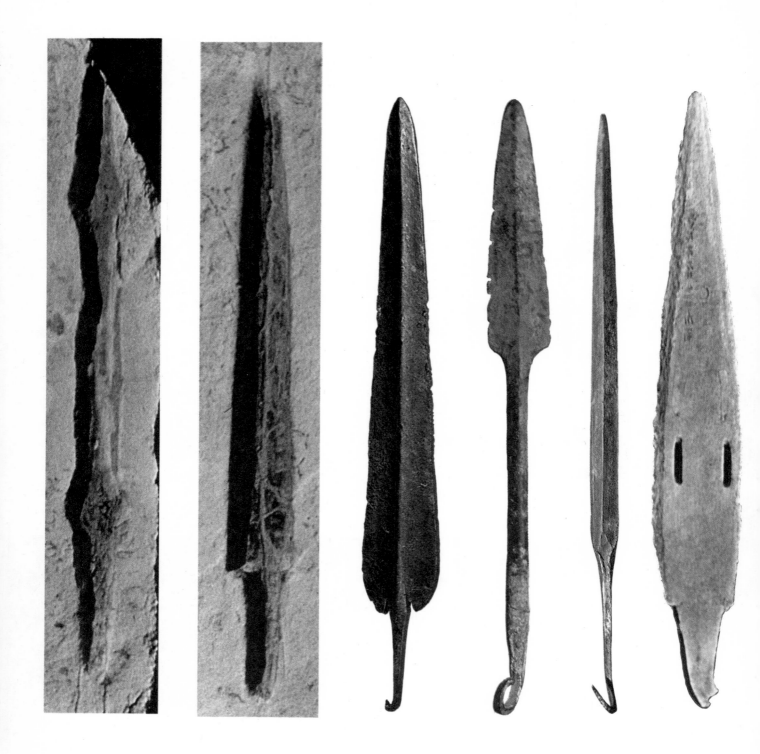

156

The tang attachment for spearheads and javelin-heads is typical
for the beginning of the period

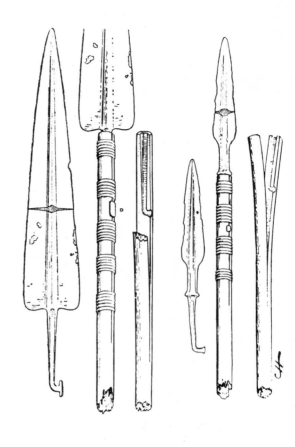

The tang by which both spearheads and javelin-heads, as well as javelin-butts, were attached to their shafts was often bent or voluted to prevent the shaft from splitting under impact. At right, drawings show how the fastenings were made. Above are typical examples of both types. At the left is a mold for casting spearheads and javelin-heads.

Photographs, right to left: Javelin-head from Ugarit, Middle Bronze I (2100–1900 B.C.). Louvre. Two double-pierced spearheads from Alaca Hüyük, Anatolia (c. 2300 B.C.). Hittite Museum, Ankara. Double-pierced spearhead of King Anittas from Kültepe, Anatolia (c. 1800 B.C.). Javelin-butt from Barkai, Israel, Middle Bronze I (2100–1900 B.C.). Spearhead from Megiddo, Israel, Middle Bronze I (2100–1900 B.C.). Spearhead from Vounnous, Cyprus, erroneously termed the "Cypriot dagger," Middle Bronze I (c. 2000 B.C). Limestone mold from Hazor, Israel (c. 1900 B.C.).

157

158

The earliest known battering-ram

The wall painting above (colors reconstructed) from the tomb of Khety shows a besieged city being attacked by Egyptian warriors armed with axes and double-convex bows and carrying medium-sized shields. In the middle register, three Egyptian soldiers within a covered enclosure thrust a long pole toward the upper part of the fortifications—a crude forerunner of the battering-ram. At left, two painted models of leather shields like those depicted in

the painting above incorporate such details as a piebald skin pattern and stitching at the edges.

Wall painting from Beni-hasan (c. 1900 B.C.). Page 158, right: A 28-inch-high wooden model of Egyptian shield from Assiut, XIIth Dynasty (c. 20th century B.C.). Metropolitan Museum of Art. Left: Wooden model of Egyptian shield, Middle Kingdom (c. 20th-19th centuries B.C.). Louvre.

Buhen—the most complete example of a XIIth Dynasty fortress

Buhen, on the west bank of the Nile in modern Sudan, was excavated as recently as 1957. This reconstruction of the c. 1900 B.C. fortification is based on the wall paintings of Beni-hasan (pages 158–159) as well as on the plans of the citadel as discovered at the excavation.

The defenses of the city consisted of a main wall with rectangular bastions; an outer wall with semicircular bastions; a deep moat; a defensive wall on the outer lip of the moat; and a steep glacis sloping outward from this last wall.

The mode of attack and of defense is seen here as paralleling the action of the Beni-hasan painting, and it may therefore be presumed that its conquest was also achieved with the help of battering-rams, which made their appearance in this period. The storming force was aided by heavy archery units, whose function was to neutralize the defending archers.

161

The slightly double-convex simple bow of Egypt at the time of the Middle Kingdom

At left, a 21st-century B.C. funerary stele of a Theban noble shows him holding a double-convex bow in his left hand and reed arrows in his right, Below it are four similar bows (c. 2000 B.C.) made of acacia wood from Beni-hasan, Assiut, and Thebes. The archer of the army of Mentuhotep II (above right) holds a bow of the same type, as do the Nubian archers (right)—part of a wooden model from the same period depicting a column of four ten-man files.

Left: Limestone stele from Thebes, XIth Dynasty. Metropolitan Museum of Art. Four bows, Middle Kingdom. British Museum. Right, bottom: Wooden model from the tomb of Mesehti at Assiut, Middle Kingdom. Cairo Museum. Top: Relief from the funerary temple of Mentuhotep II at Deir el-Bahri, XIth Dynasty. Metropolitan Museum of Art.

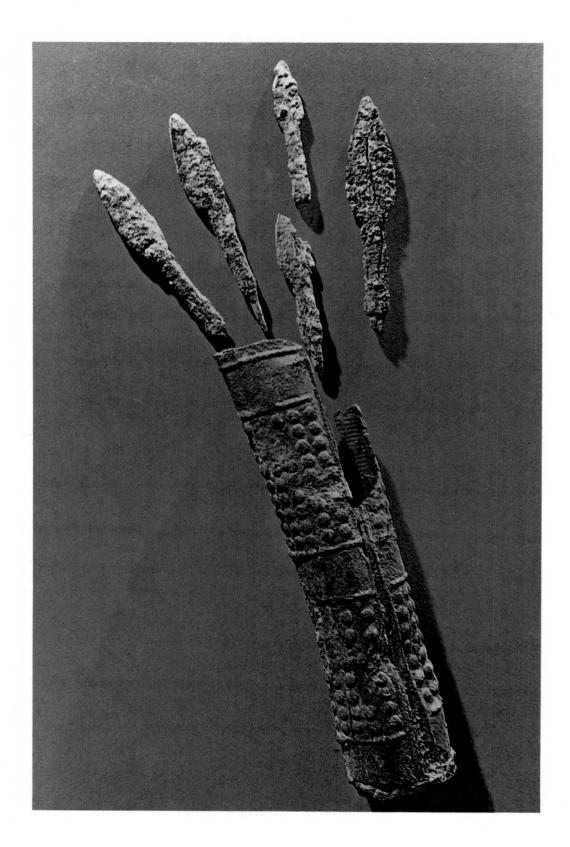

164

The quiver— introduced into Egypt from Syria and Palestine

The c. 16th-century B.C. metal quiver and arrows on page 164 are from Mari on the Euphrates. At right are two wooden models of bull-hide quivers, both dating from c. 20th century B.C. (The model at far right comes from the same Assiut tomb as the spotted shield on page 158.) Below, a Beni-hasan wall painting from the Middle Kingdom shows a workshop in which bows and arrows are being made.

Left: Metal quiver with arrows from Mari, c. 16th century B.C. Louvre.

Right: Wooden model of quiver, XIIth Dynasty: Louvre. Far right: Wooden model of quiver, XIIth Dynasty. Metropolitan Museum of Art.

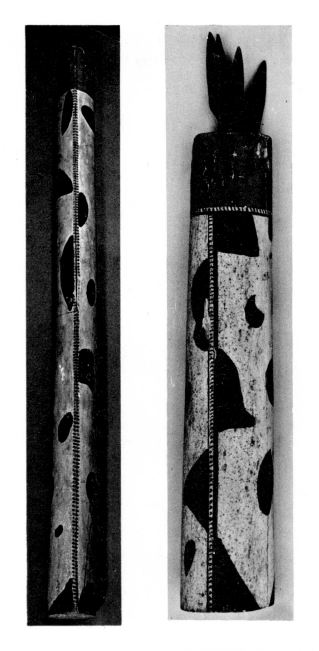

The duck-bill axe—developed as an effecti

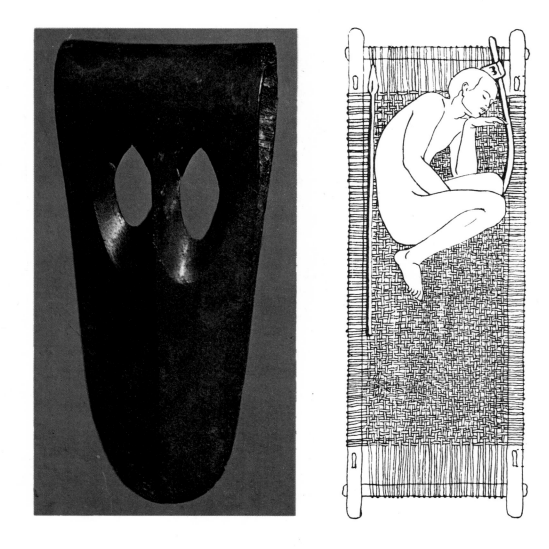

ercing instrument by lengthening the blade
and narrowing the edge
of the eye axe

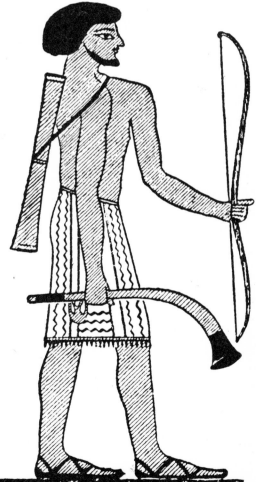

The painting above from a tomb at Beni-hasan
dating from c. 1900 B.C. shows a caravan of
Semites *en route* to Egypt, armed with the
typical weapons of Canaan in the period of
the patriarchs. The figure at the extreme left
carries an axe with a duck-bill blade (see detail
of figure at right), a double-convex bow, and a
quiver. Other men are armed with spears,
bows, and hurling-sticks.

The drawing on page 166 shows a reconstruction of a Syrian burial chamber with a duck-
bill axe near the head of the warrior and a
spear at his back. A photograph of a duck-bill
axeblade is shown at far left.

Above: Wall painting from tomb of Khnum-
hotep III at Beni-hasan, Middle Kingdom.
Right: Enlarged detail of the above wall
painting done by the Champollion expedition,
showing clearly the "duck-bill" blade. Left:
Reconstruction of burial chamber from
Baghouz, Middle Bronze II (19th–18th centuries B.C.). Far left: Duck-bill axeblade,
Ugarit (19th century B.C.). Louvre.

167

The eye axe—
developed as a
piercing weapon
with a socket,
often reappears
in socketless
form in Egypt

The eye axe was necessitated by the appearance
of helmets and armor. The one on the left
(c. 1900 B.C.) from Megiddo shows how the
form gives a new look to the shallow epsilon
axe and makes it a more effective weapon.
Above, an Egyptian version of the eye blade
remains socketless, the bronze blade being
inserted into a hollow bronze haft.

Left: Bronze eye axe from Megiddo. Depart-
ment of Antiquities, Archaeological Museum,
Jerusalem. Above: Egyptian axeblade, Middle
Kingdom. British Museum.

On page 169, above, an older type of Egyptian
axeblade incorporates eyes but remains
socketless; and below, in a Beni-hasan wall
painting, Semitic mercenaries carry a socketless
eye axe, hurling-sticks, and spears.

Page 169, above: Eye blade, Middle Kingdom
(c. 20th century B.C.). British Museum.
Below: Painting in the tomb of Amenemhet,
XIIth Dynasty (20th century B.C.).

168

These ceremonial axes all date from the XIIth
Dynasty (c. 1900 B.C.). At the right, the blades
are attached to a short gold sheath at the top
of the wooden haft. Beirut Museum.

Gold ceremonial eye
blades from the Obelisks
Temple at Byblos

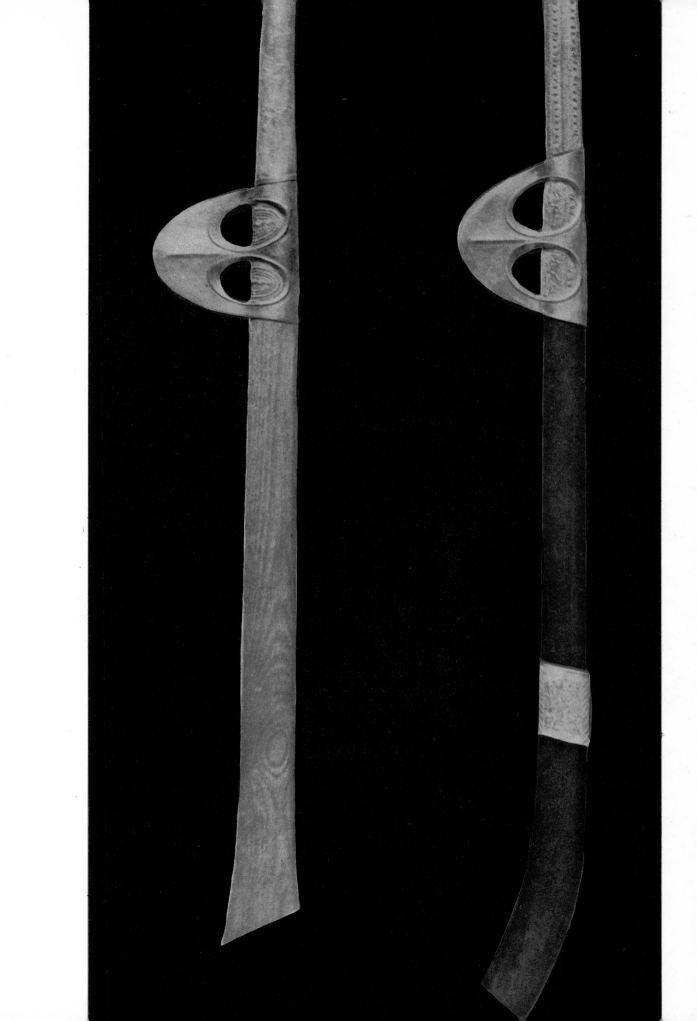

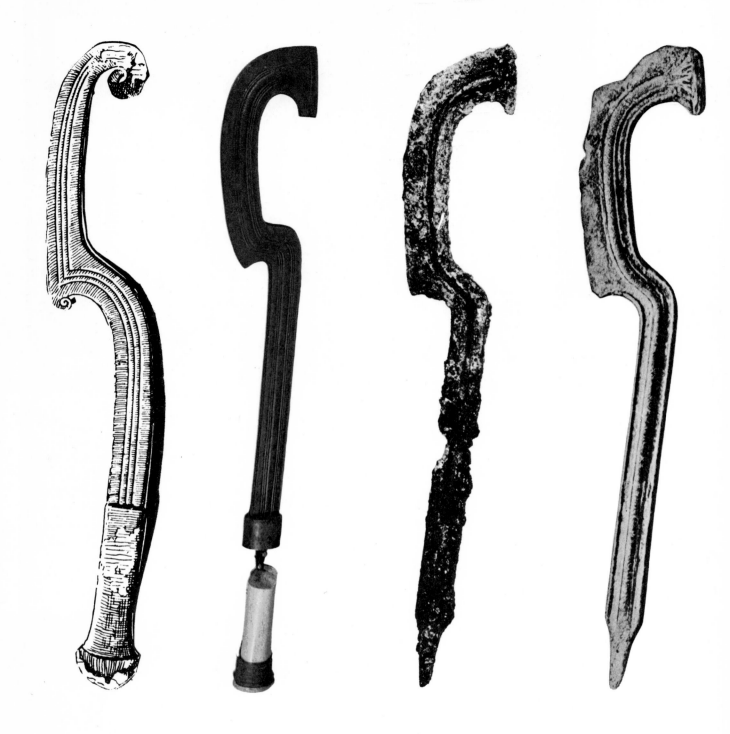

The sickle sword—developed
from the axe as a cutting, rather
than a thrusting, weapon

These four Middle Bronze Age sickle swords at left have a characteristically long handle and short blade. Only later, when the blade was made as long as the hilt, can it be said that a true sword was developed. These examples are actually closer to the shallow crescent axe —whose. function they could perform more effectively.

Swords, left to right: From Lagash, Ur III period. From Abydos (c. 19th century B.C.), Museum of the Oriental Institute, Chicago. From Byblos, XIIth Dynasty (19th century B.C.), Louvre. From Shechem (Balata), Palestine, Middle Bronze II (c. 19th century B.C.) (now lost).

In the center of the wall painting above (from Mari, on the Euphrates, 18th century B.C.) the goddess Ishtar holds a weapon in her left hand which exemplifies the transition from shallow crescent axe to sickle sword. An enlarged line drawing of the panel is shown at bottom left. Beside it is a cylinder seal of the early second millennium B.C. from Larsa, in which the deity Nergal holds a sickle sword.

Weapons from the Middle Bronze II period exhibit refined effectiveness

The Palestinian weapons above and at left are so characteristic of the period that there is hardly a tomb belonging to the era in which similar examples are not to be found. The narrow-socketed axeblade (above) was a formidable weapon for piercing the metal helmet, as was the socketed javelin-head (left center). The sword-dagger blade, now strengthened with ribs, also becomes a weapon with considerable power of penetration.

Above: Axeblade from the tomb of Ginossar. Department of Antiquities, Archaeological Museum, Jerusalem. Far left: Axe. Department of Archaeology, Hebrew University, Jerusalem. Center: Javelin-head from Barkai. Left: Sword-dagger. Department of Antiquities, Archaeological Museum, Jerusalem.

On page 175: Three straight Egyptian sword-daggers of the same period, all of bronze with ivory crescent-shaped pommels.

Left to right: Middle Kingdom (c. 1800 B.C.). British Museum. Hyksos period (1720–1570 B.C.). British Museum. XVIIth Dynasty (1600–1570 B.C.). University of Pennsylvania Museum.

The "rulers of foreign countries"

The period of the XIIIth to the XVIIth Egyptian Dynasties (1778–1570 B.C.) known as the Second Intermediate period is one of decline. Within it (XVth–XVIth Dynasty) Egypt was ruled by an Asiatic people, colloquially termed the "Hyksos"—literally, the "rulers of foreign countries."

Because no illustrated monuments of the period have been found, we know little of the military characteristics of these "rulers," although from written documents we do know that they introduced the light horse-drawn chariot into Egypt; and archaeological excavations in Palestine and Syria allow us to reconstruct their own fortified cities.

This period covers the earlier part of the Biblical Sojourn of the Children of Israel in Egypt.

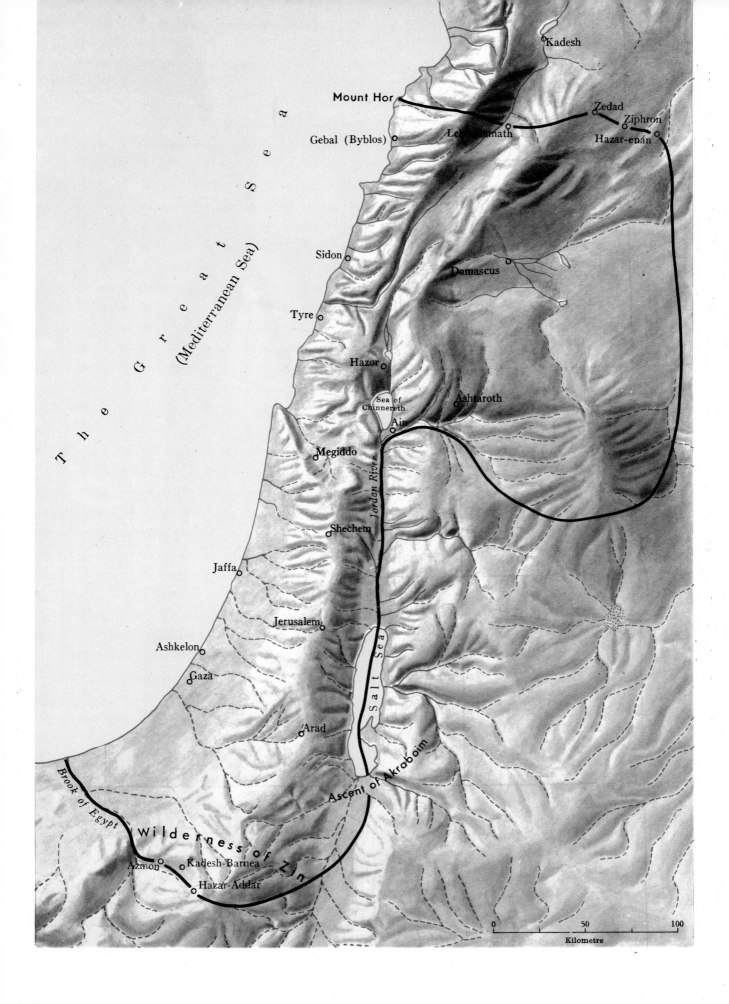

Kadesh

Mount Hor

Zedad

Ziphron

Gebal (Byblos)

Lebo-hamath

Hazar-enan

The Great Sea

(Mediterranean Sea)

Sidon

Damascus

Tyre

Hazor

Ashtaroth

Sea of Chinnereth

Ain

Megiddo

Jordan River

Shechem

Jaffa

Jerusalem

Ashkelon

Salt Sea

Gaza

Arad

Ascent of Akraboim

Brook of Egypt

Wilderness of Zin

Azmon

Kadesh-Barnea

Hazar-Addar

0   50   100

Kilometre

Hazor—fortifications that must have employed thousands of laborers over a span of several years

The great moat round the mammoth western defenses of the lower city of Hazor is 80 meters wide and reaches a depth of 15 meters. Above: the moat (looking north) and the slopes of the great earthen rampart (at the right of the photograph) resulting from its excavation. Middle Bronze II, Hyksos period (second half of 18th century B.C.).

On page 179 are shown (top) the 18th-century B.C. revetment wall of basalt boulders near the northeast gate of the lower city, and (bottom) the 17th-century B.C. stone glacis and moat in the northeast corner of the upper city.

The expulsion of Hyksos from Egypt

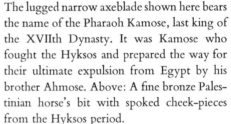

The lugged narrow axeblade shown here bears the name of the Pharaoh Kamose, last king of the XVIIth Dynasty. It was Kamose who fought the Hyksos and prepared the way for their ultimate expulsion from Egypt by his brother Ahmose. Above: A fine bronze Palestinian horse's bit with spoked cheek-pieces from the Hyksos period.

Left: Axeblade (c. 1600–1570 B.C.). British Museum. Above: Bit from Tell el-'Ajjul (17th century B.C.). The Rockefeller Museum.

Right: This ceremonial axe, presented to Queen Ahhotep by her son, King Ahmose, founder of the flourishing XVIIIth Dynasty, shows the King smiting his enemy. The bronze axehead, inlaid with gold, dates from 1570 B.C. and is now in the Cairo Museum.

Thutmose III

The expulsion of the Hyksos and the accession to the throne of Ahmose I (1570 B.C.) launched a new dynasty (the XVIIIth) and a magnificent new era in Egyptian history known as the New Kingdom.

Adopting the armaments of the Hyksos—the chariot, the sickle sword, the scaled coat of mail, and the powerful composite bow—the new Egyptian rulers developed a mighty military machine, unequaled even in the immediate periods that followed. The abundance of illustrated monuments, both from Egypt and the Asiatic countries, enable us to follow step by step the development of the art of warfare during the XVIIIth and XIXth Dynasties. This period corresponds in Palestine and Syria to the Late Bronze Age (1570–1200). The latter part of the period—the XIXth Dynasty or Late Bronze IIB (13th century B.C.)—covers the Biblical period of the Exodus and the Israelite occupation of Canaan.

Son of Thutmose II, stepson of Queen Hatshepsut, Thutmose III was one of the most powerful pharaohs of the XVIIIth Dynasty. Statue of Thutmose III (1490–1436 B.C.). Musées Royaux d'Art et d'Histoire.

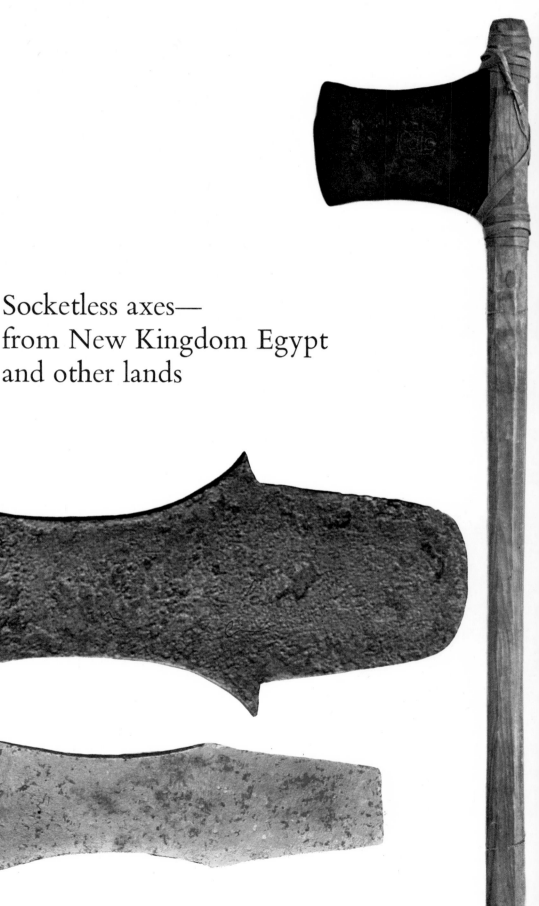

Socketless axes—
from New Kingdom Egypt
and other lands

The bronze blade of the battleaxe at the right of page 184, which bears the name of Thutmose III, is typical of the shortened head and narrower cutting edge of the New Kingdom axe form. The lugged blade is attached to its wooden haft with leather thongs. On this page a squad of Egyptian soldiers armed with typical New Kingdom weapons are led by an officer in the Expedition to the Land of Punt. Their weapons include battleaxe, short round-topped shield, and spears, and the first soldier carries a bow case like that shown on page 199. The two non-Egyptian Late Bronze axeheads at the left of page 184—the upper, with pronounced lugs, from Anatolia; the lower from Hazor—exemplify the long rear portion that differentiates them from Egyptian types.

Page 184, right: Egyptian battleaxe (1490–1436 B.C.). British Museum. Above: Reliefs from Queen Hatshepsut's temple at Deir el-Bahri (1489–1469 B.C.).

185

The Late Bronze chariots of these two hunters–

An Egyptian wall painting (c. 1430 B.C.) shows a chariot with four-spoked wheels like those of its Canaanite prototype, harnessed to two steeds. The charioteer, who is not fighting but hunting, has the reins round his waist so that his hands are free to operate his composite bow.

Painting from the tomb of Userhet, royal scribe in the reign of Amenhotep II, Sheikh Abd el-Gurnah, XVIIIth Dynasty.

e Egyptian, the other from Ugarit—are identical

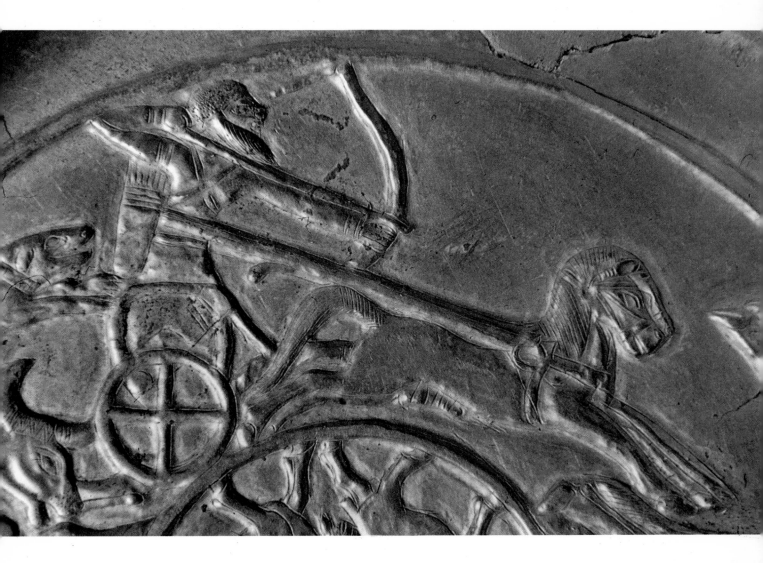

The Canaanite hunting charioteer in a similar vehicle, also has both hands free to work a powerful composite bow.

Detail from gold patera (bowl) from Ugarit (c. 1400 B.C.). Louvre.

187

Chariots of the 15th century B.C.
depicted on a tile and on the
wall of a Theban tomb

Facing page: Faience tile, XVIIIth Dynasty.
Metropolitan Museum of Art.

The gifts borne by the Canaanites depicted in
this tomb painting (above) include, at left, a
chariot that is identical with the four-spoked
one shown on page 188.

Above: Wall painting from the tomb of
Rekhmire at Thebes, XVIIIth Dynasty, reigns
of Thutmose III–Amenhotep II.

189

The surviving chariots
of the 15th century B.C.

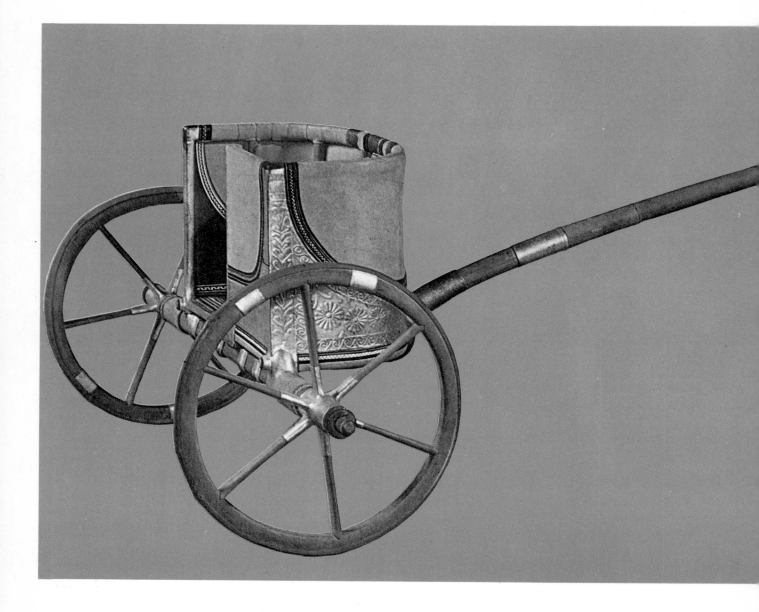

Left: Apart from its lavish gold decoration, this chariot is typical of the Egyptian chariots of the latter part of the XVIIIth Dynasty, from about 1400 B.C. onward. The diameter of the six-spoked leather-rimmed wheels is 74 cms.; the total length of the chariot is 2·45 ms.; length of the pole is 1·47 ms.; depth of the body is 90 cms. The materials are wood, leather, and metal. The wide axle, set at the very rear of the body, and the strong wheels, gave the chariot stability and enabled it to take sharp turns at high speed.

Left: Chariot of Yuya (father-in-law of Amenhotep III), discovered in his tomb (and that of his wife, Thuyu) in the Valley of the Kings. The photograph shown is of a model of the chariot in the Metropolitan Museum of Art, patterned on the original in the Cairo Museum

Above: This Early XVIIIth Dynasty chariot is much lighter than that on the facing page, and is similar to the Canaanite chariot which served as its prototype. In fact, one cannot rule out the possibility that this actually *is* a Canaanite chariot, brought to Egypt as a gift or as booty. The materials are wood, leather, and metal. Note the long pole running beneath the body to the axle (as on page 190) and strengthening an otherwise somewhat fragile construction.

Above: Chariot with four-spoked wheels. Florence Museum.

191

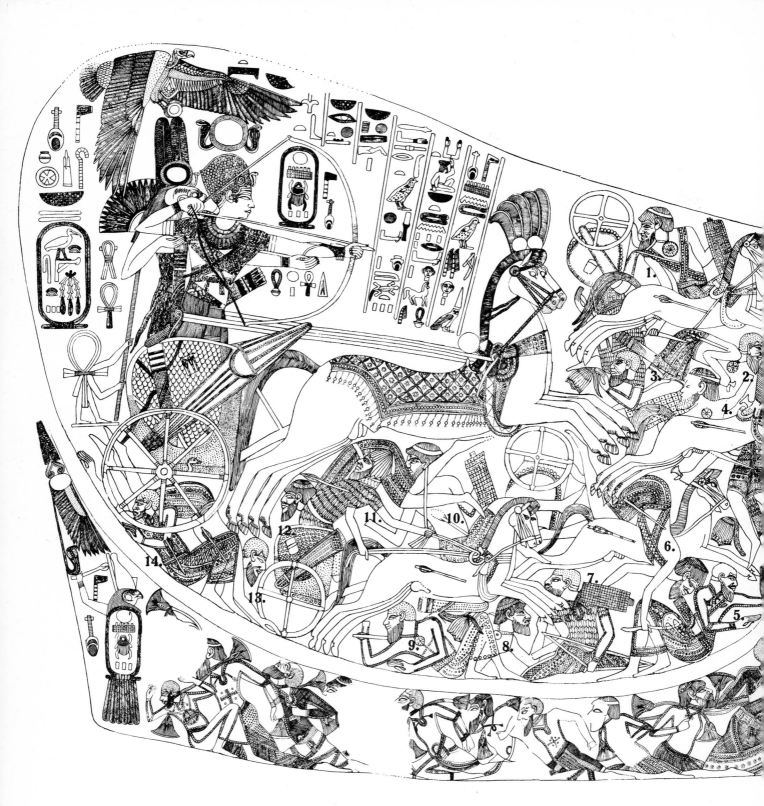

Richly revealing reliefs from the sides of a royal Egyptian chariot

192

The reliefs on the sides of the chariot body of Thutmose IV, and from the chariot itself, are highly instructive on the subject of warfare at the end of the 15th century B.C. They provide a very detailed record of the weapons, chariots, and armor used by the peoples of Syria and Palestine against whom the Egyptians fought. The King is depicted on a chariot which has eight-spoked wheels, firing his composite bow at the retreating Asiatics. The Syrian chariots

are all light, and retain the four-spoked wheels. Their charioteers wear scaled coats of mail and helmets (see page 196). Their shields are rectangular, made of wood and covered with leather, and are studded with metal nails in decorative patterns. They are armed with composite bows (see page 199). Some of the Canaanite warriors (e.g., bottom right) are bearing eye axes, but, on the basis of archaeological finds, this seems to be an anachronism.

The artist may have copied them from the extensive Middle Kingdom paintings depicting Semites with such axes (see pages 168–169). The scene is brilliantly evocative of the disorder on a battlefield.

Drawing of reliefs on chariot found in the tomb of King Thutmose IV, XVIIIth Dynasty (1411–1397 B.C.).

Weapons borne as tribute to a flourishing monarchy

In this wall painting (left), executed in the reign of Thutmose IV, an Asiatic tribute-bearer carries a quiver by a strap looped over his forearm.

Left: Detail from a Theban tomb painting (1411–1397 B.C.). British Museum.

194

Above: Tribute-bearers depicted in the reigns of Thutmose III and Amenhotep II are shown with two horses for a chariot and a triangular composite bow. Left: Tribute-bearers from the same period bear, left to right, quiver, chariot, composite bow, sickle sword, horses, and a mace.

Above: Wall painting from tomb of Rekhmire at Thebes (15th century B.C.). Metropolitan Museum of Art. Left: Wall painting from tomb of Iamanezeh, Sheikh Abd el-Gurnah (15th century B.C.).

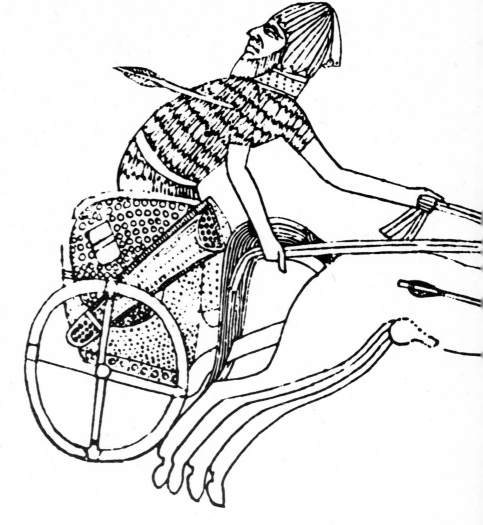

The scaled armor or coat of mail was of vital importance to warriors like the charioteer or archer whose weapons occupied both hands and who could not carry a shield. The drawing of an Asiatic charioteer at the right shows how an arrow fired from a composite bow could pierce the weak point of the coat of mail at the joint of the sleeve to the garment. (Compare the Biblical verse: ". . . and smote the king of Israel between the joints and [of] the armor . . . and the king was stayed up in his chariot . . ." (I Kings 22: 34, 35).) Below: Bronze scale armor of the 15th century B.C. from Nuzi, with scales 118 mms. × 63 mms. and 2 mms. thick. (The two rows of scales are not in their original position.) Written documents from Nuzi mention scale armor consisting of from 400 to 600 large scales and several hundred smaller scales.

Right: Detail from the reliefs on the chariot of Thutmose IV shown on pages 192–193. Below: Armor from Nuzi found at the house of Shilwi-Theshub. Baghdad Museum.

Scaled armor: essential for warriors who were unable to carry a shield

Above right: A Theban tomb painting depicts a bronze coat of mail consisting of some 450 scales, and a leather collar for neck protection similar to the one worn by the Asiatic charioteer shown on the facing page. The relics of bronze scales shown below are from a coat of mail found in the palace of Amenhotep III in Thebes. On one of the scales there was still preserved part of the cloth on which the scale was sewn. This illustration shows admirably the spine of the scale, which enabled the garment to hang well; the holes through which the scales were sewn to the cloth; and the way in which the scales were fitted to each other.

Above right: Wall painting from the tomb of Kenamon, reign of Amenhotep II (1436–1411 B.C.). Below: Bronze scales (17th century B.C.). Metropolitan Museum of Art.

197

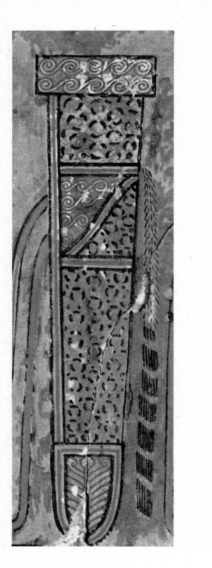

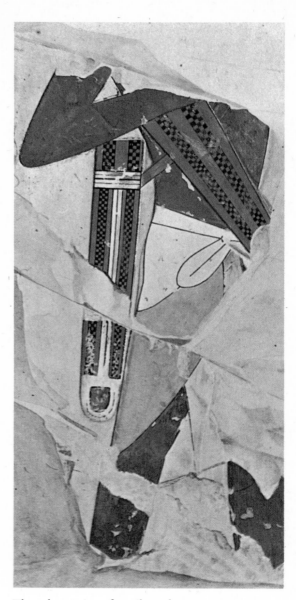

These three quivers from the 15th century B.C. show in varying degree the elaborate ornamentation to which the arrow case was now subjected.

Above, left: Detail from a wall painting in the tomb of Kenamon at Thebes, reign of Amenhotep II (1436–1411 B.C.). Center: Quiver from Thebes (?), made of leather over linen and measuring 80 cms. in length, XVIIIth Dynasty (c. 1400 B.C.). Metropolitan Museum of Art. Right: Detail from a wall painting found in the tomb of Puyemre at Thebes, Thutmose III period (c. 1450 B.C.). Metropolitan Museum of Art.

Quivers and carrying cases for the decisive weapon

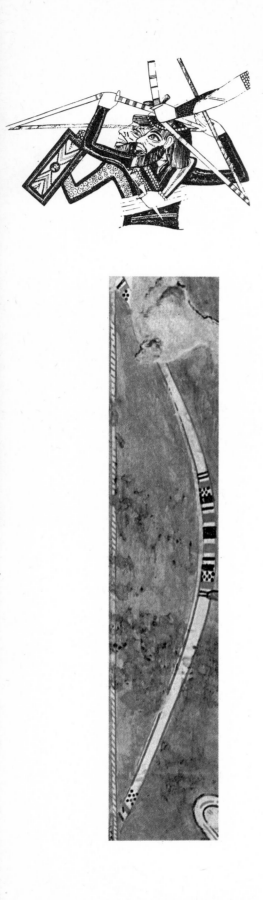

Above: A Theban tomb painting shows a servant bearing equipment that includes a very fine triangular case for a composite bow. The drawing at the upper left shows identical composite bows being used by King Thutmose IV (at right) and a vanquished Semite (at left). A detail from the same Theban tomb painting illustrated (left) depicts a composite bow in detail.

Above and left: Details from wall paintings in the tomb of Kenamon, reign of Amenhotep II (1436–1411 B.C.). Above left: Detail drawing from the relief on the chariot of Thutmose IV shown on page 193.

Above: A granite block shows Amenhotep II, the last king to use a chariot with a four-spoked wheel, engaged in firing practice. The pierced tablet at lower right of the relief, probably a copper ingot, indicates the physical prowess of the King as well as the power of the composite bow. Left: A drawing of a similar scene on a gold plaque adds a "William Tell" note, for two prisoners are tied to the copper-ingot target at which the King fires.

Above: Granite relief from the Great Temple at Karnak (1436–1411 B.C.). Left: Gold plaque from the Valley of the Kings (14th century B.C.).

The powerful composite bow in action and in training

The drawing of a cylinder-seal impression shown above depicts Rameses II firing at a copper-ingot target beneath which two Semites are tied back to back. Below: A Theban tomb painting depicts a firing range for archers. The pupil faces an ordinary rectangular target, while the instructor guides him from behind. The bow was held in the left hand—*not* as shown in the picture—while the string and tail of the arrow were held in the right. The bow on the left is composite; that on the right, representing an earlier phase of training, is a simple one.

Above: Cylinder seal, XIXth Dynasty (13th century B.C.). Rockefeller Museum. Wall painting from Sheikh Abd el-Gurnah, XVIIIth Dynasty.

201

The wooden shield of Tutankhamun, shown at the left, is covered with antelope skin and measures 72 × 51 cms. Below: A Theban tomb painting from the 15th century B.C. depicts the manufacture of similar shields in an arms workshop. On the right of the upper register a workman is stretching a piece of leather over a wooden block. In front of him lie shields already covered with leather. In the center of the upper register, a chariot wheel is being completed. Farther to the left, another worker cuts strips of leather which his mate uses to cover a quiver. A completed chariot frame with parts of the harness hanging from its shafts and with a quiver fastened to its side is shown at the left of the lower register.

Left: Shield from the tomb of Tutankhamun (1352–1343 B.C.). Cairo Museum. Below: Wall painting from the tomb of Hapu, XVIIIth Dynasty.

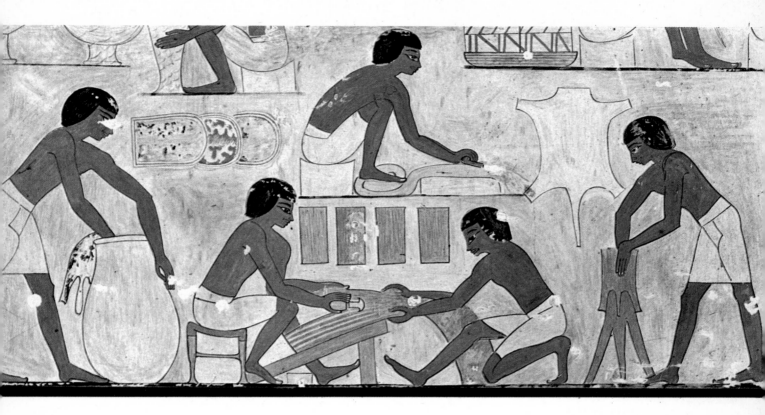

Above: A second Theban tomb painting shows the processes in the making of leather-covered shields in greater detail, with finished shields appearing at the upper left. The picture of a wooden shield covered with leather at the left is a detail from another Theban painting.

Above: Wall painting from the tomb of Rekhmire, reign of Thutmose III (1490–1436 B.C.). Left: Detail of wall painting from the tomb of Kenamon, reign of Amenhotep II (1436–1411 B.C.).

The manufacture of shields

203

This sketch shows Rameses III smiting his Canaanite enemies "with the edge of the sword," as the Bible expresses it. He uses a *khopesh*, the Egyptian version of the Asiatic sickle sword (see pages 205, 206, and 207). *Khopesh* means literally "the foreleg of an animal," and the weapon does resemble a foreleg in shape. This type of sword was introduced into Egypt during the period of the New Kingdom.

204

Painted stone from the Musées Royaux d'Art et d'Histoire, Brussels.

Warrior-gods armed with sickle swords are shown in this 13th-century B.C. Anatolian rock carving from Yazilikaya, near Boghaz-köy. *Yazilikaya* means literally "the carved rock."

The sickle sword, now with a lengthened blade, in active use from Anatolia to Egypt

By contrast with the sickle sword of the Middle Bronze period (see page 172), the later weapon has a longer blade and a shorter hilt. The Bible expression "to smite with the edge of the sword," much used in the record of Joshua's campaigns, suggests that the sickle sword and not the two-edged thrusting sword was the type in common use at the time.

Left: A detail from a late-13th-century B.C. Megiddo ivory carving shows an arms-bearer carrying a sickle sword; and below, a reconstruction of another carved ivory plaque from Megiddo shows infantrymen carrying round shields and sickle swords (see also pages 242–243). Four typical specimens of the Late Bronze II sickle sword are shown on page 207.

Above, left: Detail of upper plaque on page 243. Below: Reconstruction of ivory plaque, early 13th century B.C. Rockefeller Museum.

Facing page, right to left: From Gezer (first half of 14th century B.C.), Istanbul Museum. From Ugarit (14th century B.C.). From the tomb of Tutankhamun (c. 1350 B.C.). The sword of Adad-Nirari, King of Assyria (1310–1280 B.C.). Metropolitan Museum of Art.

The powerful sickle sword of the Late Bronze Age II

206

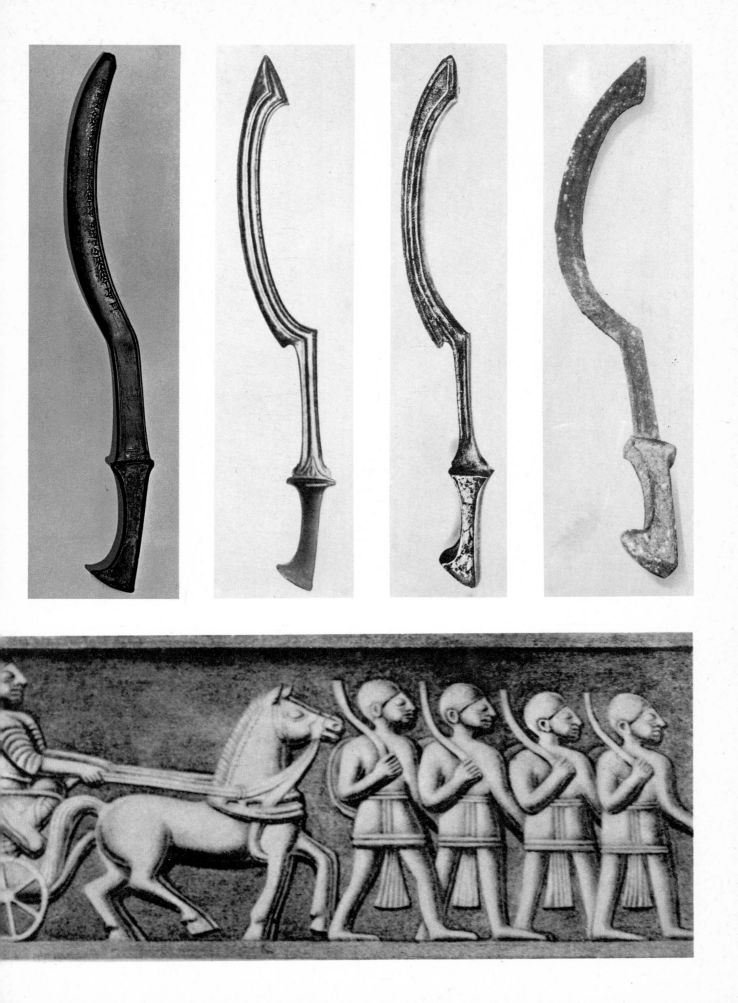

The straight sword:
the narrow-bladed
dagger gives way
to a long straight-
bladed weapon

On page 208, left, an ivory plaque from the palace at Ugarit shows a relatively long-bladed sword being thrust into the forehead of a kneeling prisoner. At right, an earlier Egyptian dagger (c. 1550–1500 B.C.) with bronze blade and gold-covered hilt.

Page 208, left: Ivory plaque (14th–13th century B.C.). Louvre. Right: Bronze-bladed dagger, Early XVIIIth Dynasty. British Museum.

These three weapons illustrate the transition from the dagger form to the long sword. Right to left: An Egyptian bronze dagger of the 14th–13th century B.C., the hilt of which was originally studded with precious materials; a c. 1350 B.C. bronze dagger from ancient Philistia; and a long straight sword from Ugarit, bearing the name of the Pharaoh Merneptah (c. 1223–1211 B.C.).

Right to left: Egyptian dagger, Late New Kingdom. British Museum. Dagger from Tell Mor, Israel. Department of Antiquities, Archaeological Museum, Jerusalem. Sword from Ugarit, XIXth Dynasty. Louvre.

This Theban tomb painting from c. 1400 B.C.
shows a harvest scene in which battle chariots,
stripped of their weapons, are being used as
transport vehicles. The wheels are the characteristic six-spoke type of Egyptian chariots of
the 14th–13th century B.C.

Wall painting from the tomb of Nebamon,
XVIIIth Dynasty. British Museum.

210

The chariot as a farm vehicle

Egyptian farming scene from c. 1400 B.C. depicts a stripped-down chariot being used as a transport vehicle.

Wall painting from the tomb of Menena, Sheikh Abd el-Gurnah, XVIIIth Dynasty. British Museum.

211

The six-spoke chariot wheel can be used as a criterion for dating an Egyptian monument after 1400 B.C.

This painted low relief showing the harnessing of the royal chariot gives clear illustration of the six-spoke wheel and the setting of the axle at the very rear of the body to give the vehicle stability on sharp turns. The pole runs beneath the body, and the two are more firmly secured with the aid of leather straps. The case of the composite bow is attached in a diagonal position.

Relief from Tell el-Amarna (14th century B.C.)

Another painted low relief from Tell el-
Amarna shows the royal chariots attended by
the grooms awaiting their masters.

Relief from the temple of Amenhotep IV.
Metropolitan Museum of Art.

und in Tutankhamun's tomb, at Thebes

This painting of a hunting scene and that of the battle scene illustrated on pages 216 and 217 are of great importance in the study of Egyptian chariots and armaments at the close of the XVIIIth Dynasty. They retain the same characteristics as the chariots and weapons depicted in the reliefs of Tell el-Amarna. The King stands in his chariot, the reins round his waist (see pages 186, 187, 192, 200), firing a powerful composite bow. The leather guard on his wrist is drawn in minute detail. He has two quivers in addition to the one fitted to the chariot body opposite the bow case. The King is followed by his royal retinue—guards in chariots and infantrymen armed with axes, spears, and bows.

Chest lid reproduced about the same size as the original (1352–1343 B.C.). Cairo Museum.

Asiatic chariots, as well as
a magnificent Egyptian one,
are depicted in this realistically
chaotic battle scene

This battle scene is painted on a side panel of the chest of which the lid is illustrated on the preceding two pages. It is similar in composition to the hunting scene, with enemy warriors replacing animals. It is also not unlike the battle scenes on the chariot of Thutmose IV (pages 192–193), although the artist here displays greater skill in capturing the chaos of a battlefield. The Egyptian soldiers are conspicuous by their shaven faces and their round-topped shields. The Asiatics, with their long hair and their rectangular checkered shields, are shown mostly at the point of death—pierced by arrows and spears and stabbed by Egyptian daggers. The Asiatic chariots, six-spoked by now too, were probably less maneuverable than the Egyptian vehicle because of the axle location midway beneath the chariot body.

Panel reproduced about four-fifths original size (1352–1343 B.C.). Cairo Museum.

Two of the earliest known representations of horsemen

Regular cavalry was introduced into armies of the lands of the Bible only at the close of the second millennium B.C. Here, a 14th-century B.C. bronze battleaxe (above) is equipped with a decorative openwork blade depicting a rider on a mare, and a wooden model of a mare and rider (right) is painted with white lines which may indicate the natural piebald pattern of the hide or reflect the Egyptian practice of chalk-marking the animals.

Above: Axe with wooden haft, XVIIIth Dynasty. British Museum. Right: Equestrian model from the el-Amarna period (c. 1350 B.C.). Metropolitan Museum of Art.

Right: W. Stevenson Smith has said of this relief from the tomb of the last XVIIIth Dynasty King: "No finer or more characteristic group has survived from the Amarna period." Its importance for us is in the rarity of its representation of a horseman at so early a period.

Right: Relief from the tomb of Horemheb at Saqqarah (second half of the 14th century B.C.). Museo Civico, Bologna.

Above: Although regular cavalry was not introduced until the end of the second millennium, horsemen are the subject of occasional graphic representations on the reliefs of the XIXth Dynasty. This mounted messenger, armed with a bow, is depicted in a scene from the Battle of Kadesh.

Above: Relief in the temple of Abu Simbel, Rameses II period (1290–1223 B.C.).

220

Rare examples of horsemen
from reliefs that predate
the end of the second millennium

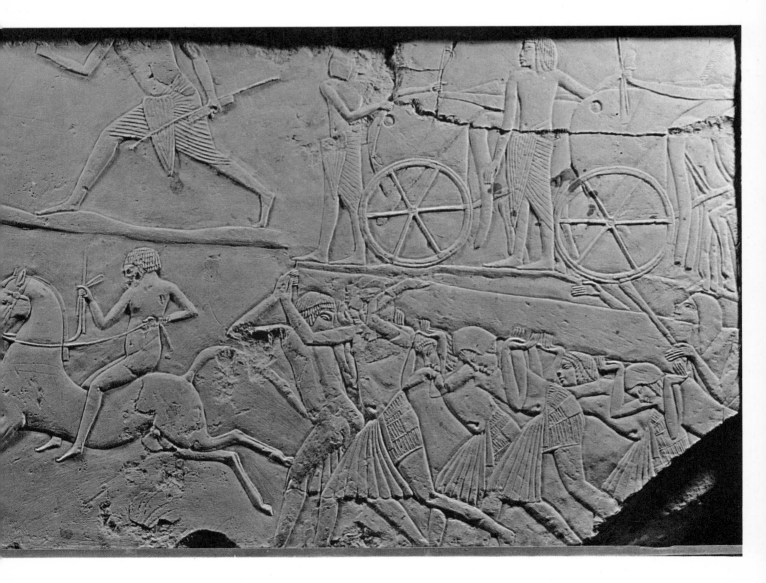

The figure depicted in the high relief at the left—a warrior, possibly a god or a deified king—is armed with a curved pointed sword and a four-pronged socketed battleaxe (see line drawing, page 77). The socketed bronze axe shown below is executed in the shape of a hand.

Left: Relief from the entrance of the King's Gate at Boghazköy (see page 224) (14th century B.C.). Hittite Museum, Ankara. Below: Bronze axe from Beth-shan (14th century B.C.). Rockefeller Museum.

The warrior-god or deified king depicted on the basalt stele above is armed with a socketed spear, and wears a helmet with curled locks. In the stele at right, the god wears a pointed helmet with two horns and locks, and is armed with a curved pointed sword, a mace, and a spear with a tree-like staff (which may possibly be a stylized representation of lightning). Before him stands a small statue.

Above: Stele from Shihan, Trans-Jordan (c. 1300 B.C.). Louvre. Right: The Baal Stele from Ugarit (c. 14th century B.C.). Louvre.

223

Above: The King's Gate of Boghazköy viewed from inside the city. (The warrior relief shown on page 222 has been removed from the gate.) This 14th-century B.C. structure has an angled approach flanked by powerful towers. A key feature was the use of monolithic jambs—two outside and two inside—tapering toward the top to give the entrance a vaulted form.

The city of Boghazköy—with its acropolis (known in Turkish as Büyük Kale), the lower inner city, and the higher outer city—was the largest and most strongly fortified city in the whole of the Middle East in the second millennium B.C.

Facing page, above: An outside view of the entrance of another 14th-century Boghazköy gate, the Lions' Gate, with its figured jambs *in situ.*

Facing page, below: A diagrammatic reconstruction of the southern defenses of the outer city of Boghazköy. This 14th-century B.C. section lies between the King's Gate and the Lions' Gate. In front of the main casemate wall with its large towers is an outer or advanced lower wall which is reached from the outside by either of two ramps, on the left and right, in which stairs have been built. In the center foreground midway between the stepped ramps is a big postern gate.

224

Boghazköy—once Hattussas, capital
of the Hittites: the finest example
of Late Bronze city fortifications

The 13th century—a crucial period in the history of the lands of the Bible

The following plates offer the military background helpful to an understanding of the historic happenings that shaped the 13th century. It was in this period that Rameses II (in the newly established XIXth Dynasty) fought, and claimed victory at, the celebrated Battle of Kadesh. The illustrated monuments represent the battle as a victory for the Pharaoh, but the ultimate result was far from victory. Indeed, the Battle of Kadesh marked the very beginning of the decline of Egyptian might. In the same period, Palestine, that permanent bridge between the great empires in the north, east, and south, witnessed one of the most spectacular and far-reaching events in its history—the gradual occupation of the country by the Israelites, led by Joshua.

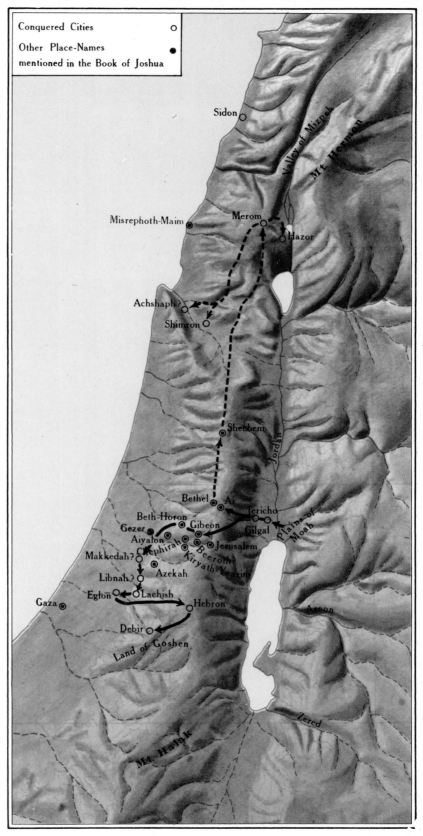

A map of the Holy Land, showing the con-
jectured lines of advance of Joshua's forces as
recorded in the Bible.

Rameses II is victorious in Palestine and Syria

"The wretched city which His Majesty took when it was wicked, Ashkelon." This is the city of Ashkelon, in Philistia, being stormed by Rameses II as depicted in a 13th-century relief. The artist uses the typical montage technique, presenting phases of the fighting in a single scene as if all were happening simultaneously. The city fortifications consist of the main bastioned wall and gates, with their battlements, and the inner citadel, in which the royal entourage prays for mercy. The Egyptian phalanx is shown on the left with its sickle swords and round-topped shields. The attack proper upon the city was made with the aid of scaling-ladders and with archers giving heavy covering fire. The assault troops protect their backs with their shields, and storm the wooden gates with battleaxes.

Drawing of relief in the temple of Karnak (1290–1223 B.C.).

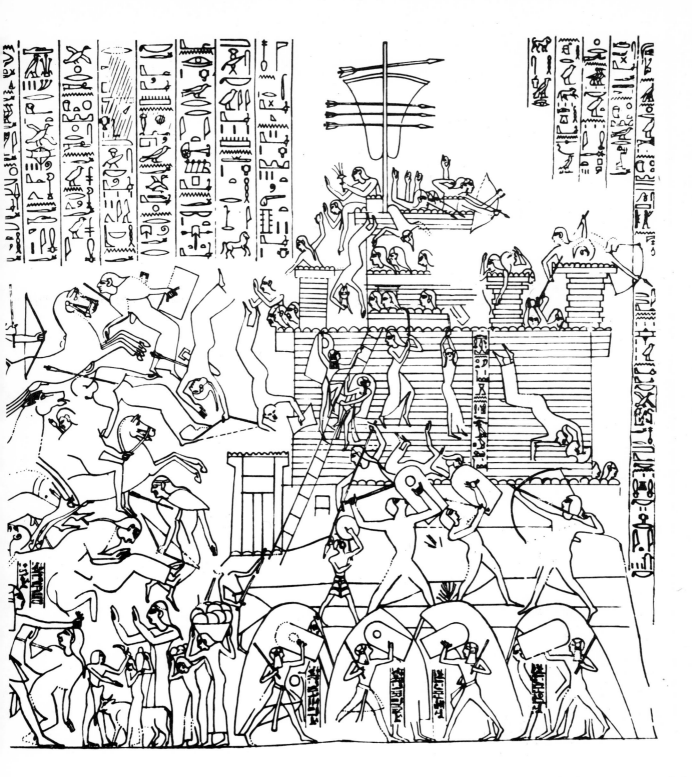

...he city which His Majesty desolated in the ...d of Amurru, Deper." The attack on this ...ongly fortified city (probably in Syria) is ...picted in this 13th-century relief in a manner ...ilar to that shown in the opposite illustra-...n. The defenders, dressed as Hittites and ...otected by the Hittite "waisted" figure-...ht shields, are gathered in the inner citadel ...neath the standard, which has been pierced ... the Pharaoh's arrows. Under strong cover-

ing fire by the archers, the assault troops scale the ladders, protecting their backs with round-topped shields. Below, in front of the four tents, are four named sons of the Pharaoh presented as fighting warriors with round-topped shields. At the lower part of the fortifications is a low outer wall built on the slope of the mound. Close to it, on the other side of the ladder, is a mercenary with his circular shield and long straight sword.

Drawing of relief in the Ramesseum at Thebes (c. 1290–1223 B.C.).

229

This relief shows the attack by Seti I on the
Shasu, "from the fort of Sile [on the border of
Egypt] to the Canaan." The artist gives a
schematic representation of a fortified city
with its bastioned and battlemented wall and
its gate flanked by towers. The upper structure
is presumably intended to portray the inner
citadel or royal fortress where the king dwelt
with his entourage. The city is built at the top

of a tell, or artificial mound, surrounded by a
moat. The Canaanites are armed with spears
and epsilon tang-type axes, which may be an
anachronistic rendering by the artist (cf.
pages 192–193).

Relief from the temple of Karnak, Seti I
(1303–1290 B.C.).

The Egyptians invade the land of Canaan

The capture of Yanoam, a city south of the Sea of Galilee, is the subject of this relief. The artist's technique is similar to that of the facing illustration, which shows the city with its moat, its main wall with bastions and crenelations, and its inner citadel. The Canaanites are still armed with rectangular shields; later in the century they were replaced by circular ones. In the upper right corner there is a rare representation of a Canaanite horseman. Note the skillful portrayal of terror-struck Canaanites trying to hide behind the bushes in the foreground.

Relief from the temple of Karnak (1303–1290 B.C.).

...... WITH THE HELP OF HIS DOG AND PROTECTED ...... THE KING IN HIS CHARIOT ......

The enemies of Rameses II fall before him

These Nubian reliefs show the Pharaoh in various attitudes of victory. Above, he is seen at left smiting a Lybian captive with a *khopesh* sickle sword and holding a triangular composite bow in his left hand. At the right of the upper relief Rameses in his chariot charges the retreating Shasu-Bedouin warriors, who seem to be armed with the sickle sword. (Note the two captives tied to the chariot pole.) At the left of the lower relief, the Pharaoh attacks a Syrian city. At the right, he is seen with a battleaxe about to smite Asiatic and Lybian captives.

Colored cast of the reliefs in the rock temple at Beit el-Weli, Nubia, south of the First Cataract (1290–1223 B.C.). British Museum.

233

The Nubians
fight and are
defeated

Additional royal victory scenes from the Beit el-Weli reliefs. In the upper relief, the Pharaoh is shown in his chariot, followed by two princes in their chariots, charging the retreating Nubians. The royal chariot is equipped with javelins as well as arrows for the bow. The Nubians wear leopard skins and are armed with bows. At the left is an impressionistic representation of a Nubian village.

The lower relief shows Nubians bringing the Pharaoh tribute of precious timber, animals, skins, and slaves. In the upper register on the right are gifts of ostrich feathers and eggs, chairs, fruit, skins, gold, bows, and leather-covered shields.

Colored casts of reliefs at Beit el-Weli (1290–1223 B.C.). British Museum.

234

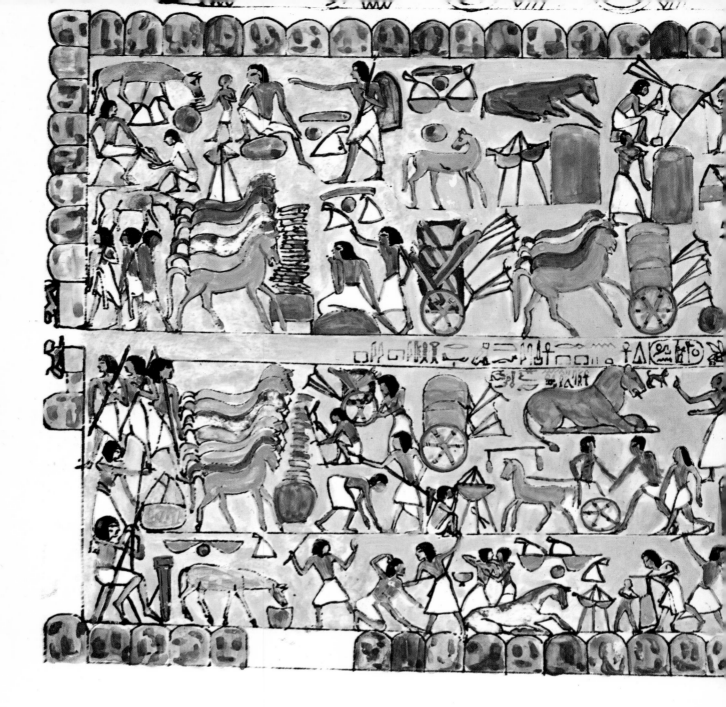

A detailed record
of Rameses'
military camp

These illustrations of the Rameses camp at the Battle of Kadesh, based on 13th-century reliefs, are the earliest records of military camps, preceding the Roman *castra* by nearly a millennium. Later Assyrian sculptures show military camps, but not in such detail. The camp, rectangular in plan, was protected by a fence made of round-topped, leather-covered, metal-studded Egyptian shields. The Pharaoh's tent was set up in a rectangular enclosure and formed a distinct element of the compound, like the *praetorium* in Roman

times. The royal enclosure and, particularly, the approaches to it were defended by the King's guard. The chariots, beasts of burden, and supplies were kept elsewhere inside the camp. Two roads ran through the compound. This scene is of added importance because it offers data on paramilitary subjects not usually treated in the illustrations of warfare on Egyptian monuments—baggage carts harnessed to oxen, the use of donkeys to carry supplies, and the mobile field equipment for watering and feeding the animals. The surprise attack on the Egyptian camp is skillfully portrayed here. On the left the ancient artist shows the calm, relaxed, almost pastoral, atmosphere of the camp; while the right bursts with action as the enemy roams through the broken fence in an assault charge (cf. pages 238–239 and text pages following page 107).

Suggested color restoration of the Rameses camp as depicted in the reliefs at Abu Simbel, Rameses II (1290–1223 B.C.).

237

Three representations of the site of a major battle

The three drawings at the left show variations in relief representations of the city of Kadesh —all differing in style, but depicting the principal features and characteristics of the city in a similar fashion. Kadesh was clearly a well-fortified city surrounded by two moats filled with water and further protected by the River Orontes. Entrance to the city was secured by two bridges spanning the moats. The city flag is shown hoisted above the inner citadel.

This presentation of the city is consistent with the general layout of Tell Nebi Mind, the modern name of the mound of Kadesh.

Top to bottom: Drawing of relief at Luxor. Drawing of relief at the Ramesseum. Drawing of relief at Abu Simbel. All three reliefs (1290–1223 B.C.).

Right: A close-up photograph of a detail of the relief at the Ramesseum, showing the charge of Rameses into the Hittite army. Only the hooves of the chariot horses are seen in the upper left corner. Near by are the fallen Hittite princes and commanders, each named in a caption engraved near his figure. Below are the Hittite chariots with six-spoked wheels (and not eight, as is shown in line drawings of the scene in some modern books; see pages 104–105). Each chariot carries three men, the charioteer, the shield-bearer, and the spearman. A color version of part of the battle scene appears on the following pages.

Rameses II charges the Hittite army at Kadesh

This color copy of a detail of the 13th-century relief in the Ramesseum is one of the finest renderings of the Egyptian chariot. Note that the Hittites wear scale armor.

241

Above: A painted sherd shows bearded Canaanite infantrymen armed with battleaxe and protected by round shield and scale armor. At center right, the reconstruction of an ivory plaque and, below it, the plaque as it was discovered at the Megiddo excavations (see also pages 206–207). The carving is of Canaanite chariots with horses in full gallop (cf. pages 132–133, lower register). The artist here has admirably captured the movement and atmosphere of the charge. The axle under the center of the body (and not at the rear) made this chariot less maneuverable than the Egyptian chariot or even the older Canaanite chariot with its four-spoked wheels. Though he is not depicted here, there must have been another man—an archer—in the crew of each chariot, for a bow case and a quiver are fitted to the chariot body.

Above: Painted sherd from Megiddo (c. 1200 B.C.). Istanbul Museum. Center and lower right: Reconstruction and ivory plaque from Megiddo (13th century B.C.). Museum of the Oriental Institute, Chicago.

This incised ivory plaque shows two independent but related scenes separated by a floral motif. At the right, the King is shown returning in triumph aboard his chariot, to which are tied two naked captive princes. He wears a coat of mail and is armed with bow (not shown, but note the quivers) and spear. Preceding him in front of the captives is an armed royal guard carrying a round shield which has replaced the earlier rectangular shield. He is followed by an armor-bearer carrying a sickle sword (see enlargement on page 204). In the scene on the left, the King is seated on his throne, flanked by cherubim, being entertained by the Queen and a musician playing the lyre.

Ivory plaque from Megiddo (c. 1200 B.C.). Rockefeller Museum.

244

A view from the excavated area of Megiddo

Megiddo, on the Plain of Esdraelon (the Valley of Jezreel), guarding the vital pass through which ran the famous Via Maris linking Egypt with the great empires of the north, was the scene of some of the most celebrated and decisive battles in the Middle East. It was the site of fierce engagements from the time of Thutmose III, Deborah and Sisera, Pharaoh Necho, and King Josiah, and has continued its role to the time of Viscount Allenby of Megiddo in his battle with the Turks, and to Israel's War of Independence.

245